THE RENEWAL AND IMPROVEMENT OF SECONDARY EDUCATION

Concepts and Practices

Herbert J. Klausmeier
James M. Lipham
John C. Daresh

UNIVERSITY
PRESS OF
AMERICA

LANHAM • NEW YORK • LONDON

This book is based upon work supported by the National Institute of Education under
Grade No. NIE-G-81-0009 to the Wisconsin Center for Education Research. Any
opinions, findings and conclusions or recommendations expressed in this publication are
those of the authors and do not necessarily reflect the views of the Institute or the U.S.
Department of Education.

Co-Published by arrangement with
The Wisconsin Center for Education Research

PREFACE

Many secondary schools are providing students an excellent education today. Much purposeful learning and effective teaching are occurring in our middle and senior high schools. However, we need a greater commitment from the public as well as from all educators to make our schools better. In addition, we need a research-validated model to guide our improvement efforts. This book and ten filmstrips and nine audiocassettes that are correlated with it present such a model. It is called a conceptual design for the renewal and improvement of secondary education. An implementation manual shows practitioners how to put the design into practice.

The design for the renewal and improvement of secondary education is very comprehensive. It is broad enough to include all possible areas of improvement. The design includes three improvement strategies and various organizational structures that facilitate implementation of the strategies. The strategies and structures are tied directly to ten components of a functioning secondary school. The design was fully validated as usable and effective through cooperative research conducted with secondary schools.

A school that does not already have a systematic improvement program in operation should not expect to be able to start more than one of the strategies or more than one of the enabling organizational structures per year. Thus, the adaptation of this design to a particular school setting and its subsequent implementation is properly regarded as a continuing process which is how the improvement of schooling should proceed. A school does not suddenly become effective in one large leap. Instead, it proceeds in an orderly, step-by-step fashion, making significant gains one year after another. In this regard, several schools that were already implementing elements of the design in 1972 are still refining them and starting others.

As the staff of a school implements the design and concurrently creates its own approaches to bettering the education of its students, it experiences renewal. The school builds its own continuing improvement capability and achieves its improvement goals. In schools in which this occurs, the majority of the staff members make a personal commitment to improving education; they work together on improvement activities; they replace day-by-day maintenance activities with improvement activities; and they find new and better ways to solve the problems of learning, teaching, advising, and administration that continuously arise. Cooperative research conducted with middle, junior, and senior high schools showed how they developed this kind of an improvement capability. Moreover, they needed little consultation and assistance from external sources.

This book was written for use in university courses and in inservice programs directed toward the improvement of secondary education. The first edition and the correlated materials were tried out in a field test conducted in universities and local schools where they were found to be easily used and highly effective. The materials were used in university courses titled Secondary Education, Secondary School Curriculum, Educational Administration, Educational Leadership, Supervision of Instruction, and Educational Psychology. They were also used in intensive, short workshops and seminars on the improvement of secondary schooling. In some courses this book was the primary text and in others a supplementary text.

The middle and senior high schools that participated in the field test used the book and the correlated materials in a number of different ways in their inservice and staff development programs to gain information and use it in their improvement activities.

The filmstrips capture exemplary practices in middle schools and high schools across the country. Although the filmstrips show exemplary individual and small group activities, there are fewer instances of whole class instruction than is desired. Our limited budget did not permit the film maker to secure the parental permission that is required for each student or to spend the large amount of time that is needed for getting only a few pictures of different classroom groups.

A teacher and another person from schools shown in the filmstrip clarify their school's practices in the school experiences audiocassettes. The practitioners focus on what they are doing, how they got started, and some of their current successes and concerns. Most of the audiocassettes describe the practices of two middle schools and two high schools in segments of 10 to 12 minutes each. Any segment can be listened to and discussed profitably without listening to the other segments. Each school is identified in the audiocassettes, as well as in the filmstrips and book. The schools continue to welcome visits and calls.

The filmstrips and the school experiences audiocassettes were not revised after the field test. This book and the implementation manual were. Besides updating this book, we re-wrote the implementation manual so that a school staff can use it and the other correlated materials on their own. A school that can conduct its own inservice program can also use these materials to plan and carry out its improvement activities. In using the material independently, the school principal and a district official first gain an overview of this comprehensive program of renewal and improvement. Next, other key staff members of the school gain the same overview. After the principal and key staff, with input from the faculty, decide on an area of improvement, such as a curricular area, instruction, advising, or school organization, the faculty members to be involved in planning and implementing the improvement activities study only the set of correlated materials related to the particular area of improvement. They do not have to familiarize themselves with the complete, comprehensive program before starting an improvement activity. The usual procedure is to use the relevant filmstrip first and then the relevant segments of the school experiences audiocassette. The inservice leader summarizes and excerpts information from the appropriate book chapter, rather than having all the teachers read it. However, a few copies of this book as well as a copy of the filmstrip and audiocassette are put in the Instructional Materials Center or the school's professional library where teachers can access them. Although some schools are able to proceed independently in using the materials, assistance from an experienced practitioner or a knowledgeable professor enables the school to progress more rapidly.

More often than not, the university professor offering a credit course on campus shows and discusses the filmstrips during regular class meetings. Only one or two audiocassette segments are used during the class period to familiarize the students with the content and to indicate how to use the audiocassettes. Copies of the textbook and audiocassettes are made available to all students. Most professors assign the textbook chapters and students listen individually to the audiocassette segments.

This book is organized into four parts to facilitate its use in different courses. Regardless of the course, Part I consisting of Chapter 1 should be studied first. Part II includes chapters on instruction, curriculum, and evaluation; Part III on administration and organization; and Part IV on community relations, support arrangements, and research. Part II and then Part IV are usually studied after Part I in courses in secondary education, secondary curriculum, and educational psychology and Part III is studied last. On the other hand, Parts III and IV usually follow Part I in courses in educational administration, supervision, and leadership. Chapter 13 summarizes the research that resulted in the operational validation of this design and should be read by everyone.

The implementation manual is used by the school principal and key faculty members, not by the entire teaching staff. Similarly, it is not used by the professor or students except when the university course includes practicum activities. Late afternoon and early evening classes and summer session courses and workshops are profitable settings for use of the materials.

The development of the design and the preparation of this book and the correlated materials required cooperation of many people across the country. Recognition of the many individuals cannot be given by name, only according to the following groups: the staff of the schools whose practices are described in this book; the students, teachers, counselors, principals, parents, and others portrayed in the filmstrips; the teachers, counselors, and principals who described their practices in the school experiences audiocassettes; the people who reviewed the revised implementation manual; the university professors and school faculties who participated in the field test; the schools that participated in the cooperative research that validated the design; and the graduate students and schools that participated with Professors Lipham and Daresh in their research on planned change, administrative leadership, and shared decision making.

Support from the Faye McBeath Foundation for the preparation of the manuscript is deeply appreciated.

The publisher, University Press of America, is recognized for its creative efforts in producing a high quality book while still keeping the retail price at a very minimum. In this regard, the authors decided not to have an index, feeling that the use made of it would not justify increasing the cost of the book.

Individuals who aided in the production of this book merit many thanks: Teri Frailey, Arlene Knudsen, and Carol Jean Roche who did the word processing, the staff of Fleetwood Graphics who did the printing, the support staff of the Wisconsin Center for Education Research who provided a variety of services, and Dan Woolpert of the Wisconsin Center who coordinated the final production.

We hope that all concerned with the improvement of secondary schools will find the design helpful both immediately and in the years ahead.

Herbert J. Klausmeier
James M. Lipham
John C. Daresh
July, 1983

CONTENTS

PART I: INTRODUCTION

PART II: INSTRUCTION, CURRICULUM, AND EVALUATION

PART IV: COMMUNITY, SUPPORT ARRANGEMENTS, RESEARCH

CORRELATED TEXTBOOK CHAPTERS, IMPLEMENTATION MANUAL CHAPTERS, FILMSTRIPS, AND SCHOOL EXPERIENCES AUDIOCASSETTES

The textbook is available from University Press of America, 4720 Boston Way, Lanham, MD, 20706. Phone (301) 459-3366. The manual, ten filmstrips, and nine school experiences audiocassettes are available from CCL Document Service, Wisconsin Center for Education Research, 1025 W. Johnson St., Madison, WI, 53706. Phone (608) 263-4214. The components of the design for the renewal and improvement of secondary education follow and the correlated materials for each component are listed.

Text Ch. 1: *Introduction and Overview of an Improvement Design.*
Manual: *Introduction and Overview.*
Filmstrip: *Introduction to the Wisconsin Program for the Renewal and Improvement of Secondary Education.*

EDUCATIONAL PROGRAMMING FOR THE INDIVIDUAL STUDENT

Text Ch. 2: *Educational Programming for the Individual Student.*
Manual Ch. 2: *Educational Programming for the Individual Student.*
Filmstrip: *Educational Programming for the Individual Student in Secondary Schools: Part I.*
Audiocassette: *Experiences of Two Middle Schools and Two Senior High Schools with Educational Programming for the Individual Student: Part I.*

INSTRUCTIONAL PROGRAMMING FOR THE INDIVIDUAL STUDENT

Text Ch. 3: *Instructional Programming for the Individual Student.*
Manual Ch. 3: *Instructional Programming for the Individual Student.*
Filmstrip: *Educational Programming for the Individual Student in Secondary Schools: Part II.*

Audiocassette: *Experiences of Two Middle Schools and Two Senior High Schools with Educational Programming for the Individual Student: Part II.*

CURRICULAR ARRANGEMENTS

Text Ch. 4: *Curricular Arrangements.*
Manual Ch. 4: *Curricular Arrangements.*
Filmstrip: *Curricular Patterns in Secondary Schools.*
Audiocassette: *Experiences of a Middle School, a Junior High School, and Two Senior High Schools with Curricular Patterns.*

CAREER EDUCATION AND EXPERIENTIAL LEARNING

Text Ch. 5: *Career Education and Experiential Learning.*
Manual Ch. 5: *Career Education and Experiential Learning.*
Filmstrip: *Work and Other Career Education Activities in Secondary Schools.*
Audiocassette: *Experiences of a Middle School, a Junior High School, and Two Senior High Schools with Work and Other Career Education Activities.*

STUDENT DECISION-MAKING ARRANGEMENTS

Text Ch. 6: *Student Decision-Making Arrangements.*
Manual Ch. 6: *Student Decision-Making Arrangements.*
Filmstrip: *Student Decision Making in Secondary Schools.*
Audiocassette: *Experiences of a Middle School, a Junior-Senior High School, and Two Senior High Schools with Student Decision Making.*

EVALUATION AND IMPROVEMENT STRATEGIES

Text Ch. 7: *Evaluation and Improvement Strategies.*
Manual Ch. 7: *Evaluation and Improvement Strategies.*
Filmstrip: *Evaluating Student Learning and Educational Programs in Secondary Schools.*
Audiocassette: *Experiences of a Middle School and a Senior High School with Evaluating Student Learning and Educational Programs.*

ADMINISTRATIVE ARRANGEMENTS AND PROCESSES

Text Ch. 8: *Administrative Arrangements and Processes.*
Manual Ch. 8: *Administrative Arrangements and Processes.*
Filmstrip: *Administrative Arrangements for Shared Decision Making in Secondary Schools.*
Audiocassette: *Experiences of a Middle School and Two Senior High Schools with Administrative Arrangements for Shared Decision Making.*

ORGANIZATION FOR INSTRUCTION AND ADVISING

Text Ch. 9: *Organization for Instruction and Advising*
Manual Ch. 9: *Organization for Instruction and Advising*
Filmstrip: *Instruction and Advisory Arrangements in Secondary Schools.*
Audiocassette: *Experiences of Two Middle Schools and Two Senior High Schools with Instruction and Advisory Arrangements.*

TEACHER-ADVISOR PROGRAMS

Text Ch. 10: *Teacher-Advisor Programs.*
Manual Ch. 10: *Teacher-Advisor Programs.*
Filmstrip: *Teacher-Advisor Programs in Secondary Schools.*
Audiocassette: *Experiences of a Middle School, a Junior High School, and Two Senior High Schools with Teacher-Advisor Programs.*

HOME-SCHOOL-COMMUNITY RELATIONS

Text Ch. 11: *Home-School-Community Relations.*
Manual Ch. 11: *Home-School-Community Relations.*
(No filmstrip or cassette.)

SUPPORT ARRANGEMENTS

Text Ch. 12: *Support Arrangements.*
Manual Ch. 12: *Support Arrangements.*
(No filmstrip or cassette.)

RESEARCH AND DEVELOPMENT

Text Ch. 13: *Research-Based Educational Improvement.*
(No filmstrip or cassette.)

PART I:
INTRODUCTION

Chapter 1: **Introduction and Overview of an Improvement Design**

CHAPTER 1

INTRODUCTION AND OVERVIEW OF AN IMPROVEMENT DESIGN

Herbert J. Klausmeier

The past few years have witnessed a marked increase in interest in improving the quality of secondary education. Hundreds of recommendations have been offered concerning what all secondary schools should do to become more effective. At the same time, there has been a pronounced dearth of information regarding how each secondary school can go about identifying its own improvement needs and then plan and carry out related improvement activities. Yet this is what must be done if a school is to develop an internal improvement capability and, in the process, experience renewal as a social organization. This book was written to enable prospective and inservice educators to understand a design for improving secondary schooling and to incorporate educational improvement in their role perceptions.

The design incorporates three closely related improvement strategies, and it also indicates the structures and processes of the school that facilitate the implementation of the strategies. Since each school is regarded as a unique social organization, the strategies and the facilitative structures must be adapted by the staff of the individual school.

The first version of the design was based on a synthesis of theory and research relevant to the improvement of secondary education. This version was reviewed by practitioners and scholars and revisions were made. The revision was tested empirically in middle schools, junior high schools, and senior high schools to assure that it indicated both desirable directions and related means for improving secondary education. It also served as a basis for conducting two kinds of research with secondary schools. Research focusing on leadership, shared decision making, and planned change was conducted by Professor Lipham and his graduate students in educational administration. The results of the research, as well as concepts related to various school organizational structures, are reported in the chapters of this book by Lipham and Daresh. The research directed toward the validation of the complete design as an effective framework for the improvement and renewal of secondary education was conducted cooperatively with five schools during a four-year period by Professor Klausmeier and a small research team, including Professor Daresh. A summary of the results of this research is given in Chapter 13, and the detailed report of the research appears in Klausmeier, Serlin, and Zindler (1983). The reader may wish to study Chapter 13 immediately after this chapter.

The design is based on my synthesis of information from three sources. One source was theory and research as reflected in the recommendations of individuals and national and state commissions. Another source was theory and research regarding learning, instruction, individual differences, school organizational structures, and improvement processes. A third source was the experiences of school practitioners and scholars who were associated with the Wisconsin Center for Education Research in a network of innovative schools.

The purposes of this chapter are to enable you to understand the kind of information that was used in developing the design and to gain an overview of it. (Middle schools that start not lower than Grade 6, junior high schools, and senior high schools are regarded as secondary schools.)

PROPOSALS TO IMPROVE SECONDARY SCHOOLING

Periodically, the improvement of secondary education receives much attention nationally. One such period was the early and middle 1970s. During this time, the focus was on achieving equality of educational opportunity and adapting schooling to meet the educational needs of the individual student. Theory regarding adaptive education underlying the recommendations of this period is incorporated in the design for the renewal and improvement of secondary education.

The next set of recommendations of the late 1970s and early 1980s focused on school effectiveness. This focus was accelerated by the publication of a book by Rutter, Maughan, Mortimore, and Ouston, with Smith (1979). After presenting the overview of the design for the renewal and improvement of secondary education, I shall relate the design to the characteristics of effective schools.

In the early 1980s a still different focus characterized the recommendations of numerous individuals and national groups, namely, reforming secondary schooling through curriculum change. The most notable of these early reports is that of the National Commission on Excellence in Education (1983) of the U. S. Department of Education. As we shall see, the present design is not prescriptive with respect to the secondary curriculum; but it does specify that the state and local district, rather than the federal government, should determine the curriculum. Accordingly, the recent recommendations regarding curriculum change are presented in Chapter 4 where this element of the present design is discussed.

Recommendations of National Groups 1973-1977

Many individuals, committees, and commissions of the 1960s and early 1970s gave serious attention to reforming the education of American youth. They tried to identify the problems of secondary education as well as the causes of the difficulties. They then recommended policy and program changes which presumably would eliminate the problems. These individuals and groups proposed that secondary schooling would be improved by changing it to meet individual students' educational needs more effectively. A synthesis follows of the major recommendations of the panels and commissions of the 1970s (Brown, 1973; Coleman, 1974; Gibbons, 1976; Hostrop, 1975; Martin, 1976; Shane, 1973, 1977; Thomson, 1975; Toffler, 1974; and Van Til, 1976):

> Schools should personalize and humanize the educative process rather than continue the three-track system of college preparation, general education, and vocational preparation.

> Multiple paths leading to high school graduation should be made available to students rather than requiring a certain number of Carnegie units for graduation and trying to enforce compulsory school attendance until age 18.

> Progress in learning and credit toward high school graduation should be based on demonstrated proficiency rather than on

the amount of time spent attending class.

Students should be given more opportunity and responsibility for planning and evaluating their educational programs.

Greater emphasis should be given to preparing youth for work, for citizenship, and for their future familial roles.

The educational resources of the community should be used much more as a means of promoting experiential learning, making career preparation more effective, and fostering adolescent interactions with children and adults.

Students, teachers, parents, and other citizens should be represented on school councils and committees that deal with curriculum and instruction, student conduct, school governance, and other educational matters.

Most persons during the 1970s probably agreed with most of the preceding proposals. However, some specific recommendations were made by the various groups which, if implemented nationally, would greatly change the character of tax-supported public secondary education. Three of these recommendations merit brief attention.

The Panel on Youth of the President's Science Advisory Committee (Coleman et al., 1974) dealt with the period of transition from childhood to adulthood, roughly age 14 to 24. A hotly debated recommendation of the Panel was to provide vouchers enabling students and their parents to choose where they will be educated and when. One means of implementing this recommendation would allocate tax monies for education to the parents rather than to the local school district. The parents would then transfer the money to the school which they select.

The National Commission on the Reform of Secondary Education, like other groups, identified many problems and made related recommendations (Brown et al., 1973). A recommendation receiving widespread attention was to drop the legal school attendance age to 14. Carrying out this recommendation presumably would get physically mature students into productive work arrangements in the community. They could return for any desired form of education at any later time. To assure this, the Commission recommended legislation to guarantee students a total of 14 years of tuition-free education. After the compulsory eight years up to age 14, they should be provided an additional six years of schooling, wherever and at such time as they decide to take the additional six years.

The Phi Delta Kappa Task Force on Compulsory Education and Transition for Youth (Gibbons, 1976) strongly supported maintaining tax-supported secondary education. However, they found so many inadequacies in current practices that a new ideal form of schooling was proposed. They recommended a complete departure from the present system of secondary education.

California Commission on the Reform of Intermediate and Secondary Education

One aim of the preceding national commissions and panels was to influence federal policies regarding education. Another was to influence local education practices as school administrators and teachers became aware of the problems and related proposals. A different and very interesting strategy was followed by the California Commission on the Reform of Intermediate and Secondary Education (Newcomber, 1975). This same strategy was subsequently employed in many other states.

In 1974 the Superintendent of Public Instruction of California formed the 37-member California Commission for the Reform of Intermediate and Secondary Education (RISE). This Commission and its work had several interesting features. Its members included students, teachers, counselors, principals, and other school personnel and also representatives of organized labor, farm groups, business, and the professions. Another feature was that intermediate as well as secondary schools were included. This made it possible to take into account the emergence of the middle school as an appropriate response to the earlier physical maturation of boys and girls. It also enabled the Commission to state aims of schooling that imply continuous progress of students from the intermediate grades through high school graduation. Perhaps the most important feature was that the California Department of Education would take responsibility for implementing the Commission's recommendations. As you read the recommendations, notice the pervasive emphasis on meeting the educational needs of the individual student.

Learners as the Most Important Individuals in the School

Each learner should be recognized and accepted as the primary client to be served by the school. Parents, the community, and the larger society are secondary clients who will benefit from schools through the education gained by the learners. As maturing learners move toward adulthood, they should progressively be able to make more educational choices and also to assume responsibility for those choices. Such choices should include where, when, and how to learn.

Progress Dependent on Demonstrated Proficiency

The strengths and weaknesses of each learner should be assessed and, based on this assessment, each learner should be able to choose and pursue an instructional program consistent with the assessment and the learner's choices. When the learner demonstrates that he/she has attained the objectives of the instructional program, appropriate credit should be received. The learning activity should not be confined to the essential skills but should encompass attainment of all of the aims of California education.

A System of Multiple Options in Programs and Learning Styles

A wide variety of choices and options in program and curriculum content should be available to learners so as to enable them to meet personal objectives in varied ways according to each learner's own learning style. The alternatives or options might include schools-within-a-school, work-study programs, regional occupational training programs, special interest schools or centers, and departmentalized traditional programs. The multiple options for learning should allow the learner to take advantage of such opportunities as learning independently, learning in groups of varying size and composition, and learning in different locations, including the traditional school setting.

Gaining Skills and Knowledge in a Variety of Locations

Multiple opportunities are needed to enable students to gain first-hand experience by means of study, observation, service, participation, and work in both the school and the wider community. Means of evaluation should be developed enabling learners to earn credit or other recognition through certain types of work situations, participation in community activities, or self-designed independent activities away from the traditional school setting.

Flexibility in Times for Learning

The hours, days, months, and school year should be flexible, extensive, and sufficiently varied to accommodate a diversity of interests, needs, and choices of individual learners. Class scheduling should be arranged to allow a learner to move freely from one activity to another on the basis of demonstrated proficiency. School sites and facilities should be available and used throughout the year and beyond the traditional school hours and five days of the week. School attendance requirements should allow a learner to leave the school system temporarily with the approval of the learner's parents and the schools. The furloughs should be of flexible duration, of educational value to the learner, and consistent with the learner's educational needs and objectives.

Personalized Instruction

The size and setting of the learning group should be based on the type of learning activity to be conducted. Groupings of learners should be small enough to offer a psychological and physical atmosphere that promotes the development of the learner's self-worth and identity within the school and community. All schools with large enrollments should be divided into several smaller schools to insure a more personalized setting. Middle schools particularly should give special attention to limiting school size because early adolescents have unique needs in learning to live and work with one another.

In addition to the preceding recommendations the California Commission proposed that all students should gain the skills, competence, knowledge, and values required to function effectively as an individual today and also as an individual and citizen during the last part of this century. Concerning proficiency in essential skills, the Commission recommended that each learner should achieve and demonstrate specified levels of proficiency in the following essential skills areas:

The communication skills of reading, writing, speaking, and listening.

Computational skills of addition, subtraction, multiplication, and division as well as in the use of decimals and percentages and in the understanding of the systems of measurement.

Ability to maintain a satisfactory level of physical conditioning and psychomotor coordination consistent with the individual's identified needs and rate of physical development. Each learner should acquire an understanding of the health practices that will serve him/her throughout his/her lifetime.

Scientific and technological literacy, including a basic understanding of scientific principles and the ability to apply the principles to everyday situations.

Knowledge of American government and institutions and an understanding of the responsibilities of a citizen in a democratic society.

The skills needed for positive interaction with others in the school and with individual groups and institutions within the larger society.

Minimum levels of proficiency in reading, writing, computation, and in other essential skill areas as a condition of completing secondary education and receiving a high school diploma.

In addition to the explicit recommendations regarding proficiency in essential skills, the RISE Commission also made recommendations for the following:

Social concepts that reflect present and future needs and concerns of society.

Cooperation, understanding of others, and mutual respect.

Processes of decision making.

Career awareness, exploration, and preparation.

Leisure time.

Aesthetic experiences.

The Commission did not assume that the preceding recommendations could be carried out, except as they are accepted by students and parents and by teachers and other school personnel. Also, mere acceptance of the desirability of the recommendations is not sufficient. Teachers and other educational workers must be given the opportunity to acquire new knowledge and skills to perform the implied activities. As the school day is currently organized and as conditions for staff development activities are arranged, there is not time, opportunity, or incentive for teachers to acquire the knowledge and skills.

In accordance with this need the Commission recommended that, in order to gain and strengthen their knowledge and skills, teachers and other school personnel should be provided with greater opportunities to design, conduct, and participate in a variety of staff development activities. A further recommendation was that the staff development programs should be designed and administered primarily at the local or regional levels so that they will be responsive to the individual learners, the staff, and community needs. Therefore, staff members should assist in identifying their specific staff development needs and programs should be designed to meet these needs. The abilities of individuals on the school staff should be identified and released time provided for them so that they may help other staff members improve their instructional techniques. Particularly needed are staff development directed toward arranging more appropriate learning activities for the individual student and techniques for evaluating student learning and instructional programs.

It is interesting to note that the various commissions emphasized adapting schooling to student needs. This followed the pattern of the social legislation of the 1960s and early 1970s. Despite this emphasis, the California Commission included the idea of each student attaining specified levels of proficiency in several essential skill areas, including the language arts, mathematics, science and technology, physical conditioning and health, and American government and institutions. This recommendation reflected the beginning emphasis on the student's responsibilities and the needs of society as well as the individual student's interests and rights.

PSYCHOLOGICAL BASIS OF THE
IMPROVEMENT STRATEGIES

In the preceding pages, I have indicated that theory regarding adaptive schooling was incorporated in the present design for the renewal and improvement of secondary education. Other information used in formulating the design is drawn from the psychology of classroom learning and the psychology of individual differences. Information from these areas provides the theoretical framework for the three improvement strategies incorporated in the design.

Principles of Classroom Learning

Many theories of learning were extant in the 1970s. Although there are many possible applications of these theories, a few principles that facilitate learning have been identified in many learning experiments that have been carried out in experimental laboratories and in school settings (Klausmeier, 1976). Teachers seem to be aware of these principles, but school and classroom conditions do not always permit successful applications of them.

The first principle is that the learner actively engages in the learning activities during the time allocated for learning. This means that the student comes to class, starts to work immediately, and continues the learning activities until it is time to start other activities.

The second principle is that the learning activities are of an appropriate level of difficulty for the learner; they are neither too easy nor too difficult. The learner does not experience a sense of accomplishment by completing very easy tasks and experiences frustration after making unsuccessful efforts to perform tasks that are too advanced or too difficult.

A third principle is that the learning session is neither too short nor too long. Too little time means that nothing is learned well and accordingly it is not retained from one session to the next. Too much time results in boredom, even for the highly motivated student.

A fourth principle involves guidance of the learner. Guidance is interpreted broadly here to include teacher activities such as providing models, confirming correct responses, aiding students in correcting errors, and providing a proper balance of teacher-directed and student-initiated individual, small-group, and large-group activities.

Effective application of these principles secures maximum learning effectiveness over a short period of time, such as during a class period. To secure the maximum amount of learning over longer time intervals, such as during a semester or across a level of schooling, there must be continuity in the learning activities.

The conceptual design encourages teachers, curriculum coordinators, principals, and other local school personnel to apply the short-term principles and also to provide for continuity in learning throughout the school years. In this regard, one serious learning problem of the 1970s was that an instructional strategy based on students' mastery of detailed performance objectives did not take into account the first four principles adequately, and there was a near total lack of continuity. No provisions were made for students to integrate, synthesize, or relearn; rather, they mastered discrete objectives once and then more often than not forgot what they had mastered.

Individual Differences

The preceding principles apply to students in general. However, their applications should take into account differences among individual students. Longitudinal research involving four groups of children and youth when in grades 1-3, 4-6, 7-9, and 10-12 indicates that the difference among the students of the same grade in their level of cognitive development are exceedingly great and that the difference increases at the successively higher levels of schooling (Klausmeier & Allen, 1978; Klausmeier & Associates, 1979). Moreover, some very rapidly developing students in grade 3 were found to be as advanced cognitively as other very slow developing students were in grade 12. Cognitive development as measured in this longitudinal study included understanding of concepts and principles drawn from the fields of English, mathematics, and science, and the ability to solve problems.

An intensive study of six rapid and six slow developers of grades 6 and 12 participating in this longitudinal study was undertaken (Mize & Klausmeier, 1977). The main purpose of the study was to identify conditions related to each student's individual and personal characteristics, school and education, and home and family that might contribute to rapid or slow cognitive development. The hypothesis was that one pattern of conditions contributed to rapid development and another to slow development.

Comprehensive information was gathered on each of the 12 students in order to answer the following questions:

1. Do students of rapid and slow cognitive development differ in
   a. Intellectual abilities?
   b. Self-directedness of behavior?
   c. Peer relations?
   d. Educational aspirations and life goals?
   e. Attitudes toward school and teachers?
   f. Rapport with teachers?
   g. Attributions of responsibility for academic performance?
   h. Use of leisure time (e.g., television viewing, reading, interests)?
   i. Home orientation, responsibilities, and perceptions of family?

2. Do parents and families of students of rapid and slow cognitive development differ in
   a. Demographic characteristics (e.g., divorce, education, number of children)?
   b. Family structure and family life (e.g., cohesiveness)?
   c. Attitudes and perceptions of the child?
   d. Attitudes toward children and child rearing?
   e. Attitudes toward school, teachers, and education?
   f. Values, goals, and aspirations for the family and for their child?

3. Do the school programs and educational backgrounds of students of rapid and slow cognitive development differ in
   a. Schools attended?
   b. Courses taken?
   c. Activities pursued?
   d. Grades made?
   e. School attendance?
   f. The teachers' perceptions of the student's attitudes toward school and education, achievement motivation, school behavior, self-esteem and self-perceptions, peer

relations, and values and goals? (Mize & Klausmeier, 1977, p. 3)

The variables that contribute to rapid and slow cognitive development of the Grade 12 students follow. Variables that do not differentiate between them are not indicated. The rapid developers have above-average IQ scores and good school achievement as represented by high grades. They have a low rate of school absenteeism and pursue an academic curriculum in high school. They enjoy reading and manifest strong achievement motivation, self-esteem, and positive attitudes toward school, education, and teachers. They actively engage in school activities and hold positive attitudes toward parents, family, and home, and their social skills with peers and adults are good. More often than not they come from upper-middle or middle-class homes characterized by a good intellectual climate. Their parents have completed high school and possibly some college, have high aspirations and expectations for their child, hold positive attitudes toward school and education, and are concerned and actively interested in their child's school, teachers, and curriculum.

Slow developers, in contrast, have average or below average IQ scores and make low grades in school. They have a high rate of school absenteeism and pursue nonacademic subjects in high school. They are not interested in reading but depend on television for information and sedentary recreation. They have low self-esteem, low motivation for learning, and negative attitudes toward school, education, and teachers. They do not engage in extracurricular school activities regularly. They have less positive attitudes toward family and home and have poor social skills and peer relations. Slow developers are more likely to come from a lower-middle-class home with an impoverished intellectual climate and parents who did not complete high school. The parents or guardians have low expectations for their child, show little involvement with the child, express negative attitudes toward school and education, and exhibit little understanding of or interest in their child's school, teachers, and curriculum.

It should be pointed out that the slow developers identified in this study in Grade 12 undoubtedly represent the high end of the range of slow developers at the high school level. These seniors were all sufficiently successful to complete four years of high school and receive a diploma. Other students who dropped out of school before their senior year were not available for inclusion in the study.

Many of the conditions associated with slow development are probably preventable if changes can be made in the home and family situation, in the school curriculum and instruction of the child, and in the relations among teachers, parents, and the student. Moreover, conditions such as absenteeism, lack of interest in reading, low self-esteem, low achievement, and negative attitudes toward school, teachers, and the curriculum must be changed if the student is to achieve reasonably well. Personalizing the instruction and advising of students and arranging a more suitable educational program for each student are two possible means of aiding the slow developer, as well as other students. These and other ideas derived from the longitudinal research, as well as from other research on individual differences, were taken into account in formulating the design for the improvement of secondary education.

EXPERIENCES OF SCHOOL PRACTITIONERS

The first draft of the design was prepared in 1976. This draft was submitted for review and input by scholars and practitioners from across the nation who attended a workshop on the improvement of secondary education held at the Wisconsin Center for Education Research. Input was received regarding the substance of the design and also its applicability to schools of greatly different characteristics. The present author prepared a revision of it, taking into account this input.

The revision was used in two doctoral studies conducted under the supervision of Professor Lipham. Klausmeier (1978) reported that the faculties of innovative middle schools and junior high schools regarded the design as indicating desirable directions and means for improving education. The participating faculties were already implementing a considerable number of the design components. Maier (1978) reported similar results in the high schools included in his study.

Only minor changes were made in the design after 1977. Accordingly, the design that is now described was implemented in the four-year cooperative research. Based on the very positive research findings, the design is regarded as providing a powerful and practical theoretical framework for improving secondary schooling.

AN OVERVIEW OF THE DESIGN

The design indicates 10 components of secondary schools, one for each major component of a functioning secondary school. For each component there is a comprehensive objective. The 10 comprehensive objectives indicate desirable directions for the improvement of secondary education. The enabling objectives for each comprehensive objective provide illustrative means of achieving the comprehensive objective. Chapters 2 through 13 of this book are devoted to the 10 components.

The 10 comprehensive objectives and the enabling objectives for Component 1 of the design, Educational Programming for the Individual Student, follow. This component incorporates two closely related improvement strategies. The third strategy is built into the component dealing with evaluation.

Educational Programming for the Individual Student

Comprehensive Objective:

An individual educational program of course work and other activities is arranged for each student each semester that satisfies the student's developmental needs and characteristics and that also meets district and state requirements.

Illustrative Enabling Objectives:

Each student's individual educational program which includes all courses and other activities:

Is planned each semester or year by the student and the student's advisor.

Takes into account the student's aptitudes for learning different subject matters, interests, motivation, learning styles, career goals, and other personal and social characteristics.

Provides for experiential learning, including work experience in the community, for students who will benefit from it.

Is monitored cooperatively by the student and the student's advisor throughout the semester.

Is changed as necessary during the semester to assure high quality education for the student.

Comprehensive Objective:

An individual instructional program is arranged for the student in each course and other activity that is part of the student's total educational program that takes into account the student's aptitudes, interests, motivation, learning styles, career goals, and other personal and social characteristics.

Illustrative Enabling Objectives:

The instructional program of the student:

Is planned by the student and the teacher of the course at the beginning of the course.

Includes course and unit objectives that are appropriate for the student in terms of the student's aptitude, entering achievement level, and career goals.

Provides an appropriate amount of time in class and during or outside school hours to suit the student's rate of achieving his/her objectives in the course.

Provides for appropriate individual attention by the teacher to take into account the student's motivation and other personal characteristics.

Provides for an appropriate amount of *teacher-directed* individual, pair, small-group, and large-group activity to take into account the student's need for independence and preferences for mode of instruction.

Provides for an appropriate amount of *student-initiated* individual, pair, small-group, and large-group activity to take into account the student's need for independence and preferences for mode of instruction.

Provides for appropriate use of printed materials, audio-visual materials, and direct experiencing to take into account the student's preferred styles of learning—visual, auditory, tactual, or kinesthetic.

Arranging an appropriate *educational program* for each student requires a school person to have a conference at least three times per semester with each student. Accordingly, there must be many counselors in the school to meet with the students or each teacher must serve as an educational advisor to 15 to 20 students to plan their programs and to monitor and evaluate their progress.

Providing an appropriate *instructional program* for each student in each course requires both teacher-directed and student-initiated activities to be arranged to take into account the differing educational needs and characteristics of students. Similarly, individual, small-group, and whole-class activities must be matched to the individual student's learning capability for the particular subject matter, learning styles, and other characteristics. Neither all teacher-directed whole-class instruction nor all individual assignments and activities can possibly provide for the educational needs of all students.

We see that an appropriate educational program cannot be arranged for a student if the student cannot get appropriate instruction in each course. Similarly, the student's instructional program cannot be effective in a course that is not suited to the student's educational needs. Accordingly, the instructional practices in each course as well as the curricular arrangements of the school are critical for implementing either strategy.

Curricular Arrangements

The curriculum is structured to meet state and district requirements but it can be adapted by the school and individual teachers to take into account the differing educational needs of students.

Three sets of changing conditions point to the importance of a structured but flexible curriculum. State and federal agencies are making ever-increasing demands and regulations related to all aspects of the curriculum inasmuch as the curriculum can be changed more easily than instructional, advising, and administrative practices. Adults' perceptions of the developmental needs and the rights and responsibilities of students are changing, and the students' own perceptions regarding these matters are evolving also. Knowledge in all subject fields continues to accrue rapidly. The school's curriculum attempts to take into account these and other societal conditions so that an excellent individual educational program can be arranged for each student.

Career Education and Experiential Learning

Career education is arranged for all students; experiential-learning activities and/or work experience in the community are arranged for each student who can profit from them. (Senior high school students, more than middle school students, require work experience and participation in community activities.)

The demands on the school for an effective program of career awareness, exploration, and preparation and also for citizenship education are increasing. Career education necessarily includes work experience for some students.

Closely related to this, many career and other educational experiences can be provided away from the school site. Most of our local communities have many potential opportunities for work and other educative experiences in which adolescents may participate with adults and also with younger children. Furthermore, many students are able to travel and study anywhere in our entire nation, as well as in foreign countries, as part of their community learning activities.

Student Decision-Making Arrangements

Students progressively assume more responsibility for planning, implementing, and evaluating their programs and activities with a lesser amount of adult direction and control.

Boys and girls in the United States mature physically about two years earlier than did their grandparents who were born at the turn of the 20th century, the time at which the Grade 7-9 junior high school was started to meet the unique needs of this age group. Although they are maturing faster, the age at which they become economically independent is delayed increasingly. Moreover, in recent decades there has been a great increase in juvenile delinquency, crippling accidents, violent crimes, alcoholism, and venereal disease among modern youth of middle school and high school age. Despite these conditions, we should not infer that students are incapable of governing themselves as individuals or in small groups. However, it is equally fallacious to assume that all of them will become socially conscious, self-governing citizens except as they receive wise guidance and learn to observe the traditions and norms of our adult society. Rules and regulations and means of enforcing them, as well as a student bill of rights are required.

Starting in the early school years, boys and girls should have many opportunities for working individually and in small groups in their classes. As they progress into middle school, they should assume increasing responsibility for making important decisions about their own education and other matters. The high school must provide them opportunities to share decision making and planning with other students and with adults as a means of preparing them for their adult familial and citizenship roles. Students need wise guidance throughout this developmental progression.

Evaluating Student Learning and Educational Programs

The individual student's progress toward attaining his/her course objectives, the student's instructional program in each course, the student's total educational program, and the school's total educational program are evaluated systematically; and the results of the evaluation are used to improve the educative processes of the school.

Teachers use a variety of measurement tools and devices to assess their students' achievements. Rarely, however, has the student's *total* educational program for a semester, a year, or for an entire level of schooling, such as the senior high school, been evaluated. One of the problems here is that the criteria have not been identified by which to evaluate the student's performances in various courses and other activities. Whether a student attains course objectives is not a sufficient criterion; the appropriateness of the program objectives and the instructional materials and activities for the student also must be evaluated.

In recent years many designs have been formulated for evaluating educational programs for groups of students, particularly programs that are federally funded. Generally, the designs call for evaluation directly related to the program objectives. Although designs are available and federally funded programs are evaluated, local schools rarely take the initiative for evaluating their own programs. Yet, annual evaluation by the staff of the local school is essential for guiding its own improvement efforts. Gathering and using evaluation information wisely provides the basis for setting realistic goals for individual students and for groups of students and then planning and carrying out related improvement activities to achieve the goals. This is the third improvement strategy built into the design.

Administrative Arrangements

The school's administrative arrangements provide for cooperative planning and shared decision making by the persons responsible for implementing the plans and decisions that are made, mainly administrators, counselors, teachers, and students.

Decision-making groups that include administrators, teachers, counselors, and, in some instances, students and parents are formed to enable persons to participate in formulating the programs and plans that they are responsible for carrying out. Areas of shared decision making include aims and philosophy, curriculum, instruction including its evaluation aspects, and student advisory arrangements. The primary outcome of these administrative arrangements is that students, teachers, and counselors work enthusiastically to implement programs and plans that they help formulate. Other outcomes include favorable student attitudes, community involvement and support, high staff morale, and high work satisfaction.

Organization for Instruction and Student Advising

The faculty and students are organized into groups so that an effective educational program is arranged for the individual student each semester and advising is personalized.

Organizing students and teachers into smaller units makes it possible to provide an excellent individual educational program for each student and to personalize and humanize the instructional and advising processes. A team of teachers having the same students for a considerable period of time during the day permits much flexibility in using time, materials, and space to arrange the best possible instruction for the students in the subject or subjects taught by the team of teachers. When each teacher of the academic team also serves as an advisor to some of the students, the teacher advisor is aware of the progress and problems that the advisees are experiencing in the classes of all the team members. Furthermore, close and continuing contact is established between the advisor and the parents of the advisee.

Teaming for instruction in the academic subjects and team members serving formally or informally as student advisors is widely practiced in Grades 6 through 9. However, the number of elective courses from Grade 9 onward increases. This makes it difficult after Grade 9 to organize academic teams of four or five teachers that offer all the instruction in the academic subject fields to a group of 100-120 students. In turn, an organization for advising is called for while maintaining a non-team approach to instruction. Accordingly, interdisciplinary advisory groups are formed for each high school grade or across grades. Interdisciplinary advising greatly facilitates implementation of the three improvement strategies.

Home-School-Community Relations

Effective communication and cooperative educational efforts between the school and the community are carried out as part of a program of home-school-community relations.

We are all aware of the rapidly changing conditions in our neighborhoods and in family living. In general it may be more difficult now than before to initiate and maintain communication and other desired relationships with the local community, but it is imperative to do so. As one example, high quality career education is impossible for many students except as they participate in community activities.

The traditional family where father, mother, and one to four children live in the same home may no longer be the prevalent family unit. New patterns in family and home life will probably continue to emerge, and the school will be called upon to provide more effective communication and interaction between the parents of students and their teachers. Regardless of changing family life, parents should participate at least once each semester in educational planning with the student and the student's advisor. In a corollary fashion, the advisor should be able to meet at other times with parents who wish to discuss the education of their child.

Internal and External Support Arrangements

The environment for learning and instruction in the school and for work and other educative experiences in the community is enriched through the intellectual, technical, and material support provided by school and school district groups, and by external agencies, such as the state education agency, intermediate agencies, teacher-education institutions, and professional associations.

Administrative and organizational arrangements in the school and school district as indicated earlier in comprehensive Objectives 6 and 7 are necessary for creating a desirable learning environment throughout the school. These arrangements require support by the principal in arranging class schedules and work loads of groups of teachers so that they can meet together at regularly scheduled times during their working hours. Adequate spaces must be found for their meetings. Counselors, too, can aid teachers in serving as educational advisors to students. Many other kinds of support in terms of providing assistance to teachers are required of the principal.

The role of the district office, the state education agency, teacher-education institutions, and professional education associations require reappraisal with respect to how they can contribute to an excellent learning and teaching environment in the schools. The educational talent exists in our schools and educational agencies for creating and maintaining good secondary schools. The working relationships between local schools and the external agencies need redirection and improvement.

Continuing Research and Development

Student learning and personality development, instruction, advising, administrative arrangements, and other educational processes become better understood and are improved through continuous research and development conducted by school personnel and cooperating individuals and agencies.

One problem associated with educational research today is that many researchers use the students and the school faculty as objects of theoretical research rather than conducting cooperative research with the schools to identify and help solve critical problems that the schools are experiencing. A related unresolved problem is for researchers to get potentially useful results of educational research into forms that students and teachers can use. These continuing problems suggest that any major renewal and improvement effort will require the local school staff to develop a capability for carrying out its own research and also to participate in cooperative problem-solving research with external agencies that are interested in identifying and solving current problems of the local schools.

RELATIONSHIP TO SCHOOL EFFECTIVENESS

Lipham (1981) and Lipham and Rankin (1982) reviewed the research pertaining to leadership, shared decision making, and change processes. They arrived at a number of conclusions regarding school effectiveness that are reported in later chapters of this book.

Edmonds (1982), drawing on his own studies (Edmonds, 1979) and those of Brookover and Lezotte (1979) and Rutter, Maughan, Mortimore, and Ouston, with Smith (1979), identified five major characteristics of effective schools. The characteristics are as follows:

The principal's leadership and attention to the quality of instruction.

A pervasive and broadly understood instructional focus.

An orderly, safe climate conducive to teaching and learning.

Teacher behaviors that convey the expectation that all students are expected to obtain at least minimum mastery.

The use of measures of pupil achievement as the basis for program evaluation.

Edmonds indicated that research has not determined which one of these characteristics is more or less the cause of schools being effective. Therefore, a school should implement all of them concurrently.

Purkey and Smith (1982) also synthesized theory and research regarding school effectiveness. Their conclusions combined with those of Edmonds regarding effective schools may be summarized as follows. In all effective schools there are high expectations for student achievement on the part of school staff members, and there is strong instructional leadership on the part of the school principal or another staff member. A large number of effective schools have six other features: well-defined school goals, staff development on a schoolwide basis, control by the staff over instructional and staff development decisions, a sense of order, a system for monitoring student progress, and good discipline. Purkey and Smith also indicate that most successful change results from collaborative efforts that involve schoolwide reforms, the participation of staff members on all levels, and a focus on the overall culture of the individual school.

All of the preceding conclusions regarding effective schools are compatible with the present design for the renewal and improvement of secondary education. There are, however, two important differences between the preceding conclusions and the design. One is that the design is a process approach to improvement rather than a set of indicators of effective schools. The design when implemented provides a means for a school to become increasingly effective in attaining its improvement goals rather than describing what an effective school is. The second difference is that the improvement strategies of the design, as well as the facilitative school organizational structures, have been validated through research in secondary schools conducted over a period of four years. Most of the school effectiveness research has been conducted in elementary schools and is generally not carried out for more than a year.

References

Brookover, W. G., & Lezotte, L. W. *Changes in school characteristics co-incident with changes in student achievement.* East Lansing, MI: Institute for Research on Teaching, College of Education, Michigan State University, 1979.

Brown, B. F., et al. *The reform of secondary education.* New York: McGraw-Hill, 1973.

Coleman, J. S., et al. *Youth: Transition to adulthood* (Report of the Panel on Youth of the President's Science Advisory Committee). Chicago: The University of Chicago Press, 1974.

Edmonds, R. R. Some schools work and more can. *Social Policy*, 1979, *9*, 28-32.

Edmonds, R. R. Programs of school improvement: An overview. *Educational Leadership*, 1982, *40*(3), 4-11.

Gibbons, M. *The new secondary education.* Bloomington, IN: Phi Delta Kappa, 1976.

Hostrop, R. W. (Ed.). *Education . . . beyond tomorrow.* Homewood, IL: ETC Publications, 1975.

Klausmeier, H. J. Continuity in learning: Long-range effects. In K. H. Hansen (Ed.), *Learning: An overview & update* (A report of the Chief State School Officers 1976 Summer Institute). Washington, D.C.: U.S. Office of Education, 1976.

Klausmeier, H. J., & Allen, P. S. *Cognitive development of children and youth: A longitudinal study.* New York: Academic Press, 1978.

Klausmeier, H. J., & Associates. *Cognitive learning and development: Information-processing and Piagetian perspectives.* Cambridge, MA: Ballinger, 1979.

Klausmeier, H. J., Serlin, R. C., & Zindler, M. C. *Improvement of secondary education through research: Five longitudinal case studies* (Program Report No. 83-12). Madison: Wisconsin Center for Education Research, 1983.

Klausmeier, T. W. *Desirability and implementation of IGE/secondary schooling: Middle and junior high schools* (Technical Report No. 461). Madison: Wisconsin Center for Education Research, 1978.

Lipham, J. M. *Effective principal, effective school.* Reston, VA: National Association of Secondary School Principals, 1981.

Lipham, J. M., & Rankin, R. E. *Change, leadership, and decision making in improving secondary schools.* Madison: Wisconsin Center for Education Research, 1982.

Maier, M. J. *Desirability and implementation of IGE/secondary schooling in selected innovative high schools* (Technical Report No. 493). Madison: Wisconsin Center for Education Research, 1978.

Martin, J. H., et al. *The education of adolescents* (The final report and recommendations of the National Panel on High School and Adolescent Education). Washington, D.C.: U. S. Government Printing Office, 1976.

Mize, G. K., & Klausmeier, H. J. *Factors contributing to rapid and slow cognitive development among elementary and high school children* (Working Paper No. 201). Madison: Wisconsin Center for Education Research, 1977.

National Commission on Excellence in Education. A nation at risk: The imperative for educational reform. *The Chronicle of Higher Education*, 1983, *26*(10), 11-16.

Newcomer, L. B., et al. *The RISE Report* (Report of the California Commission for reform of intermediate and secondary education). Sacramento: California State Department of Education, 1975.

Purkey, S. C., & Smith, M. S. Too soon to cheer? Synthesis of research on effective schools. *Educational Leadership*, 1982, *40*(3), 64-69.

Rutter, M., Maughan, B., Mortimore, P., Ouston, J., with Smith, A. *Fifteen thousand hours: Secondary schools and their effects on children*. Cambridge, MA: Harvard University Press, 1979.

Shane, H. G. *The educational significance of the future*. Bloomington, IN: Phi Delta Kappa, 1973.

Shane, H. G. *Curriculum change toward the 21st century*. Washington, D.C.: National Education Association, 1977.

Thomson, S. D. *Secondary schools in a changing society: This we believe* (A statement on secondary education prepared by the Task Force on Secondary Schools in a Changing Society). Washington, D.C.: The National Association of Secondary School Principals, 1975.

Toffler, A. (Ed.). *Learning for tomorrow: The role of the future in education*. New York: Vintage Books, 1974.

Van Til, W. (Ed.). *Issues in secondary education* (75th Yearbook, Part II, National Society for the Study of Education). Chicago: University of Chicago Press, 1976.

Suggestions for Further Reading

Cremin, L. A. *Traditions of American education*. New York: Basic Books, 1977.

Cremin presents a short account of the main trends in American education from 1607 through 1976. He provides a good perspective for interpreting the design for the renewal and improvement of secondary education as well as other proposals.

Edmonds, R. R. Programs of school improvement: An overview. *Educational Leadership*, 1982, *40*(3), 4-11.
Edmonds describes local-, district-, and state-administered school effectiveness programs. Unfortunately, the outcomes of the programs were not available at the time he wrote the article. (The entire issue is devoted to school effectiveness and includes the article by Purkey and Smith cited in the chapter.)

Fenstermacher, G. D., & Goodlad, J. I. (Eds.). *Individual differences and the common curriculum* (Eighty-second yearbook of the National Society for the Study of Education. Part I). Chicago: University of Chicago Press, 1983.
Four authors delineate areas in which students differ. Five other authors outline a common curriculum in mathematics, natural science, language and literature, aesthetics and the fine arts, and social studies and indicate means of providing for the differences.

Goodlad, J. I. A study of schooling: Some implications for improvement. *Phi Delta Kappan*, 1983, *64*(8), 552-558.
Goodlad sets forth a set of recommendations based on his extensive study of American schools. In general, the recommendations are compatible with the improvement strategies and organizational structures incorporated in the present design.

Hodgkinson, H. L. What's STILL right with education. *Phi Delta Kappan*, 1982, *64*(4), 231-235.
Hodgkinson points to a vast amount of information that indicates that our educational system is regarded as one of our strongest American institutions. He finds much support for the following conclusion:

> The U.S. public education system is a remarkably successful institution. It is designed for every student, and yet its very best students are as good as those of any nation in the world. It provides a high return on dollars invested. The future of America depends on investment in human resources. American public schools are obviously the best place to find the highest return on that investment. (p. 235)

James, T., & Tyack, D.   Learning from past efforts to reform the high school. *Phi Delta Kappan*, 1983, *64*(6), 400-406.
These authors survey the effects of reform movements, starting in 1893 with the Committee of Ten and concluding with those that started in the 1960s and extended through mid-1970s to assure equal educational opportunity for all students.

Kirst, M. W.   How to improve schools without spending more money. *Phi Delta Kappan*, 1982, *64*(1), 6-8.
This article shows how organizational structures can be changed to improve education without increasing the costs of schooling.

Klausmeier, H. J., & Allen, P. S.   *Cognitive development of children and youth: A longitudinal study*. New York: Academic Press, 1978.
This is a report of a longitudinal study carried out for four years with students, kindergarten through Grade 12. We found that some Grade 12 students were performing cognitively at the same level as elementary school children and that their cognitive and educational growth stopped at Grade 9. School and home conditions contributing to rapid and slow cognitive development are identified.

Klausmeier, H. J., Serlin, R. C., & Zindler, M. C.   *Improvement of secondary education through research: Five longitudinal case studies* (Program Report No. 83-12). Madison: Wisconsin Center for Education Research, 1983.
This monograph is the final report of the cooperative research conducted over a period of four years with five cooperating secondary schools. Detailed information is presented regarding the implementation of the improvement strategies and making operational the facilitative organizational structures of the design for the renewal and improvement of secondary education. The effects of each school's improvement activities on student outcomes are described and documented.

Lieberman, A., & McLaughlin, M. W. (Eds.). *Policy making in education* (Eighty-first yearbook of the National Society for the Study of Education. Part I). Chicago: University of Chicago Press, 1982.
Various aspects of policy making are discussed in each of 10 chapters. Lieberman has a particularly insightful discussion regarding the tensions involved in actually bringing about improvement in a school.

Minton, H. L., & Schneider, F. W. *Differential psychology.* Monterey, CA: Brooks/Cole, 1980.
Differences among individuals in intelligence, achievement, special aptitudes, and personality are discussed. Sex, age, social class, and racial differences are also indicated.

Rowan, B., Bossert, S. T., & Dwyer, D. C. Research on effective schools: A cautionary note. *Educational Researcher*, 1983, *12*(4), 24-31.
The authors point to the deficiencies of most of the research on effective schools, including the measures of effectiveness used, the research designs employed, and the fact that only global, rather than analytic, comparisons are made between effective and ineffective schools. (This issue of this journal is devoted entirely to effective schooling and has two other good articles.)

Willerman, L. *The psychology of individual and group differences.* San Francisco: W. H. Freeman, 1979.
This book reports the major areas of differences among individuals, including intelligence, achievement, special aptitudes, and personality. Sex, age, and racial differences are also discussed. There are separate chapters on handicapping conditions and on intellectual superiority.

PART II: INSTRUCTION, CURRICULUM, AND EVALUATION

EDUCATIONAL PROGRAMMING FOR THE INDIVIDUAL STUDENT

Herbert J. Klausmeier

Students of the same chronological age vary greatly in their achievement of the knowledge and skills of any subject field. The variability among the students tends to increase with each successive year of schooling. Students also differ with respect to their career goals. Some students of middle school age have quite clearly defined goals, while many high school seniors are undecided about what to do upon graduation. Because of these and other differences among students, there is general acceptance of the idea that education should be tailored to meet the needs of the individual student. At the same time, we recognize that the student should also meet district and state requirements since these requirements reflect societal needs and demands. Although the goal of meeting individual student and societal needs is widely accepted, it has not yet been attained well in many secondary schools. Individual *educational* programming and individual *instructional* programming are two closely related strategies that are designed to help local schools address this problem.

The individual *educational* programming strategy involves arranging an appropriate educational program of courses and other activities for each student each semester. Implementing the individual educational programming strategy throughout a school provides an alternative to the three-track system of secondary schooling and the accompanying lack of a personalized approach to the educative process. It also provides an alternative to permitting students to elect only easy courses and by other means to avoid learning essential knowledge and skills.

Individual *instructional* programming involves arranging an appropriate instructional program for the student in each course in which the student is enrolled. Implementing the individual instructional programming strategy is an alternative to employing all whole-class group instruction, all small-group instruction, or all individualized instruction. None of these modes of instruction meet the learning needs of all the students enrolled in a course, particularly a course that is required of all students. Chapter 3 describes individual *instructional* programming, although some attention is given to it in this chapter because of its close relationship to individual *educational* programming. The desirable effects of individual *educational* programming and individual instructional programming are presented in Chapter 13.

Study of this chapter will enable you to understand the comprehensive and enabling objectives of Component 1 of the improvement design that deal with *educational* programming for the individual student.

Comprehensive Objective:

An individual educational program of course work and other activities is arranged for each student each semester that satisfies the student's developmental needs and characteristics and that also meets district and state requirements.

Illustrative Enabling Objectives:

Each student's individual educational program which includes all courses and other activities:

Is planned each semester or year by the student and the student's advisor.

Takes into account the student's aptitudes for learning different subject matters, interests, motivation, learning styles, career goals, and other personal and social characteristics.

Provides for experiential learning, including work experience in the community, for students who will benefit from it.

Is monitored cooperatively by the student and the student's advisor throughout the semester.

Is changed as necessary during the semester to assure high quality education for the student.

NEED FOR INDIVIDUAL EDUCATIONAL PROGRAMMING

The problem of adapting education to meet individual student needs while at the same time meeting societal demands is not of recent origin. Secondary education during the 1930s was experiencing this problem as is indicated in the report of the "Eight-year Study" (Aiken, 1942). One major difficulty was that students feared that they would not be admitted to college if they did not follow the pattern of subjects prescribed by the colleges. Another was that only half of the students who entered high school graduated and of those who did graduate only one of three went to college. Students were not being prepared adequately for the responsibilities of community life. Other conclusions of the study were that the high school seldom challenged the students of high ability to work up to the level of their intellectual powers. In general, the schools failed to create the conditions necessary for effective learning by most of the students. Furthermore, the school staffs neither knew their students well nor guided them wisely. Large school plants had been built and high school enrollment had increased dramatically, but the three-track curriculum and the pattern of undifferentiated group instruction did not work well for many students.

Scholars and researchers of the 1970s also identified several educational problems and generated many reform proposals. For example, the President's Science Advisory Committee (Coleman et al., 1974) grappled with the issue of how to group students for instruction as a means of promoting more effective education for the individual student. The Committee considered physical maturation, mental ability, social level, and chronological age and indicated that grouping students homogeneously on the basis of any one characteristic resulted in great variability among the students on the other three. The conclusion was that, regardless of the grouping basis that may be employed, no one identical set of instructional activities and materials will meet the needs of all the students enrolled in a course.

The National Panel on High School and Adolescent Education (Martin et al., 1976) found that the three-track system dominates grouping practices in secondary education. According to the Panel:

The typical comprehensive high school provides three streams, or tracks, which are major divisions of the curriculum—the academic track, the vocational track, and the general track. Although moving from one track to another is possible, it rarely happens. The tracks themselves often function as dead end options. Thus, even in the schools which have "real" programs in all three tracks, one finds a separation of students, a "three-track culture" in the school. (p. 27)

The Panel concluded that students are given unequal opportunities to develop their potential. The school environment exacerbates the differences among students from different socioeconomic, racial, and ethnic backgrounds. Big schools with large enrollments tend to be inhumane, bureaucratic, and unsuited to recognizing and meeting the needs of the individual student. The near 50 percent of the students in the general track are prepared neither for college nor for job entry.

The California Commission for the Reform of Intermediate and Secondary Education (Newcomer, et al., 1975) indicated that staff responsibilities should be redefined so as to promote personalized education for all learners. The following recommendation indicates the strategy to be employed:

The strengths and weaknesses of each learner should be assessed by means of a systematic process that includes teacher observations, testing, and other evaluative procedures. Each learner should then be able to choose and pursue an instructional program consistent with the findings of the assessment and the learner's choices. (p. 8)

Goodlad (1983) indicates three aspects of individuality in particular that call for attention, including (a) differences among students in rate of learning, (b) styles of learning, and (c) interests, goals, and life styles. He suggests that each school should have a good program of general education for all students in the areas of literature and language, including English, mathematics and science, society and social studies, the arts, the vocations, and physical education and health. Moreover, within each of these areas the school must provide for all three kinds of differences if in fact each student is to receive a good general education.

Because we have been unable to provide well for individuality, special education programs are developed periodically for particular groups of students, for example, the gifted, talented, and creative and those with handicapping conditions. In regard to the gifted, Reis and Renzulli (1982) make a strong plea for schools to adopt less restrictive identification criteria so that fewer gifted students will be eliminated from special programs for the gifted. My own research (Klausmeier & Allen, 1978) suggests that practically every child has a gift. Moreover, the individual educational programming strategy can be applied not only to the student with a clearly identified gift and to those with handicapping conditions but to every student.

Public Law 94-192

The need for individual educational programming is recognized in Public Law 94-142, The Education for All Handicapped Children Act of 1975. This law specifically states that a free and appropriate public education must be extended to every handicapped child and that this education must be at no cost to the child's parents or guardians. Moreover, it specifies that individual educational planning must be implemented.

The law requires each local education agency to develop an individual educational plan for each handicapped child. This plan is to be developed in a meeting that includes an expert in special education, the teacher or teachers of the child, the parents or guardian, and, whenever appropriate, the child. Essentially, the individual educational plan is a contract between the school, the child, and the child's parents or guardians. The law requires that the individual educational plan be written.

The written plan must indicate the child's present level of performance, the annual goals and the short range instructional objectives, the educational services that the school will provide to ensure that the goals and objectives are met, the extent to which the child will be able to participate in the school's regular educational program, and the objective criteria and evaluation procedures which are to be used in determining the effectiveness of the child's program. The individual education plan must include an annual evaluation schedule to determine whether the instructional objectives are being achieved.

Part of the individual educational plan of a middle school student with a learning disability follows. When this plan was developed, the student had a grade equivalent of 1.5 in word recognition, 1.5 in spelling, and 3.9 in mathematics. The first part of the plan consists of the long range goals, in this case for a school year, that were developed and recommended by a multidisciplinary team of teachers. This team included a special teacher of students with learning disabilities. The goals are for reading, handwriting, spelling, and written expression, the areas judged to be related to the disability. The second part of the plan, objectives and methods, gives more explicit objectives related to these four areas and indicates the materials and activities that will be used to aid the student to achieve the objectives.

Individual Educational Plan of a Student with a Learning Disability

Annual Long Range Goals:

> The child will be able to read and comprehend materials on a 3.0 grade level.
>
> The child will improve his handwriting.
>
> The child will be able to spell words from a given level 3.0 word list.
>
> The child will be able to improve his written expression skills.

Two points are in order regarding individual educational programming for children with handicapping learning conditions. The first is that many persons are involved in both planning the child's program and monitoring the child's progress. Accordingly, a great deal of personnel time is involved, including the teachers in whose classes the child is mainstreamed. The second concern is that the performance objectives are highly detailed and specific. Similarly, the instructional materials and methods and the evaluation procedures are highly prescriptive. In general, there is insufficient flexibility to adjust to desired improvement by the child and to changing conditions in the home or school. Needless to say, individual educational programming with normally developing (and gifted) secondary school students is designed to avoid these problems.

ARRANGING INDIVIDUAL EDUCATIONAL PROGRAMS OF NORMALLY DEVELOPING AND GIFTED STUDENTS

The individual educational programming strategy for normally developing students involves assessing the student's educational needs, planning a program of courses and other educational activities with the student and the student's parents, monitoring the student's progress, and evaluating the student's attainment of goals. Also, after the student has completed a program, it is to be evaluated in terms of its appropriateness and value to the student. As indicated earlier, the planning process and the characteristics of the plan and the program are very different from those employed with students having a learning handicap. However, involving the student and the parents in planning the program and later in evaluating it is a most critical aspect of the strategy.

Developing the Plan

Developing an educational plan for a student who does not have exceptional educational needs is typically carried out in conferences involving the student and either a counselor or a teacher advisor. It is desirable for the parent to participate in the planning process. However, specialized personnel are rarely involved.

The nature of the planning process will become more clear by examining the steps for developing a student's educational plan. The application of the steps necessarily varies for middle schools and high schools.

1. The advisor analyzes information about the student's educational history and the cognitive, affective, and psychomotor characteristics that will be useful in developing the student's educational plan. Much of this information is supplied by a counselor or other school person on a planning form that is used by the advisor. Additional information is gained in the first planning conference with the student. Figure 2.1 lists information that is helpful in planning an individual educational program with the student. The information in Items 1, 3, 4, 5, and 10 should be provided on a form used when planning the program with the student.

Figure 2.1   Student Characteristics for Developing a Student's Educational Plan

1. Identifying Characteristics: age, sex, physical characteristics and appearance, health status, any disability or other condition that would affect the student's educational program, any unusually high ability, talent, etc. that would affect the student's program, main strengths of student (personal, social, academic).

2. Family Situation (optional): number of siblings, occupation of parent(s), marital status of parents, number of conferences or other school activities parent(s) typically participate in during a year.

3. Most Recent Mental Ability or Aptitude Test Score(s).

4. Most Recent Standardized Educational Achievement Test Scores.

5. Achievement During Prior Semester or Year: Courses taken and grades earned (or other indicators of achievement), co-curricular activities of prior semester, work experience for pay during prior semester, experiential learning in community under supervision of school during prior semester, school attendance, and tardiness.

6. Self-concept: ____Very strong, ____strong, ____weak, ____very weak.

7. Attitudes:

   Toward peers: ____Very favorable, ____favorable, ____unfavorable, ____very unfavorable.

   Toward teachers: ____Very favorable, ____favorable, ____unfavorable, ____very unfavorable.

   Toward classes: ____Very favorable, ____favorable, ____unfavorable, ____very unfavorable.

   Toward non-academic aspects of going to school: ____Very favorable, ____favorable, ____unfavorable, ____very unfavorable.

8. Motivational Characteristics:

   For academic Subjects: ____Very high, ____high, ____average, ____low, ____ very low.

   For extracurricular and other noncredit activities: ____Very high, ____high, ____average, ____low, ____very low.

   ____Ascribes own successes and failures to own ability and effort.

   ____Ascribes own successes and failures to luck, chance, or other external conditions.

9. Subject Interests, General Interests, Hobbies.

10. Career Interest(s) and/or Career Field and the Option Selected such as College Preparatory, Technical, Job Entry.

11. Profile of Learning Styles (See Figure 3.1 in Chapter 3 for a listing of learning styles).

2. The advisor makes sure that he or she understands the local school and school district requirements. These are often prepared by a counselor. In some schools the requirements are placed in a guide for advisors; in others they are part of the planning form.

3. The advisor meets with his or her advisor group to acquaint them with school requirements and with possible electives and extracurricular activities for the ensuing semester or year. The teacher advisor may administer a checklist or a questionnaire to secure information from the students regarding their interests, learning styles, or other characteristics.

4. The advisor meets in a conference with the student and the student's parents. In this conference the plan for the ensuing semester or year is prepared. This plan includes each course and other educational activity, one or more goals for each course, and other information indicated in (1). The student, the parents, and the advisor get a copy of the student's educational plan. This plan is used by the student and the advisor in monitoring the student's progress. The plan should also be accessible to each teacher who has the student in a class.

Hood River Valley High School of Hood River, Oregon, has developed a form to be used in planning the student's courses for all high school grades, starting with Grade 9. In Grade 9, a counselor, the student, and the parents meet in a conference in which the student tentatively makes a career choice. The planning form includes a list of the courses and also the units of courses that the student plans to take in each grade, 9 through 12, a list of extracurricular activities that the student plans to participate in each year; and a place for indicating post-high school planning. Other information provided to aid the student and the advisor includes a list of the competency requirements and other requirements for graduation, the required and elective courses related to different career choices, and an outline of an honors program. Provisions are made for changes in the plan during Grade 10 and each year thereafter.

Monitoring Student Progress

In the typical secondary school today, no one staff member monitors the progress of the student in all of his or her courses and other activities. Students are assigned grades in each course by the different teachers, none of whom typically is aware of how the student is progressing in the other courses. Sometimes a guidance counselor or assistant principal examines the report card and, if time is available, confers with the student who has failing grades, is tardy or absent often, or who misbehaves seriously. Eliminating this kind of practice is a central purpose of monitoring student progress. The monitoring process is based on the student's educational plan for the semester and information regarding the student's progress related to the plan. The monitoring typically is conducted in conferences by the advisor and the student.

Holding a conference at the end of each grading period is an appropriate timing arrangement. The conference may be very short with students who are achieving up to expectancy, and it serves mainly to reinforce the student's effort and accomplishments. More attention is required for the student who is achieving below expectancy in any course. With this student the central purpose is to identify the cause of the low achievement and to find means of remedying it. In many cases this can be accomplished without calling in the student's teachers, other school personnel, or the parents. How to proceed with the more difficult cases depends upon the particular case as well as the policies and practices of the school.

Figure 2.2 is the individual educational plan of a Grade 10 student of Cedarburg High School, Cedarburg, Wisconsin. The courses and extracurricular activities were selected in March of Grade 9 and the goals were set early after school opened in Grade 10. The goals that are included in the plan provide information for monitoring the student's progress at the end of each grading period. The school reports grades four times per semester.

We should be aware that goals may be stated in terms other than those indicated in Figure 2.2. For example, the student may indicate the percentage of minimum competency objectives that will be mastered, the typing speed that will be achieved, the number of themes that will be written, the kind of painting that will be produced, the science experiments that will be undertaken, and many others.

To be able to generate goals, the student must know what the possible goals are in each course.

Figure 2.2   Educational Plan of a Grade 10 Student

Student's Name: _____

Standardized Test Results:

English	99 percentile	Reading	97 percentile
Mathematics	99 percentile	Science	98 percentile
Mental Ability	97 percentile	Social Studies	93 percentile

Grade 9 GPA: 3.8

Career goal: Scientist

Motivation: High, self-starter, persistent.

Attitudes: Favorable toward learning and school.

Self-concept: Positive regarding academic, peers, home.

Learning styles: Analytic and reflective rather than global and impulsive. Convergent rather than divergent thinking. No preference for individual, pair, or small-group work. No preference for a sensory modality.

Courses:

Advanced Literature: Writing
      Goal: Complete 5 units for .5 credits; make an A.

Chemistry
      Goal: Complete 6 units for .6 credits; make an A.

Advanced Algebra
      Goal: Complete 6 units for .6 credits; make an A.

Social Studies
      Goal: Complete 5 units for .5 credits; make an A.

Intermediate German
      Goal: Complete 5 units for .5 credits; make an A.

Wind Ensemble
      Goal: Complete course for .5 credits; make an A.

Physical Education
      Goal: Complete course for .25 credits; make an A.

Extracurricular Activities
      German club   Student government
      Jazz ensemble   Wrestling

Program Approved by:

Student _____   Date _____
Parents _____   Date _____

Advisor _____   Date _____

Program Changes: Approved by:

_____ Date _____   Student _____
_____ Date _____   Advisor _____

Evaluating the Completed Program

One purpose of evaluating the student's completed program is to ascertain the extent to which the goals were attained. Another is to determine how appropriate and how worthwhile the course activities and other learning experiences were for the student. This information is useful in planning subsequent programs with the student. Procedures and instruments to be used in evaluating student's individual educational programs are described in Chapter 7.

At Steuben Middle School of Milwaukee, Wisconsin, the Grade 8 students take English, reading, mathematics, social studies, either an exploring course or computer-assisted instruction, physical education, and an allied arts course daily. The classes meet for 48 minutes per day, five days per week. To clarify what is meant by evaluating the appropriateness of an educational program in terms of its taking into account the learning characteristics of the student we shall examine the characteristics of two students and the programs that they completed in English, mathematics, and exploring or computer-assisted instruction. For each course, information is provided regarding the content studied, the kinds of instructional materials used, and the proportion of class time spent in individual, pair or small group, and whole class activity. (This information describes the instructional program in each of these courses.)

Brad's Characteristics

Brad is in Grade 8 and is 14 years old. His percentile ranks on a recent standardized educational achievement test were 84 in reading, 86 in language, and 99 in mathematics. Brad is motivated by good grades and achieves at an above-average level in all of his classes.

Brad is proud of being a newspaper carrier, is interested in sports, and likes working with various types of electronic equipment. He maintains an awareness of current social, political, and economic problems. Brad plans to go to college after high school graduation but is uncertain about any particular career.

Related to learning styles, Brad can ignore most noises in the classrooms or labs when studying, prefers dim or shaded light, prefers to feel cool rather than warm, and studies best at a desk or sitting on a hard chair. He regards his classes as interesting and important. Brad finishes nearly all the things that he starts, thinks that it is important to do things as well as he can, and prefers classes where he selects most of the materials and activities and there are few directions. He learns best alone and likes to learn in several different ways rather than by any single method. Brad likes something to eat or drink when he studies, and he studies best in the afternoon. He likes to sit in the same place through most of the class period and likes to do things the way most other people do them.

Lucy's Characteristics

Lucy is 13 years old and is in Grade 8. On a standardized educational achievement test, she scored at the 34th percentile in reading, the 30th in language, and the 30th in mathematics. She has a moderately low level of conceptual development and low motivation to achieve in her academic subjects, but her motivation and achievement are high in both artistic and physical endeavors.

Lucy expresses her attitudes and opinions regarding films, clothing materials, and styles in a sophisticated, mature way. Her primary interests as shown during the school day, in after-school activities, and outside of school are in artistic, gymnastic, and modern dance activities.

Lucy cannot study in a noisy environment. She prefers bright light for studying, warmth rather than coolness, and she studies best lounging in an informal arrangement. She regards academic classes as not very interesting or important but feels that art and physical education are great. Lucy voluntarily finishes only the things in which she is interested, thinks it is all right to do just enough to get by, and prefers classes where she is told exactly what to do. She learns academic subject matter best with a friend or two and prefers to learn visually, tactually, and kinesthetically. She likes something to nibble on when studying. She studies best in the morning and prefers to move around during the class period. Lucy prefers to do things her own way.

Brad's Program in English

Content Studied:

> Composition: Emphasis on the development of thesis statements in composition.
> Literature: Study of the novel for plot, theme, and character development.
> Spelling improvement.
> Creative dramatics: Write and produce an original play with a small group.

Instructional Mode Proportions (to nearest one-tenth in each instructional mode): individual .6, pair or small group .2, whole class .2.

Instructional Materials Usage (to nearest one-tenth): books .8, newspapers and magazines, .1, films and filmstrips .1.

Alternative Activities in English:

> Brad was assigned to the language arts/reading lab for 3 weeks instead of this English class. In the lab, he studied Greek and Roman nature myths with an emphasis on vocabulary, comprehension skills, and composition skills. The instructional modes were .4 individual, .3 pair or small group, and whole class .3. The use of instructional materials was books .4, films and filmstrips .2, records and cassettes .2, and teacher-prepared materials .2.

Lucy's Program in English

Content Studied:

> Composition: Emphasis on development of basic sentence patterns and paragraph format.
> Literature: Using mainly short stories, learn how characters are developed by the author.
> Spelling improvement.
> Creative dramatics: Write and produce an original short play with a small group of students.

Instructional Mode Proportions: individual .1, pair or small group .7, whole class .2.

Instructional Materials Usage: books .5, newspapers and magazines .5.

Alternative Activities: None.

Brad's Program in Mathematics

Content Studied:

Brad worked independently in two commercial math programs titled *Key to Algebra* and *Key to Geometry*. In algebra, he completed basic concepts through the factoring of polynomials. In geometry, he worked on definition of geometric shapes and procedures for construction of each shape.

Instructional Mode Proportions: Individual .8, whole class .2.

Instructional Materials Usage: books 1.0.

Alternative Mathematics Activities:

Brad attended the math lab one day during each of the three six-week periods to participate in enrichment activities relating to algebra and geometry. In addition to this lab and the regular class, Brad worked independently in math. On the locally-developed math competency test administered in September, Brad scored 91%. A conference with the math lab teacher determined that the missed problems resulted mainly from calculation errors, not from a lack of concept understanding. The outcome of the conferences with the math lab teacher and unit math teacher was that Brad took programmed algebra and geometry courses which are used only by the highest level math students.

Lucy's Program in Mathematics

Content Studied:

Measurement: Use of rule to nearest 1/16 inch.
Review of four basic mathematic functions with whole numbers.
Introduction to four basic functions using integers.
Use of tables in mathematics to solve problems.
Introduction to comparing, reducing, and factoring fractions.

Instructional Mode Proportions: individual .5, pair or small group .3, whole class .2.

Instructional Materials Usage: books .7, learning packages and commercial kits .3.

Alternative Activities: Spent 1 day during each of the three six-week periods in the mathematics lab. Used manipulative materials to reinforce concepts from math class.

Brad's Program in Exploring Course

Content Studied:

Exploring is a 6-week mini-course which the student elects. Each six weeks, the student may take a different course. No grading or evaluation of any kind is done in this class. Brad's 6-week courses were musical theater—study of Broadway musicals, their plot, musical style, and writers; comic books and cartooning— study of techniques of drawing cartoons and development of plots for comic books. He elected to remain in his unit for the other six weeks and help the teachers with a candy sale fund-raising activity.

Instructional Mode proportions: individual .5, whole class .5.

Instructional Materials usage: records and cassettes .4, current materials .6.

Lucy's Program in Computer-Assisted Instruction
(In lieu of exploring course)

Content Studied:

Math, reading, and writing. Lucy worked about 20 minutes with the teacher and spent 10 minutes on the computer on math exercises and 10 minutes on reading.

Instructional Mode Proportions: individual .8, pair or small group .2.

Instructional Materials Usage: books .2, computer terminal, calculator, teacher prepared materials .8.

A question may be raised regarding the difference between individual educational programming in the middle school and in the high school. In the middle school, students have very few elective subjects and few choices of extracurricular activities. However, not all students typically attempt to attain the same objectives of each unit or course. Thus, rapid learners work on enrichment or acceleration objectives while slow learners sometimes need additional time and help to attain the objectives that are required of all students. Accordingly, the plans and programs of the middle school students are differentiated in this manner rather than through election of courses. Arranging for teachers to have time to carry out advising and arranging the schedules of the teacher advisors and advisees for advising purposes is relatively simple if an academic team has its students for a block of time and does most of the advising during the block period. If this is not the case, then these matters must be resolved as for the high school, to be discussed next.

We have seen what goes into the educational plan of the high school student. Teacher advisors typically have five classes in a seven-period day, one period for preparation and one period for other activities. Their work day includes some time before students arrive at school and some time after the students leave. The typical work week at school is about 40 hours. Most teach about 240 minutes per day, about 20 hours per week. The amount of time required to do an excellent job of advising 20 students regarding their educational programs as outlined in this chapter is about 60 hours per semester (three conferences of 50 minutes each), or slightly under four hours per week. The usual procedure is for this advising time to come from the approximately 20 hours per week that the teacher is not teaching. In some schools, teaching schedules and students' programs are arranged so that each advisor can spend a considerable portion of one day every two weeks in advising activities. It is also possible to have only one or two individual conferences with the advisee each semester and a few group sessions. This, of course, reduces the amount of advisor time.

A STATE PROGRAM OF INDIVIDUAL EDUCATIONAL PLANNING

In the previous pages we examined educational programming practices in schools of Oregon and Wisconsin. In these states employment of the individual educational programming strategy is optional, except for students with handicapping learning conditions.

In 1977, the Utah State Board of Education adopted a statewide policy regarding individual educational planning (Robinson, 1982). The policy provides that an individual education plan will be developed cooperatively by each secondary school student, designated school personnel, and parents. The individual educational plan is developed annually in a conference attended by the parents, the teacher or counselor, and the student.

The written plan varies somewhat from school to school, but it generally contains five kinds of information: vital statistics about the student and identification of family members; a list of graduation requirements and competency examinations; tentative career interests and choices of careers at each grade level; class schedules of courses proposed and taken at each grade level; and dates of all individual educational planning interviews and signatures of those present.

The Utah State Office of Education undertook an evaluation of the program in the summer of 1980 (Robinson, 1982). Principals, teachers, students, and parents were surveyed to determine how worthwhile the program had been in their schools.

The principals agreed almost unanimously that it had been effective in improving school/parent relations, in helping to diagnose student strengths and weaknesses, and in making the work of counselors more effective. They were divided about whether or not it had actually brought about changes to meet student needs or encouraged teachers to modify their methods and techniques of teaching.

Seventy percent of the students rated the program as excellent or good. A high percentage stated that the school helped locate the courses and activities they had selected, that the conferences helped them learn more about the school program, and that because of the conferences they felt that the school was interested in them. Eighty-six percent endorsed the program.

About 58% of the parents considered the program excellent or good, and about 40% considered it fair or poor. Two-thirds of the parents thought that the program should be continued but could be made more meaningful.

As of 1982, 31 of the 40 Utah school districts were conducting individual educational planning conferences in Grades 7 through 12, and three districts were conducting the conferences only between the ninth and 12th grades. The teacher serving as the advisor had emerged as the predominant means of planning with the students. This arrangement provided for a workable advisee/advisor ratio and thereby promoted a personal, caring relationship that could be sustained throughout a student's years in school. In small schools the teacher advisor had an average of 12 to 15 students and in larger ones, between 25 and 30.

Robinson (1982) regarded individual educational planning only as good as those who used it. Some resentment persisted among some teachers who viewed the process as an added burden they ought not to bear. Some parents remained either uninterested in planning their children's experiences or simply wished the schools would mind their own business.

Robinson (1982) concluded that individual educational planning had dramatized the fact that the quality of a student's public school education is a shared responsibility of teachers, parents, and students. She concluded that Utahans believe that, to derive the maximum value from the years they spend in school, all students need guidance from their parents as well as school personnel to help them set realistic, appropriate, carefully chosen educational goals.

We should point out that as described in the article the Utah program does not include the monitoring of progress nor evaluation of the student's completed program. Based on this author's observations, much value is lost when this is not done. When an advisor cannot do it for all advisees, monitoring the progress of a high, middle, and low achiever and then annually evaluating the appropriateness and value of these students' completed programs provides very helpful information for improving individual educational programming for all students from year to year.

References

Aikin, W. M. *The story of the eight-year study*. New York: Harper & Row, 1942.

Coleman, J. S., et al. *Youth: Transition to adulthood* (President's Science Advisory Committee). Chicago: University of Chicago Press, 1974.

Goodlad, J. I. Individuality, commonality, and curricular practice. In G. D. Fenstermacher & J. I. Goodlad (Eds.), *Individual differences and the common curriculum* (Eighty-second yearbook of the National Society for the Study of Education. Part I). Chicago: University of Chicago Press, 1983.

Klausmeier, H. J., & Allen P. S. *Cognitive development of children and youth: A longitudinal study.* New York: Academic Press, 1978.

Martin, J. H., et al. *The education of adolescents* (The final report and recommendations of the National Panel on High School and Adolescent Education). Washington, D.C.: U. S. Government Printing Office, 1976.

Newcomer, L. B., et al. *The RISE Report* (Report of the California Commission for reform of intermediate and secondary education). Sacramento: California State Department of Education, 1975.

Reis, S. M., & Renzulli, J. S. A case for a broadened conception of giftedness. *Phi Delta Kappan,* 1982, *63*(9), 619-620.

Robinson, D. The IEP: Meaningful individualized education in Utah. *Phi Delta Kappan,* 1982, *64*(3), 205-206.

Suggestions for Further Reading

Cervone, B. T., & O'Leary, K. A conceptual framework for parent involvement. *Educational Leadership,* 1982, *40*(2), 48-49.
These authors outline a continuum of parental involvement that starts with passively receiving information and extends into participating in decision making regarding their child's individual educational program and also in teaching students.

Goldberg, M. F. What's happening in . . . Shoreham-Wading River High School? *Phi Delta Kappan,* 1982, *64*(2), 132.
This author identifies the following requirements for maintaining innovations in his high school, including individual educational advising of students by teachers: support by the superintendent, support by the administrative team, support by the large majority of the teachers, and a continuing program of staff development.

Goodlad, J. I. Individuality, commonality, and curricular practice. In G. D. Fenstermacher & J. I. Goodlad (Eds.), *Individual differences and the common curriculum* (Eighty-second yearbook of the National Society for the Study of Education. Part I). Chicago: University of Chicago Press, 1983, 300-318.
Goodlad recommends that all high school students should take 18

percent of their total high school program in literature and language (English and other), 18 percent in mathematics and science, 15 percent in each society and social studies, the arts, the vocations, and 10 percent in physical education. To provide for differences in interests and ability, he would permit a variation of up to 20 percent in each area, e.g., 12 to 18 percent in the arts. Other means of providing for individuality include having the faculty and students arranged in small groups and using a variety of instructional activities and materials in the required courses.

CHAPTER 3

INSTRUCTIONAL PROGRAMMING FOR THE INDIVIDUAL STUDENT

Herbert J. Klausmeier

It is well to recall that the term, individual *educational* program, refers to the student's learning experiences in all the courses taken during a semester, as well as non-course experiences. In contrast, individual *instructional* program refers to the student's learning experiences in each course and other educational activity that is included in the student's educational program. Accordingly, a student's completed educational program for a semester or for a longer period of time consists of the student's completed instructional programs along with his or her organization and integration of the various instructional programs. Although there is this close relationship between the completed programs, the processes and persons involved in planning, monitoring, and evaluating a student's complete *educational* program and the student's *instructional* program in each course are very different.

In the preceding chapter, we have examined the individual educational programming strategy. This chapter clarifies the comprehensive and enabling objectives of individual instructional programming that are incorporated in the design for the renewal and improvement of secondary education.

Comprehensive Objective:

An individual instructional program that takes into account the student's aptitudes, interests, motivation, learning styles, career goals, and other personal and social characteristics is arranged for the student in each course and other activity that is part of the student's total educational program.

Illustrative Enabling Objectives:

The instructional program of the student:

Is planned by the student and the teacher of the course at the beginning of the course.

Includes course and unit objectives that are appropriate for the student in terms of the student's aptitude, entering achievement level, and career goals.

Provides an appropriate amount of time in class and during or outside school hours to suit the student's rate of achieving his/her objectives in the course.

Provides for appropriate individual attention by the teacher to take into account the student's motivation and other characteristics.

Provides for an appropriate amount of *teacher-directed* individual, pair, small-group, and large-group activity to take into account the student's need for structure and preferences for mode of instruction.

Provides for an appropriate amount of *student-initiated* individual, pair, small-group, and large-group activity to take into account the student's need for independence and preferences for mode of instruction.

Provides for appropriate use of printed materials, audiovisual materials, and direct experiencing to take into account the student's preferred styles of learning—visual, auditory, tactual, or kinesthetic.

PLANNING AND MONITORING STUDENTS' INSTRUCTIONAL PROGRAMS

The preceding objectives imply that there is no one method of instruction that is equally applicable to all students, all teachers, and all subject fields. For example, neither totally individualized instruction in all subject fields in which each student proceeds through a given course at his or her own rate, nor all teacher- directed group instruction in which all students receive the same information and carry out the same assignments meets the learning needs of all students. Similarly, no two teachers may be equally effective with a given method of instruction. Moreover, no one method of instruction is equally applicable to all subject fields, such as American literature, algebra, art, chemistry, conversational French, history, and personal typing. Clearly, then, the individual instructional programming strategy, though designed to meet the needs of the individual students, is not a form of individualized instruction.

Rothrock (1982) indicated that interest in individualized instruction had peaked by 1975 and that it has declined markedly since. Contributing to the decline was too much instruction guided by individual contracts, computer-assisted instruction, and other forms of individualized instruction based on detailed behavioristic performance objectives. In this regard, Rothrock included Individually Guided Elementary Education, which was developed under my direction, as a form of individualized instruction. This is an unfortunate misinterpretation of Individually Guided Elementary Education (Klausmeier, 1977). The fact is that I conceptualized this form of elementary education as an alternative both to totally individualized instruction and total class-size group instruction. I tried to make this idea clear in the following statement:

> Instruction may be arranged so that students proceed through units of instruction by means of independent study, on a one-to-one basis with a teacher or another student, as members of small groups, as members of large groups, or in a combination of these modes. . . . One-to-one instruction of a child by a teacher as the sole mode is possible only for a limited number of children. The use of large groups with 25 or more students also is limited because children typically cannot work effectively in large groups, and rarely do they need the same identical information from their teachers. Therefore, the use of small groups is common in IGE schools and within the small groups there is some one-to-one instruction by the teachers, peer tutoring, independent study, and subgrouping. The two large categories of small instructional groupings in IGE are learning-station groups and teacher-directed small groups. (p. 66)

The preceding quotation indicates that some but not only class-size group instruction is appropriate at the elementary school level. The instructional programming strategy implies the same conclusion at the secondary level. However, Goodlad (1983) found that teacher-directed group instruction is used almost exclusively in secondary schools today, as it has been for decades. He indicated that this form of instruction does not enable secondary schools to achieve many of the widely accepted goals of secondary education.

In Chapter 1, areas of differences among students that cannot be met with only identical assignments and class-size group instruction were indicated. In a similar vein, Good and Stipek (1983) propose that the two main differences among students that should be taken into account are their capability for learning the particular subject matter and their learning styles. Good and Stipek state that most schools have not been successful in adapting instruction to these differences and that there is no one method for doing so. They also propose that improving instruction will be advanced if we focus on providing a better quality of education rather than on having all teachers use a given method of teaching, such as all individualized or all class-size teacher-directed group instruction. They suggest that in attempting to improve instruction, teachers should adapt instruction to individual student's educational needs, first, by using methods that they already are able to implement effectively and, second, by using a problem-solving approach to enable them to adjust quickly to the needs of the students enrolled in their classes. This same point of view underlies the individual instructional programming strategy. In addition, however, the strategy recognizes that to be as effective as they could be and would like to be, teachers must have more facilitative support from the principal, district officials, and parents than they are receiving at present and also that curriculum reform is needed. These concerns are addressed in later chapters of this book.

Before turning to the implementation of the individual instructional programming strategy, we should recognize that planning prior to meeting the students is required, as well as competence in more than one method of instruction, such as lecturing, guiding small-group activities, or using individualized assignments. As a minimum, the teacher must be familiar with the objectives and content of the entire course and must have outlined a more detailed plan for the first unit of the course.

Planning the Program

A common procedure in planning an instructional program with each student is to present an overview of the course on the first day of class and complete information regarding the first unit of the course. The unit information is typically presented in written form, such as in a learning guide, and it is placed in the hands of the students. The guide indicates the unit objectives; individual, pair, small-group, and whole-class activities and assignments to attain the objectives; instructional materials to be used; and the evaluation procedures to be employed. Information regarding the preparation of learning guides is presented later in this chapter.

The learning guide is discussed with the students. Each student identifies the unit objectives that all the students are required to attain and also appropriate enrichment or acceleration objectives. The activities and materials that will be used in attaining the objectives are clarified by the student. The student then sets one or more goals related to the unit objectives. The teacher checks the goals with the student.

When pre-planning has been carried out properly, no more than two class periods are needed for planning each student's program, including goal setting. In addition, at least one short and interesting learning activity can be carried out each period. The desirable effect on student motivation resulting from this process is truly noteworthy.

Monitoring Progress

After each student is clear about his or her unit program, the teacher and the students engage in teaching and learning activities. The teacher informally monitors each student's progress on a daily basis. Students' goals and the teacher's plans and activities may be modified on the basis of this monitoring. Formal evaluation of attainment of course goals is carried out at the end of the unit for all the students or for each student at the time the student thinks the goals are achieved. Evaluation related to instructional programming is discussed in Chapter 7.

As was indicated earlier, implementing the individual instructional programming strategy varies greatly from one course to another. Similarly, the amount of preparation that must precede use of the strategy depends upon how instruction is arranged in each particular course. These and other considerations involving the learner's characteristics are addressed in the remainder of this chapter.

COURSE PATTERNS AND INDIVIDUAL INSTRUCTIONAL PROGRAMMING

The nature of each individual student's program in a course is related to three critical matters dealing with the course and to the units of instruction within the course: (1) Are all the students required to attain identical objectives or are some of the objectives different for some students? (2) Must the objectives of each unit be mastered before the student can progress to the next unit? (3) Must the units be taken in a fixed order? Related to these questions, there are eight different course patterns that affect the kind of instructional program that is arranged for each student enrolled in the course. The eight patterns are shown in Figure 3.1.

Common objectives, full mastery, and fixed sequence. In this pattern all students' instructional programs for each unit have identical objectives; every student is required to attain the objectives to a mastery criterion before progressing to the next unit; and the units of instruction in which the objectives are incorporated are taken in a fixed order. Following this pattern in courses where students are not equally capable for learning the particular subject matter has two possible outcomes. One is that not all the students complete the same number of units during a semester. Another is that all students complete the same number of units but spend different amounts of time to complete them. The slower achievers spend more time (in or out of class); the rapid achievers spend less. In this situation the rapid achievers may profitably engage in course-related enrichment activities.

We should pause briefly to consider why units are organized in a fixed order. A fixed order for learning some subject matters, such as mathematics or physics, is followed because it is felt that learning certain knowledge and skills is prerequisite for learning later knowledge and skills. In other cases, the fixed order is followed merely for convenience; learning the content of one unit of the course is not actually prerequisite for learning the content of any other unit. It is well to recognize, too, that there is not consensus among educators as to whether a mastery criterion should be applied in a particular course or subject field. At the present time, it is being applied widely in courses in which students are to attain a minimum level of proficiency in mathematics, reading, spelling, or writing.

Common objectives, full mastery, variable sequence. This pattern

Figure 3.1   Patterns of Objectives, Criteria of Attainment, and
Sequencing of Units

Pattern	Objectives	Criterion	Sequence
1	Common objectives	Full mastery	Fixed order for taking units
2	Common objectives	Full mastery	Variable order for taking units
3	Common objectives	Variable attainment	Fixed order for taking units
4	Common objectives	Variable attainment	Variable order for taking units
5	Variable objectives	Full mastery	Fixed order for taking units
6	Variable objectives	Full mastery	Variable order to taking units
7	Variable objectives	Variable attainment	Fixed order for taking units
8	Variable objectives	Variable attainment	Variable order for taking units

is the same as the preceding one except that the units of instruction are taken in a variable order. Thus, mastering the unit objectives is established as requisite for completing a unit, but the student, upon mastery of any unit, may progress to any other unit included in the semester course. Literature and biology are illustrative of courses in which the units may be taken in a non-fixed order.

Common objectives, variable attainment, fixed sequence. This pattern differs from pattern 1 in that the students are required to attain the objectives only to a level of achievement judged by the teacher to be adequate for that particular student. Students proceed to the next unit in the sequence if the teacher judges their achievement to be adequate. Rapid learners may complete more units than slow learners or they may complete the same number of units and engage in enrichment activities. Slow learners typically proceed through the units according to the same time schedule as other students but master fewer objectives.

Common objectives, variable attainment, and variable sequence. Courses in expressive fields, such as art and dance, sometimes incorporate this pattern. All students' instructional programs include the same objectives; the objectives need not be mastered; and the units are not taken in a fixed sequence.

Before considering the next four patterns, we should recognize that it is possible to provide for differences among students in interests, learning styles, and rate of learning in any of the eight patterns. It is, however, easier to provide for all categories of differences when objectives are variable (patterns 5-8) than when instructional programs include only identical objectives (patterns 1-4).

Variable objectives, full mastery, fixed sequence. In this pattern there may be no objectives required for all students or there may be a core of common objectives for all students and other objectives to suit the particular needs of each student. If the students are not equally capable in the subject matter, not all will complete the same number of units during a semester; or they will complete the same number of units but may spend different amounts of time on each one; or they will complete the same number of units but will engage in different amounts of enrichment or acceleration activities.

Variable objectives, full mastery, variable sequence. Students' instructional programs are arranged here as in pattern 5 except that the students are not required to take the units of instruction in a fixed sequence.

Variable objectives, variable attainment, fixed sequence. In this pattern, not all students' programs include the same objectives and mastery of the unit objectives is not required; but the units are taken in a fixed sequence.

Variable objectives, variable attainment, variable sequence. This pattern is followed widely in open education courses and in independent study where students are given much responsibility for choosing among different options and also for deciding how much effort they will expend.

In relating the instructional programs implied by the eight patterns to the total educational programs of students, we should recognize that any student's program for a semester may include courses reflecting several different patterns. Most of the courses will probably not call for both identical objectives and mastery.

Another point must be made. In each of the preceding patterns, there may be only one learning path, that is, only one identical set of learning activities and materials for achieving each objective. On the other hand, there may be two or more learning paths. It is necessary to have more than one to take into account differences among students in learning styles, as we shall see later.

A MODEL FOR ARRANGING INDIVIDUAL INSTRUCTIONAL PROGRAMS

We have now seen how common and variable course objectives, mastery and non-mastery levels of achievement, and a fixed or a variable sequence for taking units of a course may be arranged in eight patterns. In Figure 3.2 a seven step model of instructional programming that is useable with all eight patterns is presented.

The instructional programming model is described and is illustrated with the concept of mastery learning and continuous progress as proposed by Block (1974), Block and Anderson (1975), Bloom (1976), and Carroll (1963). Many schools use mastery learning and continuous progress in an attempt to assure that every student attains a specified level of competency in mathematics, reading, spelling, and writing by the end of each grade of school. These schools arrange courses with identical objectives for all students, require each student to reach a mastery criterion before proceeding from one unit to the next, and have each student take the units of the courses in a fixed order (pattern 1).

Formulate educational objectives for the student population of the building to attain in terms of educational achievement and in terms of values and action patterns. For each subject field, objectives at three levels of comprehensiveness are required to guide mastery learning effectively: (a) program objectives that students work toward achieving throughout a level of schooling, (b) course objectives, and (c) specific objectives for each unit of a course. The program objectives are for all the courses within a subject field at a particular school level. The course objectives indicate the main outcomes that students should attain upon completion of each course. The unit objectives are more specific and indicate desired student outcomes upon completion of each unit.

Estimate the range of objectives for a curricular area or course that subgroups of the student population, such as those of a school grade, may have already mastered. This estimation is necessary to assure that the student who has mastered the fewest objectives as

Figure 3.2   Instructional Programming Model. (Source: Klausmeier, 1977, p. 16)

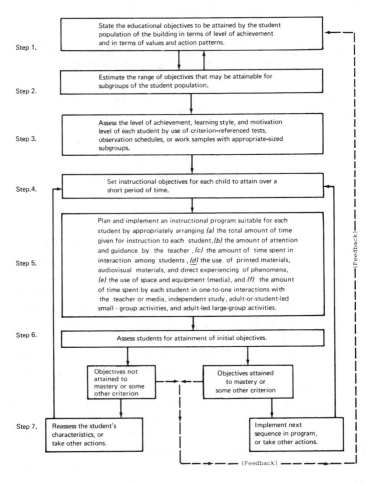

well as the one who has mastered the most objectives will be identified in the preassessment process.

Assess the student's level of achievement related to the objectives, learning styles, and motivation level. The assessment of achievement is necessary for initially placing each student in the proper unit of the sequence. It is not necessary after the students have been placed properly and have completed a unit. Ordinarily, only achievement testing is done in the preassessment process. Learning styles, motivation, and other characteristics of the student are identified from cumulative records, or they are evaluated after instruction begins.

Based on the assessment, identify instructional objectives for each student. The objectives that the student has not yet achieved to the mastery criterion and which are next in the sequence become the instructional objectives for the particular student and are used in developing the instructional plan of the student.

Plan and implement an instructional program by which the student may achieve the objectives. As was discussed earlier in the chapter, an instructional program is planned for each student at the beginning of each course. The program is planned to take into account the student's entering achievement level, learning styles, motivation, and other characteristics. To arrange an appropriate instructional program for the student, it is necessary to vary (a) the amount of time that the different students need to achieve the same objectives, (b) the amount of attention and direction that the teacher gives to the different students, (c) the amount of time that the students spend in interacting with one another and the teacher, (d) the use of printed materials, audiovisual materials, and direct experiencing of phenomena by the different students, (e) the use of space and equipment, and (f) the amount of time spent by each student in both teacher-directed and student-initiated individual, pair, small-group, and large-group activities. Some combination of individual student activity including independent study, small-group student activity including tutoring and other pairing arrangements, teacher-led small-group instruction, and teacher-led whole-class instruction appears to be necessary in most courses to take into account the preceding differences among students. Also, students generally require a considerable amount of teacher explanation, guidance, and monitoring when abstract concepts and principles are introduced for the first time.

Assess each student's attainment of the objectives. The assessment is done as soon as the individual students think they have achieved their objectives and also at the end of the regularly scheduled time for completion of a unit.

The usual procedure is for the assessment to be carried out simultaneously for all the objectives of a unit rather than separately for each single objective. This greatly reduces the amount of time required for evaluation and also for record keeping. For example, if a student completes five three-week units in mathematics during a semester, a permanent record is kept regarding the student's performance related to the five units, not for each of the separate objectives of the five units.

If the objectives are achieved to the specified criterion by the student, identify new objectives; if the objectives are not attained, determine why and take other actions that are appropriate. The student who masters the objectives proceeds to the next unit as soon as the prior one is completed. The student who does not attain mastery in a reasonable amount of time is studied to try to determine causes. Depending upon how nearly the student is to mastery and other considerations, various actions may be taken. The student may continue to work on the same unit, proceed to the next unit in the sequence and come back to the present one later, proceed to the next unit and try to achieve the objectives of both units simultaneously, or cease work on the particular unit temporarily.

Continuous progress and mastery learning (pattern 1) was used to illustrate the instructional programming model because all seven steps are required when implementing this type of instructional programming. Other patterns, however, do not require all seven steps. Steps 1, 4, 5, 6 are sufficient for planning and implementing individual instructional programming in any subject field in which students are not required to reach a mastery criterion as a condition of progressing from one unit to the next, as is indicated in patterns 3, 4, 7, and 8. Steps 2 and 3 are not necessary when student are permitted to enter a course regardless of their entering achievement levels or when they have completed a prerequisite course. Step 7 is not essential if school policy permits students to progress to the next unit or course after making a passing grade or even after having failed to achieve the objectives.

USING DEVELOPMENTAL OBJECTIVES

We should be aware that some teachers and principals have spent many hours writing behavioristic, performance objectives and they do not wish to continue the process. Moreover, they regard themselves as being familiar with all kinds of objectives and do not wish to spend more time learning about educational objectives. Despite the unfortunate experiences that many educators have had in writing instructional objectives, the public, including many parents, wants to know what schools and teachers are trying to accomplish and how well they are succeeding. Moreover, state legislatures are demanding this. Accordingly, having a good understanding of different kinds of objectives and how to use them remains an important concern of every educator.

A set of developmental objectives for a subject field includes program, course, and unit objectives. Program objectives indicate the main outcomes in the particular subject field, e.g., English or science, that student should work toward achieving at each level of schooling. This kind of objective is necessary to achieve continuity in learning during each school level and across the school levels. Typically, course objectives are formulated to guide instruction and learning during a semester. The course objectives should be relatable to one or more of the program objectives. Unit objectives are formulated to guide learning and teaching over short time periods.

Program, course, and unit objectives typically are formulated before instruction starts. The unit objectives and the related course objective, or objectives, are included in a learning guide that is prepared for each unit. The guide is then used in planning an instructional program for each student at the time instruction starts.

A handbook widely used to guide the formulation of educational objectives is Bloom, Hastings, and Madaus (1971). It includes the earlier taxonomy of objectives in the cognitive domain (Bloom, 1956). In the taxonomy, knowledge and five major intellectual skills are identified as a basis for developing objectives in any subject as follows: Knowledge, or the recall or recognition of information, comprehension, application, analysis, synthesis, and evaluation. Each successively higher skill is more complex and builds upon the prior one. Thus, a student generally can comprehend a concept or principle before being able to apply it. Similarly, a situation or event must be understood before it can be analyzed or evaluated. Application, analysis, synthesis, and evaluation objectives should be used as program and course objectives rather than only knowledge and comprehension objectives.

Program Objectives

Formulating program objectives for various subject fields is often the responsibility of a committee that includes the district curriculum coordinator in the subject field and teachers of the district. In formulating program objectives, much time can be saved by turning to statements prepared by other groups, such as textbook authors, school district committees, and state and national groups. These statements can be modified as necessary to fit the characteristics of the individual school or the school district. One good source of objectives is the Tri-County Goal Development Project (Doherty & Peters, 1978). Course objectives from this source, called goals, are given later in this chapter. Another good source of program objectives is the National Assessment of Educational Progress. It has prepared program objectives for high school and also for different age groups corresponding to the end of grade 3, grade 7, and grade 11. The objectives have been formulated for the areas of art, career and occupational development, citizenship, literature, mathematics, music, reading, science, social studies, and writing. New areas are added from time to time. These objectives are used in constructing the tests that are being used in the National Assessment of Educational Progress in the United States.

Following is an example of a program objective in science related to measurement. The primary program objective is for all levels of schooling. There are three related age level objectives:

Primary Program Objective:

Understands that measurement is an important feature of science.

Program Objectives for Age Levels:
Age 9 Understands that quantitative measurements of natural phenomena can be made.
Age 13 Describes how quantitative measurements provide clearer and more precise representations of natural phenomena than do qualitative descriptions.
Age 17 Explains or demonstrates that quantitative measurements, when feasible, provide the basis for description, hypothesis testing, and prediction; explains that

mathematics and statistics provide valuable tools for deriving information from quantitative data; explains that all data are not equally precise. (National Assessment of Educational Progress, 1972, p. 19)

Course Objectives

Course objectives are stated in general terms. Teachers use course objectives in developing instructional techniques, in identifying instructional materials, and in identifying or developing evaluation tools and procedures. There are usually several objectives for each course and at least one to which each set of unit objectives is related. The characteristics of course objectives may be inferred from the examples that follow.

Physical Science:

The student knows that dark colored materials tend to be good absorbers of radiant energy.

The student knows that shiny and bright colored materials are good reflectors.

The student is able to calculate the heat exchanged between objects (e.g., iron at one temperature is placed in water at a different temperature). (Doherty & Hathaway, 1973, p. 454)

Music:

The student is able to accept guidance and direction in solving problems of psychomotor performance.

The student is able to analyze his performance problems and to take appropriate practice measures to resolve them. (Doherty & Hathaway, 1974a, p. 126)

Social Science:

The student knows ways that consumer lending or credit policies influence demand and supply in markets for other goods (commodities, services).

The student is able to use appropriate concepts and models for analysis of interdependencies of supplies- demands-prices in financial and commodity markets. (Peters & Doherty, 1976, p. 386)

Physical Education:

The student knows the appropriate form for shots used in table tennis including forehand, backhand, chop, and smash.

The student is able to execute the skills in the table tennis using the appropriate form. (Doherty & Hathaway, 1974b, p. 386)

Second Language:

The student values the use of second language skills in leisure time activities.

The student values the role a second language plays in meeting society's needs for communication among countries and cultures. (Doherty & Hathaway, 1973, p. 19)

Unit Objectives

Unit objectives are more specific than most course objectives. Often there are several unit objectives related to each course objective. Although not recommended by the present author, some schools use highly detailed performance objectives as unit objectives (see Chapter 4 for a more complete analysis). Below is a course objective and a set of related unit objectives.

Course Objective:

The learner will develop the skills needed for writing unified and well-developed paragraphs.

Unit Objectives:

The learner will:

Analyze the way in which a sentence is developed from a core pattern.

Write three sentences using at least three levels of development and label each level (developmental level refers to increasingly complex sentences structurally).

Analyze the levels of development used in four sample paragraphs provided by the teacher.

Select three suitable topics for paragraph writing.

Write topic sentences for each of the topics which he/she selected and have them approved by the teacher.

Write three paragraphs, using the topic sentences, which contain at least three levels of development and label those levels.

Minimum Competency Objectives

Two sets of objectives are needed in some courses in order to arrange an appropriate instructional program for each student. One is the set that indicates the minimum level of competency that each student should achieve as a condition of proceeding from one unit to the next. These objectives are included in the program of every student. The other set includes additional objectives that are appropriate for the more able students and even for the most rapid achievers.

Steuben Middle School of Milwaukee, Wisconsin, developed 100 objectives in mathematics and specified which ones should be attained to mastery by every student by the end of grade 8. These are the minimum competency objectives. Students who do not master these objectives in grade 6 attempt to do so in grade 7, or still later in grade 8. Four of the most advanced *minimum competency* objectives in mathematics are:

Be able to recognize similar and congruent polygons.

Make a scale drawing.

Use mean, median, and mode to describe a set of data.

Be able to plot a set of ordered pairs.

Two of the most advanced grade 8 mathematics objectives which are not a part of the minimum set are:

Given the dimensions of one triangle of a pair of two similar triangles, and one side of the second, find the other two sides.

Estimate the probability of an event based upon previously collected data.

Steuben is an inner-city school that has heavy student turnover. No one method of teaching can be used uniformly by all teachers with all students. Teachers therefore use the minimum competency and other unit objectives in a variety of ways, depending on the preferences of either teams of teachers or individual teachers within teams. Some teachers employ a considerable amount of whole-class instruction in which all the students have the same objectives in their individual programs. Other teachers use much individual activity. Still others use a combination of activities.

TAKING INTO ACCOUNT THE STUDENT'S LEARNING CHARACTERISTICS

The student's learning characteristics must be considered when planning an instructional program for the student. The most important characteristics of the student are (1) the student's capability for learning the subject matter, (2) interests, (3) learning styles, and (4) motivation. Some teachers attempt to assess their students on one or more of these characteristics prior to starting instruction and then arrange the instructional program of the student accordingly. Others have the students take much initiative in selecting the activities in which they will engage, assuming that the students will select activities which reflect their capabilities, interests, learning styles, and motivational characteristics.

To arrange instruction to suit the particular characteristics of each student, teachers vary the following (step 5 of the instructional programming sequence):

The amount of time that students use in completing each unit.

The instructional materials the students use.

The instructional space(s) and equipment that the students use.

The amount of attention and direction the teacher gives to the students.

The amount and kind of teacher-directed individual, pair, small-group, and large-group activities in which the students participate.

The amount and kind of student-initiated individual, pair, small-group, and large-group activities in which the students engage.

Consider how the four categories of student characteristics are related to the six instructional variables.

Capability for Learning New Material

A student's capability for learning new subject matter may be estimated by various techniques. One is to examine the prior achievement of the student in the same subject. Another is to give a criterion-referenced test. A third is to examine the aptitude test scores of the student.

We may relate student capability for learning the subject matter to the amount of time required for instruction and also to the amount of teacher assistance and guidance that may be required. In general, the higher the capability of the student for learning the new material as estimated by any of the three techniques, the lower the amount of time required to achieve any given objective; and conversely, the lower the achievement or aptitude, the greater the time required. The same relationship exists between student capability and the amount of teacher attention and guidance required. Students with high capability generally require less teacher guidance to achieve a particular unit objective than do students with lower capability. Teachers can find more time for slower students by assigning them work during study periods and at other times outside the regularly scheduled time. In addition, the student may be given more days or weeks to complete the unit. The rapid learners may be given enrichment or acceleration activities after completing their program objectives.

Interests

Teachers usually are able to recognize how the general interests and the career interests of the student may be related to the activities in which the student engages, the materials the student uses, and the elective activities the student pursues. The major difficulties in responding to student interests are matching the interests with the course requirements and the availability of space and materials. An instructional materials center stocked with print materials, audiovisuals, and three-dimensional objects is especially helpful to the teacher and the student in utilizing the student's present interests and in developing new ones.

Learning Styles

Learning style refers to the way a person prefers to learn. It is different from the person's aptitude or capability for learning particular subject matter. Dunn and Dunn (1978) identified 18 learning styles that suggest that learners are affected by four sets of conditions and needs: (a) conditions in the immediate learning environment—sound, light, temperature, and design of the room and furniture; (b) their own emotional states and conditions—motivation, persistence, responsibility, and structure; (c) sociological preferences for learning—individually, pair, peers, team, adult, or varied; and (d) their own physical characteristics and needs—sensory modalities and other preferences related to intake, time of day, and mobility. Each student has preferences related to the elements of each of the four preceding categories. The Dunns indicate that the student learns most effectively when the student's profile of learning styles is identified and a learning environment is arranged that takes into account the student's learning styles.

An inventory has been constructed that is administered to students and scored by computer. A computer-generated learning style profile is prepared for each student with recommendations concerning how to arrange the environment for the student (Dunn & Dunn, 1978). Groupings of students with similar profiles are also identified by computer and made available to the school.

Messick and Associates (1976) have also identified learning styles. Three of their styles are not directly reflected in those of Dunn and Dunn. Two of these learning styles, analytic versus global and reflective versus impulsive, are closely related. Persons with analytic, reflective styles size up a situation carefully, analyze it into its relevant elements, and then respond. Those with global, impulsive styles, on the other hand, tend to get a quick overview of the total situation and respond without careful deliberation. Independent study and research activities seem to work well for those with analytic, reflective styles, whereas small group work with questions directed toward encouraging analysis and reflection seems to gain better results with students with global impulsive styles.

A third style described by Messick and Associates (1976) involves divergent production versus convergent production. Persons with divergent production styles are creatively inclined. They seek new and different solutions to problems. Students with convergent styles hesitate to produce a novel idea or product. They seek correct and socially approved solutions.

Figure 3.3 represents a synthesis of both sets of learning styles. Completing the checklist mentally as you read through it will aid you in understanding the styles. You may wish to think about the styles of a student whom you know well.

The teacher who tries to take each student's profile of learning styles into account must make several decisions. One is to determine which styles can be accommodated with a reasonable amount of teacher effort. A second decision is to ascertain which styles can and cannot be accommodated in terms of the available space, instructional materials, and time. Finally, the teacher must determine which student learning styles to attempt to change.

Much experimenting remains to be done to determine how to relate learning styles to arranging an excellent instructional program for each student. Thus far, we have made some progress in providing for the sensory modality preferences—hearing, seeing, tactual, or kinesthetic—and the grouping preferences—individual, pair, or small

Figure 3.3   Learning Styles

Directions: People learn and study in different ways. Each question in this checklist describes how a person might like to learn or study. First read all the parts of the question. Then for each question, put a + in the ( ) to indicate your preference (or that of a student you have observed).

1. ( ) Prefer quiet; sounds such as   ( ) Can ignore most sounds when
         records, TV, or conversation   studying.
         are distracting when studying.
2. ( ) Prefer bright light.   ( ) Prefer subdued light.
3. ( ) Prefer cooler temperature.   ( ) Prefer warmer temperature.
4. ( ) Prefer formally arranged   ( ) Prefer informally arranged
         furniture and room with fixed   furniture and room where
         desk or chairs.   lounging is possible.

Check only one.

5. ( ) Prefer to learn things outside the school environment, not things
         included in regular classes.
    ( ) Eager to learn new material and skills included in classes.
    ( ) Will learn new material and skills only if incentives and reasons
         are provided.
6. ( ) Persist until activities that   ( ) Do not complete many tasks
         are started are completed.   that are started.
7. ( ) Take much responsibility for   ( ) Do not assume much responsi-
         doing things well without   bility for doing things well.
         supervision.
8. ( ) Prefer clear guidelines   ( ) Prefer unstructured situa-
         regarding assignments and   tions without guidelines
         projects.   and prescriptions.

Check only one.

9. Prefer to study and to work on activities:
        ( ) alone.
        ( ) with one peer or partner.
        ( ) with two peers.
        ( ) with several peers.
        ( ) with an adult leader.
        ( ) in any of the preceding ways, depending on the situation.

10. Check only one.
        ( ) Prefer auditory learning activities, i.e., listening to tapes,
             records, peers, and other persons.
        ( ) Prefer visual learning activities, i.e., seeing pictures, film-
             strips, and objects, processes, and events.
        ( ) Prefer manipulating things with the fingers and hands.
        ( ) Prefer kinesthetic learning activities, i.e., doing activities
             involving total body movement.
        ( ) Have no preference for any one of the preceding.

11. ( ) When studying, prefer to have   ( ) Do not require anything to
          something to eat, chew, or   eat, chew, or drink when
          drink.   studying.

Figure 3.3 (continued)

Check only one.

12. Study best in:
    ( ) early morning.
    ( ) late morning.
    ( ) afternoon.
    ( ) evening.
    ( ) have no preference for any one of the preceding.

13. ( ) Prefer to be able to move   ( ) Prefer the same posture and
         about frequently and vary   location for a considerable
         posture and location often   period of time.
         when studying.
14. ( ) Analyze a problem into its   ( ) View situations in totality,
         parts and try to see the   or globally, and ignore the
         relationships among the parts.   details.
15. ( ) Respond to situations after   ( ) Respond to situations quickly
         some thought and reflection.   without thinking much about
                                                 the situation or the response.
16. ( ) Prefer to seek novel or unique   ( ) Prefer to seek correct or
         solutions to problems.   socially-approved solutions.

---

* Items 1-13 based on Dunn and Dunn (1978) and 14-16 on Messick and Associates (1976).

group. We achieve best results with self-motivated students. Research, as well as experience, shows that many current instructional modes do not take into account the learning styles of many students. For example, classical individualized instruction that calls for only individual activity, guided by contracts, unipacs, and programmed learning materials, does not accommodate either the grouping preference or motivational style of many students. Large undivided open spaces where 100 or more students receive all their academic instruction are not providing a physical environment conducive to learning for the many students who cannot adjust to the noise, light, student movement, and other distracting conditions. Furthermore, class-size group instruction consisting of teacher lectures, lecture-discussions, and question-and-answer recitations that may be suitable for some teacher-motivated students with auditory preferences has proved to be unproductive for students who prefer individual and small-group learning arrangements using pictures, filmstrips, films, and other visual stimuli. On the other hand, some teams of three to five teachers having the same group of students for a block of time daily are effectively arranging space, time, equipment, furniture, materials, and activities that accommodate many different learning styles.

Motivation

Motivation is included as a learning style by Dunn and Dunn (1978). It is also regarded as an integral aspect of the learning process by most motivational theorists. Two main approaches based on different theories of motivation are employed in the schools. One is behavior modification, which is based on Skinnerian learning theory and behavioristic instructional psychology. The other is cognitive, which is based on humanistic philosophy and cognitive learning psychology.

Each approach is employed with considerable success to achieve certain purposes. For example, behavior modification is employed with exceptional students to help them replace undesired forms of behavior with behavior that is more socially acceptable. The cognitive approach to motivation underlies all forms of individual goal setting and decision making (Klausmeier, 1979). It is especially important to consider here inasmuch as students are expected to set learning goals at the beginning of each unit of instruction.

According to the cognitive approach, the human being is an information-processing, stimulus-seeking organism whose thought influences action. Thought, particularly in the form of intentions, has a powerful effect on the first three of four phases of a behavior sequence: (a) its activation or instigation, (b) its direction, (c) its persistence until goal achievement, and finally, (d) the consequences following achievement or nonachievement of the goal.

DEVELOPING A LEARNING GUIDE
FOR STUDENTS

Preparing a learning guide for each unit of a course prior to starting instruction is helpful when later planning each student's instructional program in the course. The learning guide is especially helpful in courses that are required of all students. Notice that the term, helpful, is used here. Teaching can, of course, be effective without a learning guide. However, planning prior to starting instruction does contribute to more effective instruction.

The learning guide may be written by an individual teacher or by a team of teachers and a curriculum expert. It includes an introduction to the student, directions to the student, the unit objectives and the course objective to which they are related, either a list of the correlated materials or an indication of the teacher-learner procedures to identify the materials, and either the activities and assignments correlated with the instructional materials or the teacher-learner procedures to be used in planning the activities.

Before preparing the guide, key questions must be answered. How they are answered will influence the content of the guide and how it is used.

Will all or part of the objectives be required of all students?

Will the students be required to achieve a mastery criterion in order to proceed to the next unit or to receive credit for passing the unit?

Will the units be taken by all the students in a fixed sequence or will they be taken at any time during the semester?

Will the students entering the unit be required to have met specified prerequisites?

Will there be more than one learning path by which students may achieve the same objective?

Another consideration is whether the guide will list all the materials, activities, and assignments or whether it will serve only as a teaching-learning resource. Some guides include all the essential information for guiding the learning-teaching process throughout the unit. Others list only the assignments. They do not specify the individual, small-group, and whole-class activities that may be used to complete the assignments. Some guides indicate only the teaching-learning procedures to be used in identifying materials and in planning the activities. They do not list all the materials or activities.

Student's Introduction

The student introduction may include any or all of the following:

An overview of the content and activities.

Statements indicating the importance of the material or giving reasons for learning it.

An indication of how this guide is related to others in the series.

Written and/or graphic material to gain the student's attention. Graphic material that is humorous appears to be especially helpful.

Course and Unit Objectives

Either independently or as a part of the student introduction, the course objective is given, followed by the unit objectives. These objectives should be stated so that the student understands the expected outcomes. In courses such as typing, foreign language, and physical education, it may be appropriate to state part or all of the objectives in terms of observable behaviors and also to indicate the desired performance criterion. In courses where concepts and principles are the major content, it appears unwise to use objectives that specify only observable behavior or performance objectives.

Directions to the Student

As necessary throughout the guide, directions to the student are indicated. Some teachers prefer to give directions orally rather than to include written instructions. In general, it appears better to include directions in clear written form so that the student can refer back to them if, for one reason or another, he or she has not understood or has forgotten the oral instructions.

Instructional Materials

It is especially important for the teacher to identify and indicate different materials that students may use to achieve the same objectives in accordance with their aptitudes, learning styles, and interests. The materials may be listed separately early in the guide or with each activity or assignment. As noted earlier, students can be directed to identify some of the materials they will use.

Activities

The main types of learning activities are individual, pair, small group, and whole class. These can be teacher-led or student-initiated.

These different kinds of activities make it possible to take into account differences among students in rate of achieving the objectives, learning styles, interests, and motivation. As with materials, students may suggest activities; therefore, it is not necessary to list every possible activity in the guide.

Self-evaluation Procedures

In some guides, checks are placed in the guide that enable the students to determine their achievement of the objectives. These are very useful as a kind of feedback device. In the event the self-check is not placed in the guide, an indication is provided concerning how this will be carried out by the teacher, such as by a unit test of some type.

From the preceding it should be clear that learning guides differ greatly from the earlier unipacs, curriculum guides, learning activity packages, teaching-learning units, workbooks, and similar materials that were used to provide for differences among students *only in rate of learning and only through the same individual assignments that all students completed.* Some of these guides were deficient in several respects. First, only behavioral or performance objectives were included in the guide. Further, they were stated in such a manner that the higher level intellectual skills such as application, analysis, synthesis, and evaluation were not included. The students were therefore not aided in developing these higher level skills. Second, there was not continuity between successive guides inasmuch as none of the activities were directed specifically toward course and program objectives. Even though students mastered the objectives of the successive units, they forgot quickly because no opportunity was provided for review, re-learning, and integration of the separate items of knowledge and skills. For example, many students who learned all the *separate* skills of reading during their elementary school years could not, on entering middle school, read books and other materials that are appropriate for Grade 6 middle school students. They did not learn to apply, consolidate, and integrate the separate skills into the total process of reading. Similarly, many students who mastered the many separate performance-based objectives in mathematics during their middle school years were incapable of performing the computation skills necessary to learn the simplest grade 9 algebra. Recognizing these many deficiencies should enable us to prepare more effective learning guides for students.

A NOTE ON EFFECTIVE TEACHING

The individual instructional programming strategy does not prescribe a complete set of teaching behaviors nor does it imply any one method of teaching. It assumes, however, that teachers plan and conduct their instructional activities in a systematic, orderly manner and that they expect students to achieve the course objectives. Moreover, they demonstrate enthusiasm for the subject matter and for the students and make the instruction clear and meaningful. In concluding this chapter, it may be instructive to examine ways that teachers express enthusiasm and what they do to make instruction clear.

Collins (1976) identified the following eight ways that teachers express enthusiasm:

Rapid, uplifting, varied vocal delivery.

Dancing, wide-open eyes.

Frequent, demonstrative gestures.

Varied, dramatic body movements.

Varied, emotive facial expressions.

Selection of varied words, especially adjectives.

Ready, animated acceptance of ideas and feelings.

Exuberant over-all energy level. (p. 2)

Collins (1976) developed a program to teach enthusiasm. Prospective teachers who experienced the program demonstrated more enthusiasm than those who did not.

Clarity of instruction and related teaching behaviors were studied by Cruickshank, Myers, and Moenjak (1975); Bush, Kennedy, and Cruickshank (1977); Land (1979); and Land and Smith (1979a,

1979b). Part of the 32 behaviors identified in one or more of these studies follow (*Practical Applications of Research*, 1981, p. 3):

Explain the work to be done and how to do it.

Ask students before they start work if they know what to do and how to do it.

Explain something then stop so students can think about it.

Take time when explaining.

Help students to organize materials in a meaningful way.

Repeat questions and explanations if students don't understand.

Repeat and stress directions and difficult points.

Encourage and let students ask questions.

Answer students' questions.

Synthesize ideas and demonstrate real-world relevancy.

Teach at a pace appropriate to the topic and students.

Personalize instruction by using many teaching strategies.

Teach in a related step-by-step manner.

Use demonstrations.

Use a variety of teaching materials.

Provide illustrations and examples.

Emphasize the key terms/ideas to be learned.

Consistently review work as it is completed and provide students with feedback or knowledge of results.

Although not stated explicitly, making clear to the students what is to be learned and the main activities for learning it is an excellent way to start a class. If students are missing either one of these, initial fumbling and loss of time throughout the class occur. We make the points here because experienced teachers often forget to carry out the procedure in one or more of their daily classes.

References

Block, J. H. (Ed.). *Schools, society, and mastery learning.* New York: Holt, Rinehart, and Winston, 1974.

Block, J. H., & Anderson, L. W. *Mastery learning in classroom instruction.* New York: Macmillan, 1975.

Bloom, B. S. (Ed.). *Taxonomy of educational objectives. Handbook I: Cognitive domain.* New York: McKay, 1956.

Bloom, B. S. *Human characteristics and school learning.* New York: McGraw-Hill, 1976.

Bloom, B. S., Hastings, J. T., & Madaus, G. F. *Handbook on formative and summative evaluation of student learning.* New York: McGraw- Hill, 1971.

Bush, A., Kennedy, J., & Cruickshank, D. An empirical investigation of teacher clarity. *Journal of Teacher Education,* 1977, *28,* 53-58.

Carroll, J. B. A model of school learning. *Teachers College Record,* 1963, *64,* 723-733.

Collins, M. L. *The effects of training for enthusiasm on the enthusiasm displayed by preservice elementary teachers.* Unpublished doctoral dissertation, Syracuse University, 1976.

Cruickshank, D. R., Myers, B., & Moenjak, T. *Statements of clear teacher behaviors provided by 1,009 students in grades 6-9.* Unpublished manuscript, 1975. (Available from College of Education, Ohio State University, Columbus, OH.)

Doherty, V. W., & Hathaway, W. E. *K-12: Course goals in biological and physical science* (Tri-County Goal Development Project). 1973. Available from Commercial-Educational Distributing Services, P. O. Box 8723, Portland, Oregon 97208.

Doherty, V. W., & Hathaway, W. E. *K-12: Course goals in music* (Critique Edition, Tri-County Goal Development Project). 1974a. Available from Commercial-Educational Distributing Services, P. O. Box 8723, Portland, Oregon 97208.

Doherty, V. W., & Hathaway, W. E. *K-12: Course goals in physical education* (Critique Edition, Tri-County Goal Development Project). 1974b. Available from Commercial-Educational Distributing Services, P. O. Box 8723, Portland, Oregon 97208

Doherty, V. W., & Peters, L. B. *K-12: Program goals and subject matter taxonomies for course goals in art, biological and physical sciences, business education, health education, home economics, industrial education, language arts, mathematics, music, physical education, second language, social science, and career education* (Tri-County Goal Development Project). 1978. Available from Commercial-Educational Distributing Services, P. O. Box 8723, Portland, Oregon 97208.

Dunn, R., & Dunn, K. *Teaching students through their individual learning styles: A practical approach.* Reston, VA: Reston Publishing Co., 1978.

Good, T. L., & Stipek, D. J. Individual differences in the classroom: A psychological perspective. In G. D. Fenstermacher & J. I. Goodlad (Eds.), *Individual differences and the common curriculum* (Eighty-second yearbook of the National Society for the Study of Education. Part I). Chicago: University of Chicago Press, 1983.

Goodlad, J. I. A study of schooling: Some implications for school improvement. *Phi Delta Kappan*, 1983, *64*(8), 552-558.

Klausmeier, H. J. Instructional programming for the individual student. In H. J. Klausmeier, R. A. Rossmiller, & M. Saily (Eds.), *Individually guided elementary education: Concepts and practices.* New York: Academic Press, 1977. Pp. 55-76.

Klausmeier, H. J. Introduction. In H. J. Klausmeier & Associates, *Cognitive learning and development: Information-processing and Piagetian perspectives.* Cambridge, MA: Ballinger Publishing Company, 1979. Pp. 1-27.

Land, M. Low inference variables of teacher clarity: Effects on student concept learning. *Journal of Educational Psychology*, 1979, *71*(6), 795-798.

Land, M., & Smith, L. Effect of a teacher clarity variable on student achievement. *Journal of Educational Research*, 1979, *72*, 196-197. (a)

Land, M. L., & Smith, L. R. The effect of low-inference teacher clarity inhibitors on student achievement. *Journal of Teacher Education,* 1979, *30*(3), 55-57. (b)

Messick, S., & Associates. *Individuality in learning.* San Francisco: Jossey-Bass, 1976.

National Assessment of Educational Progress. *Science objectives for 1972-73 assessment.* Denver, CO: National Assessment of Educational Progress, 1972.

Peters, L., & Doherty, J. *K-12: Course goals in social science* (Vol. 1, Tri-County Goal Development Project). 1976. Available from Commercial-Educational Distributing Services, P. O. Box 8723, Portland, Oregon 97208.

Practical Applications of Research (Newsletter of Phi Delta Kappa's Center on Evaluation, Development, and Research). Bloomington, IN: Phi Delta Kappa, 1981, *3*(3).

Rothrock, D. The rise and decline of individualized instruction. *Educational Leadership*, 1982, *39*(7), 528-530.

Suggestions for Further Reading

Amenta, R. What's happening in . . . Horizon High School? *Phi Delta Kappan*, 1982, *64*(3), 204-205.
Amenta gives a verbal snapshot of an alternative high school with an enrollment of 180 students. Personalized instruction as well as individual educational programming are described.

Arlin, M., & Webster, J.   Time costs of mastery learning. *Journal of Educational Psychology*, 1983, *75*(2), 187-195.
These authors found that mastery learning reduces differences among students in achievement but only when slow learners are given more time and fast learners are held back. As in other mastery-learning experiments, the mean achievement of all the students was raised dramatically. However, mastery students required twice as much time as nonmastery students to complete their study of the same material.

Brandt, R. On improving teacher effectiveness: A conversation with David Berliner. *Educational Leadership*, 1982, *40*(1), 12-15.
Berliner explains the research findings regarding teacher effectiveness and describes a kind of observation and consultation with teachers that aids them in applying the findings. He states that it is critical for students of all ability levels to experience academic success.

Dunn, R. Can students identify their own learning styles? *Educational Leadership*, 1983, *40*(5), 60-62.
Dunn, who was instrumental in conceptualizing learning styles and also in constructing a learning style inventory, indicates that most

high school students can reliably identify their own learning styles. She also reports research that shows that student outcomes, including achievement and attitudes, are better when teachers take into account each student's learning styles.

Klausmeier, H. J.   Instructional programming for the individual student. In H. J. Klausmeier, R. A. Rossmiller, & M. Saily (Eds.), *Individually guided elementary education: Concepts and practices*. New York: Academic Press, 1977, 55-76.

Many of the instructional programming practices of Individually Guided Elementary education are relevant for middle schools of Grades 6, 7 and 8 since, with minor exceptions, students of the middle school do not have elective subjects. However, the practices are not equally applicable to the high school. This chapter presents more information regarding instructional programming for the individual student in middle school level than could be presented in the present book.

Rubin, L.   Artistry in teaching. *Educational Leadership*, 1983, *40*(4), 44-49.

Rubin explains the difference between exciting and dreary classes and shows what teachers can do to make their classes exciting for the learners and themselves. (This issue of this journal has other excellent articles on teaching.)

CHAPTER 4

CURRICULAR ARRANGEMENTS

Herbert J. Klausmeier

In recent decades federal policy has had a considerable impact on the curriculum of local schools, especially by extending equal educational opportunity to minority and handicapped students. State policy has moved in the direction of mandating minimum proficiency standards in various subject fields. School districts have provided for a more structured curriculum, and many schools have moved away from the three-track system in order to meet the educational needs of the individual student more effectively.

This chapter examines these issues and clarifies the comprehensive and enabling objectives pertaining to curricular arrangements that are included in the design for improving secondary schools.

Comprehensive Objective:

The curriculum is structured to meet state and district requirements but it can be adapted by the school and individual teachers to take into account the differing educational needs of students.

Illustrative Enabling Objectives:

The curriculum, including the required courses or competencies and the amount of time allocated for instruction in each course, is arranged to promote effective learning in the following areas:

Communication skills, including reading, writing, speaking, and listening.

Mathematical concepts and skills.

Scientific and technological concepts and skills, including computer technology.

Social science concepts and skills.

The expressive and performing arts, including aesthetics, art, dance, drama, and music.

Foreign languages.

Career education, including awareness, exploration, and preparation.

Health education, both physical and mental.

Family and home membership.

Leisure education, including crafts, clubs, and extracurricular activities.

Related to the preceding areas, curriculum committees, groups of teachers, and individual teachers:

Identify or prepare content outlines, organized in the form of taxonomies, other hierarchies, or topical outlines.

Identify or formulate program, course, and unit objectives.

Identify or prepare resource units and other materials for teacher use.

Identify or prepare instructional materials for student use.

Prepare learning guides that the students and the teacher use at the beginning of each course in planning each student's instructional program.

FEDERAL AND STATE INFLUENCE

The design calls for the state and local school districts, with input from educators and other citizens, to determine the curriculum of the schools of the state and the district. Each school and individual teacher should be able to adapt the curriculum to take into account the differing educational needs of students.

Local school curriculum development is constrained, however, by federal and state policies and mandates. The influence of the federal government varies somewhat across time, and there is a great variation among the states with respect to the control of local school curricula. van Geel (1979) has identified the examples of federal and state policies that follow.

Federal Policy

Curriculum policy-making refers to the establishment of limits, criteria, and guidelines but not to the actual development of materials for use by students and teachers. Constitutionally, curriculum policy-making resides in the state governments. However, in the 1960s and 1970s the federal government was heavily involved in policy-making that affected the local school curriculum and it will probably continue to be.

Federal Courts and the Constitution

A few examples will indicate the pervasive effects of the federal courts on the local school curriculum through interpretations of the Constitution. The federal courts repeatedly are filing on matters dealing with desegregation. With respect to religion, school ceremonies which have involved recitations from the Bible and the saying of prayers are prohibited. Similarly, school facilities may not be used for religious instruction. With respect to acculturation, students are required to learn English as part of their school instruction and, even though bilingual education is supported by the courts, the purpose is ultimately to lead students to the mastery of English.

Congress and the Federal Agencies

One manner in which the Congress and federal agencies determine curriculum policy is through making grants of money to state education agencies and local school districts and attaching conditions to the grants. For example, Title I of the Elementary and Secondary Education Act of 1965 provides monies to educate the disadvantaged. It also makes many requirements of local schools that receive the monies, such as evaluating the effects of the programs funded through the grants and ensuring compliance with regulations regarding antiracial and antisexual discrimination.

Public Law 94-142, the Education for All Handicapped Children Act of 1975, establishes monetary entitlements on behalf of state and local education agencies. Carrying out the provisions of the law greatly influences the curriculum not only for handicapped children, but it also impacts on the curriculum of the normally developing children who attend classes with the handicapped.

Title VI of the Civil Rights Act of 1964 includes the basic anti-discrimination provision which is attached to the use of all federal money. It provides that no person shall, on the grounds of race, color, or national origin, be excluded from participation in, be denied the benefits of, or be subjected to discrimination under any program or activity receiving federal financial assistance. The effects of Title VI have directly or indirectly led to many changes in local school attendance patterns and also in curriculum and instructional arrangements in the schools.

The purpose of Title IX of this same Act is to eliminate and prevent sexual discrimination in education. Discrimination is prohibited regarding course offerings and requirements, counseling and guidance programs, admissions to special schools and programs and to school organizations such as social and service clubs, extracurricular activities, hair and dress codes, rules with regard to pregnancy and parenthood, and athletics.

It is easy to underestimate the direct and indirect effects of these and other federal actions during the past 30 years on the present curriculum of each local school. On the positive side, a considerable amount of money has been made available to extend equal opportunity for education. On the neutral or negative side, there is increasing reliance on the federal government to provide part of the funding for any significant curricular improvement at the national level.

State Policies

Constitutionally, the state is responsible for all educational matters of the state. Therefore, the state legislatures and the state courts can exercise enormous power over the curriculum. In general, state legislatures have chosen not to exercise their full power. However, many state education agencies require that all the students of the state take certain courses.

States vary widely with respect to how much authority is allocated to local school boards regarding the curriculum and other matters. In states with a decentralized approach, local boards are delegated broad authority to control the school program while the state board and the chief school officer only advise and assist local school districts. In contrast, in states with a highly centralized approach, state officials prescribe and enforce the same course of study in all the schools. There are relatively inflexible textbook adoption policies in some states. Most states are moderately centralized, and state officials exercise some authority regarding the course of study and textbook adoption.

In recent years, the tendency is for more states to move toward greater centralization rather than toward decentralization. Representative of this trend are the mandated statewide testing and minimum competency policies. By these policies, state officials are determining the objectives, selecting the test items, and establishing the level of performance deemed acceptable for meeting the minimum standards.

The state courts increasingly are involved in determining curriculum policy through their decisions. These decisions usually are related to the constitutional right of the student to an education. The courts also are frequently involved in interpreting state statutes that affect education. The number of such interpretations is also increasing.

As a result of federal and state policies, local control of the curriculum today is much less than it was even 30 years ago (van Geel, 1979). This lesser control has been brought about by the federal government and the state governments for the purpose of protecting and defending students whom local school boards have tended to neglect in the past, especially the handicapped, the non-English speaking, racial minorities, and the politically powerless. This expansion of equal opportunity has probably been the most important factor leading to the lessening of local control. The public appears to have accepted the increased centralization in order to get more widespread equality of opportunity. It may now also be willing to accept further centralization to achieve other perceived values, such as greater effectiveness of the educational process.

CURRICULUM PRIORITIES

There appears to be consensus that the 10 curricular areas indicated in the enabling objectives at the beginning of this chapter should be included in the secondary school curriculum. Realistically, however, time does not permit all students to take courses in each area. Similarly, time and budgetary constraints limit what the school can provide in each area. Therefore, priorities among the 10 areas and within each area must be established.

Many individuals and groups are concerned with the priorities. There appears to be some agreement that there should be certain requirements for all students. This is usually referred to as general education for all students. In addition, students with different career goals should be provided for: those who enter the labor market immediately after high school graduation, those who go to a technical school or a community college, and those who enter a four-year university. A fourth group, and a very large one, is the dropout group that does not complete high school.

Recently, many individuals and groups are interested in general education and university preparation. However, we shall examine only three major proposals because of space constraints. The first one makes recommendations for university entrance in terms of competencies rather than courses while the next two consider both general education and college preparation.

Competencies for College Entrance

The College Entrance Board has exercised considerable influence on the high school curriculum for many years. The recommendations that follow (College Entrance Board, 1981) are among the first that specify competencies rather than a number of Carnegie units of credit equal to a one-year course. The recommendations assume that students who develop the competencies before high school graduation will improve their chances for success in the first year of college. Acceptance of recommendations such as these has major implications for curriculum change in local schools and, accordingly, for implementation of the individual educational programming and instructional programming strategies.

Reading Competencies

The ability to identify and comprehend the main and subordinate ideas in a written work and to summarize the ideas in one's own words.

The ability to recognize different purposes and methods of writing, to identify a writer's point of view and tone, and to interpret a writer's meaning inferentially as well as literally.

The ability to separate one's personal opinions and assumptions from a writer's.

The ability to vary one's reading speed and method (survey, skim, review, question, and master) according to the type of material and one's purpose for reading.

The ability to use the features of books and other reference materials, such as table of contents, preface, introduction, titles and subtitles, index, glossary, appendix, bibliography.

The ability to define unfamiliar words by decoding, using contextual clues, or by using a dictionary.

Writing Competencies

The ability to conceive ideas about a topic for the purpose of writing.

The ability to organize, select, and relate ideas and to outline and develop them in coherent paragraphs.

The ability to write Standard English sentences with correct:
    sentence structure
    verb forms
    punctuation, capitalization, possessives, plural forms, and
        other matters of mechanics
    word choice and spelling.

The ability to vary one's writing style, including vocabulary and sentence structure, for different readers and purposes.

The ability to improve one's own writing by restructuring, correcting errors, and rewriting.

The ability to gather information from primary and secondary sources: to write a report using this research; to quote, paraphrase, and summarize accurately; and to cite sources properly.

Speaking and Listening Competencies

The ability to engage critically and constructively in the exchange of ideas, particularly during class discussions and conferences with instructors.

The ability to answer and ask questions coherently and concisely, and to follow spoken instructions.

The ability to identify and comprehend the main and subordinate ideas in lectures and discussions, and to report accurately what others have said.

The ability to conceive and develop ideas about a topic for the purpose of speaking to a group; to choose and organize related ideas; to present them clearly in Standard English; and to evaluate similar presentations by others.

The ability to vary one's use of spoken language to suit different situations.

Mathematical Competencies

The ability to perform, with reasonable accuracy, the computations of addition, subtraction, multiplication, and division using natural numbers, fractions, decimals, and integers.

The ability to make and use measurements in both traditional and metric units.

The ability to use effectively the mathematics of:
    integers, fractions, and decimals
    ratios, proportions, and percentages
    roots and powers
    algebra
    geometry.

The ability to make estimates and approximations, and to judge the reasonableness of a result.

The ability to formulate and solve a problem in mathematics terms.

The ability to select and use appropriate approaches and tools in solving problems (mental computation, trial and error, paper-and-pencil techniques, calculator, and computer).

The ability to use elementary concepts of probability and statistics.

Reasoning Competencies

The ability to identify and formulate problems, as well as the ability to propose and evaluate ways to solve them.

The ability to recognize and use inductive and deductive reasoning, and to recognize fallacies in reasoning.

The ability to draw reasonable conclusions from information found in various sources, whether written, spoken, tabular, or graphic, and to defend one's conclusions rationally.

The ability to comprehend, develop, and use concepts and generalizations.

The ability to distinguish between fact and opinion.

Studying Competencies

This set of abilities is different in kind from those which precede it. They are set forth here because they constitute the key abilities in learning how to learn. Successful study skills are necessary for acquiring the other five competencies as well as for achieving the desired outcomes. Students are unlikely to be efficient in any part of their work without them. One further difference must be expressed: activities related to acquiring the basic studying competencies will fail unless students bear in mind the role of their attitude in the learning process. That attitude should encompass a sense of personal responsibility for one's own progress, a desire to make full use of the teacher as a resource, and a willingness to conduct themselves in ways that make learning possible for their classmates as well as themselves.

The ability to set study goals and priorities consistent with stated course objectives and one's own progress, to establish surroundings and habits conducive to learning independently or with others, and to follow a schedule that accounts for both short- and long-term projects.

The ability to locate and use resources external to the classroom (for example, libraries, computers, interviews, and direct observation), and to incorporate knowledge from such sources into the learning process.

The ability to develop and use general and specialized vocabularies, and to use them for reading, writing, speaking, listening, computing, and studying.

The ability to understand and to follow customary instructions for academic work in order to recall, comprehend, analyze, summarize, and report the main ideas from reading, lectures, and other academic experiences; and to synthesize knowledge and apply it to new situations.

The ability to prepare for various types of examinations and to devise strategies for pacing, attempting or omitting questions, thinking, writing, and editing according to the type of examination; to satisfy other assessments of learning in meeting course objectives such as laboratory performance, class participation, simulation, and products of students' evaluation.

The ability to accept constructive criticism and learn from it. (pp. 10-15)

A Flexible Curriculum

Goodlad (1983) states that individual schools have no right to deny students access to common learnings in five broad areas—literature and language, mathematics and science, society and social studies, the fine and performing arts, and the vocations. He feels that every student should have some course work in each area, that neither the college bound student nor the student preparing for job entry should be permitted, much less required, to take so much work in one or two areas that one or more of the other areas is squeezed out. The design for the renewal and improvement of secondary education also incorporates this point of view and in addition implies a need for computer literacy.

Goodlad (1983) first specifies a desired percentage of the high school curriculum that should be given to each of the five areas and then indicates the amount of flexibility that is necessary to meet the needs of students with different subject matter interests and career goals. He specifies the following: 18 percent of a student's program in literature and language (English and other); 18 percent in mathematics and science; 15 percent in each social studies, the arts, and vocations; and 10 percent in physical education. This gives a total of 91 percent of a student's total curricular time. However, he would permit a variation of plus or minus 20 percent in each area, for example, as much as 18 percent or as little as 12 percent in the arts. Also, two students of quite different abilities and interests might both give 18 percent of their time to mathematics and science, one taking an advanced course or two and the other seeking mastery in the common part of this domain.

By electing a downward variance of 20 percent in two or more domains, a student could take much more than 20 percent in one of the other domains. This could be used for talent development in the arts, an academic subject such as mathematics, or sports. In addition to the course work, students should be provided vouchers for purposes of purchasing instruction in the public or private sector, for example, college classes for advanced mathematics, a private tutor for instruction in singing, a professional trainer for swimming.

Goodlad recommends that, beyond the preceding curricular arrangements for commonality and diversity, other provisions for individual differences should be in the organization of groups and in pedagogy. Regarding organization, he specifies that teams of teachers and aides (up to six or seven full-time equivalents in secondary schools), each including a head teacher and a group of from 100 to 150 students, should be organized into clusters over the entire four-year span of the high school. Each cluster should provide the entire curriculum, except for talent development.

An Inflexible Curriculum

In April of 1981 an 18-member commission was appointed by Secretary of Education Terrel H. Bell to examine the American educational system and to recommend reforms. In April of 1983, the Commission's report (National Commission on Excellence in

Education, 1983) was made public as an open letter to the American people. The letter was titled "A nation at risk: The imperative for educational reform."

The risk implied in the report was that America had fallen behind the other industrialized nations of the world in many areas of productivity during the last two decades. Although the lack of productivity was not related directly to national defense, the perceptive reader recognizes that a low level of productivity that cannot maintain a strong defense capability puts a nation at risk. The commission attributed the cause of the decline in productivity to the failure of the American educational system and indicated that the system should be reformed, and very quickly, to eliminate the risk of falling farther behind.

The letter includes the commission's findings regarding the content of education, or the curriculum, the expectations of school staffs and students regarding student learning and achievement, the use that schools and students make of time for education, and the quality of teaching. The findings are all negative: The content is too easy and much of it is inappropriate; the expectations are too low; not enough time is given to education and the available time is not used well; too few able students are attracted to teaching; teachers salaries are too low; and there is a serious shortage of qualified teachers, particularly in mathematics and science.

Few observers of American education, including myself, would disagree with any of the preceding findings. However, some of the recommendations of the panel for eliminating the difficulties are debatable.

With respect to the curriculum, the panel recommended that at a minimum all students should be required to complete four years (credits) of English, three credits of each mathematics, science, and social studies, and one-half credit of computer science, a total of 13 1/2 credits, in order to receive a high school diploma. Two years of a foreign language in high school and two to four years prior to high school were recommended for the college-bound student. Another recommendation was that the high school curriculum should provide "students with programs requiring rigorous effort in subjects that advance students' personal, educational, and occupational goals, such as the fine and performing arts and vocational education." No mention was made of physical education and health or any applied arts.

We observe that these minimum requirements provide for no flexibility in meeting any of the unique characteristics of students or of local schools, such as differences in enrollment or the nature of the student population.

With respect to standards and expectations, the panel recommended more rigorous and measurable standards and higher expectations. This recommendation implies that all students will be able to meet the standards set by teachers and the schools in implementing the curriculum recommendations. Accordingly, the panel did not deal with the possibility that many failures might occur and that the dropout rate might increase.

A 220-day school rather than 180 was recommended as well as a longer school day, at least a seven-hour day. The panel recommended that the local district and the state should pay for the increased cost of the longer school year and school day.

Seven recommendations were made to improve teaching as follows:

1. Higher achievement standards for those who would be teachers and improvements in teacher-preparation programs;

2. Higher teacher salaries that are professionally competitive, market-sensitive, and performance-based;

3. An 11-month teacher contract to ensure higher salaries and time for curriculum and professional development;

4. A three-part career ladder for the teaching profession, which would include the beginning teacher, the experienced teacher, and the master teacher;

5. Use of master teachers to design teacher-preparation programs and to supervise beginning teachers;

6. Immediate attention to the shortage of mathematics and science teachers, through the employment of mathematicians and scientists, graduate students, and retired scientists in the schools; and

7. Financial incentives such as grants and loans, to attract outstanding students to teaching.

I, as many others, strongly support most of these recommendations regarding teaching. However, the probability of implementing them in the near future is limited since the needed funding is also to come from the local district and the state, not the federal government.

As with many reports of national panels and commissions, no provision is made for determining the extent to which the recommendations will be implemented or the effects of implementing them. My research and observations indicate that the federal education legislation of the 1960s and early 1970s contributed substantially to the decline in student achievement between 1965 and 1980. Our schools and our teachers were not prepared to take on the many new responsibilities that resulted from this massive legislation. Moreover, the change in family living and of society in general has greatly increased the demands placed on the schools to meet needs of students that were previously met by the family, the neighborhood, and the church. The panel's recommendations do not address these matters.

SCHOOL DISTRICT CURRICULUM DEVELOPMENT

Regardless of external prescriptions, it is essential for curriculum development to be carried out at the district level to assure continuity in student learning from one school level to the next. Six of the most important items to deal with at the district level involve (a) educational philosophy, (b) the scope and sequence of each curricular area, (c) the time allocations for the various curricular areas, (d) experiential learning including work experience in the community, (e) instructional methodology including materials, and (g) evaluation tools and procedures. In the author's view, district curriculum policy should not result in uniform and detailed prescriptions for all the schools of the district; rather, it should provide guidelines and limits for use by each local school, such as those suggested by Goodlad.

General Strategy

The manner in which school districts proceed in curriculum development varies greatly. Like state governments some districts follow a highly centralized pattern in which most of the important curricular decisions are made by district officials. Other districts are highly decentralized, placing much responsibility on each local school. The remaining districts are centralized on certain matters, such as instructional material selection, and decentralized on others, such as objectives. Furthermore, some districts have central office personnel who can be very helpful to the local school while others do not.

Tri-County Goal Development Project

The purpose here is not to identify the many school district curriculum development activities that are possible. Rather, a summary is presented of a locally funded Tri-County Goal Development Project (Doherty & Peters, 1978). This project, in which 55 school districts of three counties of Oregon participated, is presented in order to clarify three important outcomes of school district curriculum development, namely, program and course objectives, subject matter taxonomies, and evaluation tools.

Program and Course Objectives

Figure 4.1, taken from the science collection, illustrates four possible levels of objectives (goals) in the Tri-County Project: system, program, course, and instructional. The board of education of the school district is responsible for approving the broad statements of purpose that are indicated in the *system goals. Program goals* serve as guides to planning and organizing programs at the district level. *Course goals* serve as guides to planning courses in the local schools.

Behavioral and performance objectives are also given in Figure 4.1, but these types of objectives are not included in the collections of the Tri-County Project. The behavioral objective includes and specifies the desired behavior as well as implying the method of measurement. The performance objective adds the desired level of proficiency to be attained by the student.

The Tri-County Goal Development Project chose to produce only the program and course goals since these are suitable for educational planning at the local school level. The project personnel prefer-

Figure 4.1   Six Categories of Goals and Objectives. (Based on
Doherty & Peters, 1978, p. iv)

System Goal:	The student knows and is able to apply basic scientific and technological processes.
Program Goal:	The student is able to use the conventional language, instruments, and operations of science.
Course Goal:	The student is able to classify organisms according to their conventional taxonomic categories from observations, illustrations, or descriptions.
Instructional Goal:	The student is able to correctly classify as needle-leaf cuttings of the following trees: hemlocks, pines, spruces, firs, larches, cypresses, redwoods, and cedars.
Behavioral Objective:	Given cuttings of ten trees, seven of which are needle-leaf, the student is able to correctly identify which of the trees are needleleaves.
Performance Objective:	Given cuttings of ten trees, seven of which are needle-leaf, the student is able to correctly identify at least six of the seven as belonging to the class of needleleaves.

red not to constrain teachers by the measurement demands of behavioral and performance objectives. Thus, teachers who decide to use the course goals and instructional goals are provided statements of possible student learnings for which they can accept responsibility for attaining in ways most suitable to their instructional circumstances. The teachers are free to select those methods for achieving selected goals which seem most promising within the constraints of their resources and capabilities. This provides for more flexible teaching and learning since behavioral and performance objectives force decisions about how to teach and how to measure.

We can get a better idea of how program goals and course goals may be stated by examining a few examples. Five of the total of nine program goals for health education follow:

The student has positive feelings about himself and all people.

The student has the knowledge and skills needed to insure the physical and mental health of himself and others.

The student makes decisions and acts in ways which contribute to good personal and community health.

The student has a basic knowledge of human growth and development.

The student has knowledge and skills relative to safe living, accident prevention, and emergency care. (Doherty & Peters, 1978, p. 44)

Two of the course objectives for the mental health program goals are as follows:

The student knows that discussing problems and concerns with family members can bring about understanding and aid in problem-solving.

The student knows that effective communication among family members concerning sexuality can lead to personal understanding and understanding of the feelings of others. (Doherty & Hathaway, 1974, p. 74)

Subject-Matter Taxonomies

The taxonomy for each subject field is an outline of subject matter that is organized in an appropriate form for use both by subject matter experts and by teachers and students (Doherty & Peters, 1978). The taxonomy in each subject matter field represents an effort to classify the content of the particular field of study into categories with which teachers are most familiar.

There are four major concepts in the health education taxonomy: mental health, physical health, community health, and safe living. The first five of eight subclasses of concepts in the major category, mental health, follow to illustrate how a taxonomy is organized and what is included in it. A taxonomy of this kind permits teaching and learning to focus on any particular level of the taxonomy and on topics of the taxonomy that may be desired.

1. Mental health
   1.1 Definition of mental health
   1.2 Relationship to physical health
   1.3 Relationship to community health

1.4 Determinants of mental health
  1.41 Physiological determinants—physical and hereditary
  1.42 Environmental determinants—physical and societal
  1.43 Psychological determinants
    1.431 Concept of self and others
    1.432 Psychological needs and motivation
    1.433 Sources and expression of emotions
    1.434 Outlook on life and values

1.5 Behavior influenced by mental health
  1.51 Communicating
  1.52 Decision making
  1.53 Risk-taking—positive or negative
  1.54 Behaving responsibility or irresponsibly
  1.55 Adjusting—adapting
  1.56 Problem solving
  (Doherty & Peters, 1978, p. 45)

Comprehensive taxonomies of this kind are useful to any local school that has not recently identified and organized the subject matter of the content field. You can compare it with your own ideas of the content of the field and how it should be organized.

LOCAL SCHOOL CURRICULUM DEVELOPMENT

The comprehensive and enabling objectives related to curricular arrangements call for two levels of curriculum development by the local school staff. At one level the school staff continuously adapts the district curriculum to the needs of the student population of their school. For example, the reading curriculum of a school in which all the students have met the minimum competency level in Grade 9 is very different from that of another school in which 50 percent of the Grade 9 students have not met it. A second area of local school curriculum development is the preparation of learning guides, or curriculum guides, to be placed in the hands of students at the beginning of each unit of a course. The guide is needed to expedite the planning of individual student's instructional programs in the course.

The development of learning guides was described in Chapter 3.

A procedure that is used in many schools to plan and carry out curriculum improvement activities at the school level involves a school curriculum committee for each school of the district. The committee includes a representative teacher from each curricular area, a counselor, an administrator, and the school curriculum coordinator. Consultants from the district office and sometimes an external agency are invited to the committee meetings. A curriculum development plan generated by this committee that involves a particular subject field is referred to the faculty of the subject field. A representative group of teachers from this subject field and from the school committee carry out the related curriculum development. When experiential learning activities in the community are considered, persons from the community participate, usually to provide information to the committee, not to prepare curricular materials.

There are many ways of improving the curricular arrangements of a school. In the remainder of this chapter, the focus is on the curricular arrangements of a middle school and a senior high that employ the committee procedure just described.

MIDDLE SCHOOL CURRICULAR ARRANGEMENTS AND INDIVIDUAL EDUCATIONAL PROGRAMMING

Sennett Middle School of Madison, Wisconsin, enrolls approximately 600 students in Grades 6, 7, and 8. The students and their academic teachers are organized into six instruction and advisory units, with about 100 students in each unit. There are also 30 students with learning disabilities enrolled in the school, and there are three learning disabilities teachers. Each learning disabilities teacher serves as an advisor to approximately 10 students, while each academic team teacher is an advisor of about 25 students. About one-third of the students of each instruction and advisory unit are enrolled in Grade 6, another one-third in Grade 7, and another one-third in Grade 8. Each teacher advises the same students for the entire three-year period they are enrolled at Sennett and periodically plans an educational program with the student and the student's parents.

Sennett Middle School has a program for academically talented students. Grade 8 students who are mathematically talented take algebra in the nearby LaFollette Senior High School. There are also opportunities for talented students to extend their interests and accelerate their competencies in creative writing, foreign language, and other areas. An example of adapting this school's curriculum and instructional practices to arrange an appropriate individual educational program for an academically talented student and an LD student follow.

Individual Educational Program of a Student Talented in Math

Jim is in Grade 8, age 13. He is tall, slim, and vigorous. His health is excellent. He has unusually high ability in mathematics. He is kind to others, highly motivated, and well liked. He attends school regularly and is always on time. His parents are living together and he has two siblings. His parents participated in two conferences during the first semester of the school year.

On recent standardized educational achievement tests his percentile ranks were as follows: 98 in reading, 97 in language, 99 in mathematics, and total battery, 99. Jim has achieved high in all subject fields thus far and completed the Grade 8 math requirements while in Grade 7. During the present semester his extra-curricular activities are basketball and intramural sports. His hobbies are collecting postcards and beer cans. He wants to be a basketball player when he goes to college, and he is definitely interested in a college preparatory program in high school.

Jim's self-concept is regarded as very strong. His attitudes toward peers, teachers, classes, and toward the non-academic aspects of going to school are all regarded as very favorable.

Jim has an interesting profile of learning styles. He is eager to learn new materials and skills, persists until activities are completed, takes much responsibility for doing things well without supervision, and prefers clear guidelines regarding assignments and projects. He has no preference for working alone, with a partner, in a small group, or with an adult leader. Jim has an analytic style, is reflective, and prefers correct or socially-approved solutions rather than seeking novel or unique solutions to problems.

Jim's individual program for the first semester of Grade 8 included academic and exploratory courses. In language arts, Jim took units in speech, independent study, paragraphing, spelling, study skills, elements of literature, and intensive writing. He performed in an outstanding manner in all of the units. In language arts, Jim was given much responsibility for selecting varied materials, a variety of activities, and individual, pair, or small-group activity to take into account his interests and learning styles. He had the same options in his other subject fields.

Jim's science units included drug education, sex education, and human body systems. His social studies units were map skills, human relations, introduction to cultural diversity, analysis of prejudice, analysis of human relations, and immigration—wave 1. His performance in these units was regarded as outstanding.

Jim took Grade 9 algebra at an adjoining senior high school. The units included uses of algebra, operations on real numbers, sentences and problem solving, graphing relations and linear functions, and systems of sentences.

Jim's other classes included woodshop for 12 weeks and art for the next 12 weeks, each class having alternate meetings two or three times per week. Jim took physical education on alternate days throughout the semester and an extra-curricular activity, sports, one day per week throughout the semester

The program of the Madison School District for students with learning disabilities is generally regarded as among the very best in the United States. At Sennett Middle School, each learning disabilities teacher meets with the child and the parents at the beginning of each semester to plan the student's educational program for the semester. Before this meeting, the LD teacher has already met with the academic team of teachers to consider with them the kind of program which will be best for the student in each of the academic areas.

The student is mainstreamed as much as possible. LD students in Grades 7 and 8 get most of their instruction in the academic subjects with the other students. During this time the LD teacher works with the LD students, the academic teachers, and the other students. The LD student whose deficiency requires special attention meets with the LD teacher in the LD resource room during the student's scheduled study period.

Individual Educational Program of a Student with a Learning Disability

Sue is in Grade 8, 13 years of age. She is of moderate height, slender, and well developed. Her health is excellent. She has a learning disability that affects her performance in mathematics. She has unusually good ability in physical education, works very hard, and has many friends. She is occasionally absent from school but is rarely tardy. Sue's parents are both employed and there are three children in the family. Her parents attended two conferences with her and her teacher advisor during the semester.

On recent standardized educational achievement tests Sue's percentile ranks were as follows: 51 in reading, 31 in language, 8 in math, and 27 for total battery. Up to the present time she has achieved reasonably well in all curricular areas except mathematics. She is interested in horses and is talented in athletics. She engages in many kinds of sports, including intramural activities.

Sue's advisor rates her self-concept as strong. Her attitudes toward peers, teachers, classes, and the non-academic aspects of going to school are regarded as favorable.

Sue will learn new academic material and skills only if incentives are provided. In some academic activities she persists and in others she does not. She prefers clear guidelines regarding assignments and projects and frequently needs attention and encouragement from her teachers. She does not assume much responsibility for doing things well except in physical education and sports. Sue has no preference for learning alone, with a partner, or with a small group. Her preferred sensory modality is visual. She tends to be impulsive. She prefers to seek novel and unique solutions rather than correct or socially- approved solutions.

Sue's program in language arts includes reading, spelling, listening, and writing at a level typical of other Grade 8 students enrolled in the school. Inasmuch as mathematics is where her disability is reflected, she completed three units which most Grade 8 students had completed in earlier grades. The three units were whole number computation, number theory, and fraction computation. She spent about 75% of the total instructional time in mathematics in individual activity, closely monitored by the special education teacher or another team teacher. She also received individual instruction from the LD teacher in the regular classroom and occasionally in the LD resource room that was specifically designed to overcome her disability.

The units which Sue completed in science were drug education, sex education, and human body systems. The units which she completed in social studies were map skills, human relations, introduction to cultural diversities, analysis of prejudice, analysis of human relations, and immigration—wave 1.

Sue took home economics during the first 12 weeks of the year and art the next 12 weeks, alternating these two courses two or three times per week. She took physical education throughout the semester two or three times per week and was in sports for her extra-curricular activity. She excelled in these activities and enjoyed them very much.

HIGH SCHOOL CURRICULAR ARRANGEMENTS AND INDIVIDUAL EDUCATIONAL PROGRAMMING

Cedarburg High School is the only high school in the school district of Cedarburg, Wisconsin. It enrolls approximately 1,200 students in Grades 9 through 12. It has a teacher-advisor program by which each academic teacher works out individual educational plans with about 20 students.

All Cedarburg High School students must complete 20 credits for graduation. The required credits (years) are 4 in English, 2 in math, 2 in science, and 4 in social studies, a total of 12.[1] Two of these in each subject field must be taken in Grades 9 and 10. Another requirement is 2 credits of physical education. This makes a total of 14 required credits.

We see that all students must take English, math, science, and social studies in each Grade 9 and Grade 10. This arrangement facilitates taking into account each student's capability for learning different subject matters in two ways. First, when in Grade 9 students may be enrolled in one of four different levels of algebra, from pre-

---

[1] The total was increased after 1980-81.

algebra through accelerated algebra and in science in either biology or chemistry. When in Grade 10, the student may choose courses of different difficulty levels in most of the four required academic subject fields. Second, the amount of time students may use to complete the same units of a course during the class period and outside the class period, including study halls, is varied.

Within a particular course in Grade 9 and Grade 10 each student's learning styles and interests are taken into account by varying the instructional activities, instructional materials, and physical arrangements. An instructional materials center and other facilities outside the regular classroom spaces are available.

In Grades 11 and 12 each student's career interests and goals are reflected in the student's choice of courses within the required subjects and in the student's choice of electives. There is much more election in Grades 11 and 12 than in Grades 9 and 10. Experiential learning, including work experience in the community, has a major role in the senior year for some students.

The characteristics of two Cedarburg sophomores follow. The courses they completed during a semester reflect the results of implementing individual educational programming.

Kim is in Grade 10, age 15. Her health is normal and she has no disability or other condition that would affect her educational program. She is rarely absent or tardy. Her parents live together and are both employed. She has two brothers.

On a recent mental ability test, Kim's percentile was 93. Her percentiles on a standardized educational achievement test were 85 in reading, 71 in language arts, 61 in mathematics, 87 in social studies, and 94 in science. Kim is not engaged in any extra-curricular activities. She does baby sitting as part-time work. Her hobbies include music and being with friends. Her career interests are fashion modeling or preschool teaching.

Kim does not regard herself as having a strong self-concept. She regards her attitudes as favorable toward peers, teachers, her classes, and the non-academic aspects of going to school.

Kim indicates that she finishes most of her assignments on time, thinks it is important to do things as well as she can, and prefers classes where the directions are clear. She prefers to study with several classmates rather than working alone or with one other classmate. She regards herself as analytic, reflective, and likes to find new and different ways to do things.

During the first semester of her sophomore year, Kim completed the following courses with the following amount of credit:

Literature: Writing	.5 credit
Biology	.3 credit
Geometry	.5 credit
Social Studies: Man and His Social World	.5 credit
Typing	.5 credit
Physical Education	.25 credit

In addition to taking the six preceding courses, Kim had two study halls during the eight-period day of Cedarburg High School.

Penny is in Grade 10, age 16. She is 5'4', very talented academically, and highly sociable. She attends school regularly and is not tardy. Penny has one sibling. Her father and mother are both teachers. They participated in two conferences with Penny and her teacher advisor during the first semester.

On a recent mental ability test, Penny scored at the 99th percentile. On recent standardized educational achievement tests, her percentile ranks were 99 in reading, 99 in language arts, 97 in math, 98 in social studies, and 99 in science. During the semester her extra-curricular activities included cheerleading, French club, student government, ski club, pet club, and chorus. She did not work for pay. Her hobbies and interests include piano, guitar, cheerleading, skiing, swimming, and modeling. Her career goal is to be an MD.

Penny regards herself as having a strong self-concept and very favorable attitudes toward peers, teachers, classes, and the non-academic aspects of going to school.

Penny indicates that most of her subjects are interesting and she regards them as important. She finishes nearly all things that she starts, thinks it is important to do things as well as she can, and prefers classes where clear directions are given. Penny indicates no preference for learning alone, with a partner, or with a small group. Penny regards herself as analytic rather than global, reflective rather than impulsive, and as liking to find new and different ways to do things rather than to do things the way most other people do them.

During the first semester of her sophomore year, Penny had one study hall and took the following courses and earned the following credits:

Advanced Literature: Writing	.5 credit
Chemistry	.5 credit
Advanced Algebra	.5 credit
Social Studies: Man and His Social World	.5 credit
Intermediate French	.5 credit
Mixed Choir	.5 credit
Physical Education and Driver Education	.25 credit

References

College Entrance Examination Board. *Preparation for college in the 1980s: The basic academic competencies and the basic academic curriculum*. New York: The College Board, 1981.

Doherty, V. W., & Hathaway, W. E. *K-12: Health education*. Tri-County Goal Development Project, 1974. (Available from Commercial-Educational Distributing Services, P.O. Box 8723, Portland, Oregon 97208).

Doherty, V. W., & Peters, L. B. *K-12: Program goals and subject matter taxonomies for course goals in art, biological and physical sciences, business education, health education, home economics, industrial education, language arts, mathematics, music, physical education, second language, social science, and career education*. Tri-County Goal Development Project, 1978. (Available from Commercial-Educational Distributing Services, P.O. Box 8723, Portland, Oregon, 97208).

Goodlad, J. I. Individuality, commonality, and curricular practice. In G. D. Fenstermacher & J. I. Goodlad (Eds.), *Individual differences and the common curriculum* (Eighty-second yearbook of the National Society for the Study of Education. Part I). Chicago: University of Chicago Press, 1983.

National Commission on Excellence in Education. A nation at risk: The imperative for educational reform. *The Chronicle of Higher Education*, 1983, *26*(10), 11-16.

van Geel, T. The new law of the curriculum. In J. Schaffarzick & G. Sykes (Eds.), *Value conflicts and curriculum issues: Lessons from research and experience.* Berkeley, CA: McCutchan Publishing Corp., 1979, 25-71.

Suggestions for Further Reading

Cawelti, G. Redefining general education for the American high school. *Educational Leadership*, 1982, *39*(8), 570-572.
Cawelti's model includes five areas of general education: learning, communicating, and thinking skills; cultural studies; citizenship and social studies; science and technology; and health, recreation, and leisure. The area of learning, communicating, and thinking skills is novel and especially interesting. (This issue of this journal has other penetrating articles on general education.)

Combs, A. W. Affective education or none at all. *Educational Leadership*, 1982, *39*(7), 494-497.
An excellent account of the relationship between affective learning and learning in general. (There are other excellent articles on affective education in this issue of this journal.)

English, F. W. (Ed.). *Fundamental curriculum decisions* (1983 yearbook). Alexandria, VA: Association for Supervision and Curriculum Development, 1983.
Various writers present their views regarding the nature of the curriculum, curriculum planning, curriculum implementation, and curriculum evaluation.

Fenstermacher, G. D., & Goodlad, J. I. *Individual differences and the common curriculum* (Eighty-second yearbook of the National Society for the Study of Education. Part I). Chicago: University of Chicago Press, 1983.
Romberg, Munby and Russell, Early, Broudy, and Crabtree present a common curriculum for all students, and provisions for individual differences in mathematics (Ch. 6), natural sciences (Ch. 7), language

and literature (Ch. 8), aesthetics and fine arts (Ch. 9), and social studies (Ch. 10). There is a considerable difference among these authors with respect to the precision with which the common curriculum can be specified. However, all of them agree that there must be some variation in the common curriculum and a considerable amount in the use of instructional activities and materials in each class.

Goodlad, J. I. A study of schooling: Some findings and hypotheses. *Phi Delta Kappan*, 1983, *64*(7), 465-470.
Goodlad reports his in-depth study of 1,016 classrooms, about half of which were high school classes. He shows why planned improvements have become so difficult to start and maintain. (Most of the other articles in this issue of the journal are reactions to his study, both positive and negative.)

Grady, M. T., & Gawronski, J. D. (Eds.). *Computers in curriculum and instruction*. Washington, D.C.: Association for Supervision and Curriculum Development, 1983.
This short handbook has concisely written selections on choosing computers, using computers, computer literacy for teachers, computer literacy for students, computer uses by subject areas, and the future of computers.

Johnson, M. *Toward adolescence: The middle school years* (Seventy-ninth yearbook of the National Society for the Study of Education. Part I). Chicago: The University of Chicago Press, 1980.
This *Yearbook* focuses on the middle school years. The first part of the book deals with the relationship of this age group and the family, the school, the mass media, and other aspects of the milieu. The second part describes interventions and the third part indicates approaches to research. A final chapter identifies tasks for the middle school.

Schaffarzick, J., & Sykes, G. (Eds.). *Value conflicts and curriculum issues: Lessons from research and experience*. Berkeley, CA: McCutchan Publishing Corp., 1979.
This book, the product of a task force appointed by the National Institute of Education, Department of Health, Education, and

Welfare, is interesting reading for the person concerned about the role of the federal government in determining the curriculum of the local school and also for the person who wishes a quick overview of the great changes that have occurred in curriculum development since the mid- 1800s.

Trump, J. L., & Miller, D. F. *Secondary school curriculum improvement: Meeting challenges of the times* (3rd ed.). Boston: Allyn & Bacon, Inc., 1979.
Directed toward practitioners in middle schools, junior and senior high schools, this book considers general issues in curriculum and instruction first and then more specifically in business and distributive education, English language arts, fine arts, foreign languages, home economics, industrial arts, mathematic, physical education, health and safety education, science, social studies, and vocational and technical education. Major concepts and practices that cut across the curricular areas are included.

Wallace, D. G. (Ed.). *Developing basic skills programs in secondary schools.* Alexandria, VA: Association for Supervision and Curriculum Development, 1982.
Various scholars give their views concerning the basic skills that all students should develop, including oral communication, reading, writing, and mathematics. Teaching strategies are described.

CHAPTER 5

CAREER EDUCATION AND EXPERIENTIAL LEARNING

Herbert J. Klausmeier

What is the place of career education and experiential learning in the curriculum? How are course work at school and experiential learning in the community combined effectively? How do local schools incorporate various aspects of career awareness, career exploration, and career preparation into the individual educational programs of their students?

This chapter addresses these questions and clarifies the comprehensive and enabling adjectives related to career education and experiential learning that are incorporated in the improvement design.

Comprehensive Objective:

Career education is arranged for all students; experiential learning activities and work experience in the community are arranged for each student who can profit from them.

Illustrative Enabling Objectives

District and local school policies and practices have been developed that facilitate effective:

Career awareness, exploration, and preparation, including work experience.

Student participation in cultural, recreational, service, or other nonwork activities in the community.

Participation of community personnel in school activities and of school personnel in community activities.

Use of community resources and facilities.

Preparation of community personnel who participate in the educative process.

The local school staff, with appropriate participation by school district personnel and others:

Identifies program, course, and unit objectives to guide its career education activities.

Uses effective counseling and advising procedures in planning each student's individual educational program, including career education.

Uses instructional methods, materials, and community resources in courses and other educational activities that facilitate the individual student's attainment of his/her goals related to career education.

EXPERIENTIAL LEARNING

We shall examine the nature of experiential learning before turning to career education. Effective career education requires a considerable amount of experiential learning.

Gibbons (1976) indicated that the formal study of subject matter in courses of one semester length is the basic mode of school learning, and it is clearly a very important one. By itself, however, it is not sufficient to provide high quality education. Two other elements are required: concrete sensory experiencing and productive activity. Gibbons regards the combination of these two as experiential learning.

Concrete experiencing involves the sensory modalities of seeing, feeling, and movement. This kind of experiencing brings reality to the abstract concepts that are learned in the classroom. The kind of experiencing desired is modeled after that of the artist, medical intern, or scientist. Some students gain this kind of concrete experiencing informally as part of their family and neighborhood activities. Others require both opportunity for it as well as wise guidance of the process. For example, in the study of physical geography, most students should have opportunities to experience the landscape of the community and should be guided in exercising all their senses.

Gibbons stated that for truly powerful learning, productive activity must be added to concrete experiencing and formal study, that is, the outcomes of concrete experiencing and formal study must be used in activities that yield a product. The product might be an idea, a song, a building, a critique, a garden, a service. This kind of productivity requires knowledge to be consolidated and used. From an educational standpoint, the product is not desired so much as a product but for the processes that are learned and used in creating it. In this sense, work performed by students, whether at the school site or in the community, is a constructive form of experiential learning when it is guided properly. Gibbons strongly endorsed experiential learning in school and in work and other experiences in the community.

CAREER EDUCATION FOR ALL STUDENTS

Vocational education associated with preparing some students to take jobs upon high school graduation has been accepted as an appropriate task of the comprehensive high school for many decades. Unfortunately, it is also associated with a three-track system of education in which many students do not receive any kind of career education. More recently, emphasis has been placed on career education for all students. The goals of career education are now seen as aiding every student to become aware of different kinds of careers, to explore the nature of a few different kinds of careers; and, for some students, to prepare for work immediately after high school graduation.

Brown, et al. (1973) captured the spirit of the current emphasis on career education. The main ideas are summarized in the few statements that follow:

> Career awareness programs should be incorporated in the curriculum to assure that all students will gain an appreciation of the dignity of work.

> Opportunities for exploring a variety of career clusters should be available to students in Grades 8 through 10.

> Students should have opportunities to acquire skills in a career area of their choice in Grades 11 and 12. This education should involve experience in the world outside school and should equip the student with job-entry skills.

Job placement should be an integral part of the career education program for students planning to enter the labor force
upon leaving school. Secondary schools should establish an
employment office staffed by career counselors and clerical
assistants. The office should work in close cooperation with
the state employment services.

The National Panel on High School and Adolescent Education
(Martin et al., 1976) recommended making work opportunities
available to all youth as part of their high school education. One
benefit of work experience is alleviating some teenagers' pressing
economic needs to make their own way as well as to help their
families. Other values include promoting a sense of independence
and self-esteem, reducing isolation from older and younger people,
and providing many non-academic learning experiences that are not
available in the school.

The Panel also indicated that with a few notable exceptions, the
vocational courses in both comprehensive high schools and vocational schools fail to attain their stated objectives of preparing youth
for work. They felt that, although business education generally appeared successful, most other in-school job preparation curricula
were severely limited by the unrealistic nature of the course work
and the related isolation from the larger economy and community.
The Panel strongly endorsed work-study and cooperative work-
education programs for adolescents. In these programs, students
should receive high school credit and diplomas for a combination
of school work and part-time employment.

The California Commission for the Reform of Intermediate and
Secondary Education (Newcomer et al., 1975) recommended that
learners should have extensive and continuing opportunities for
career awareness, exploration, and preparation. Specifically, they
proposed that instructional programs should aid each learner in
developing self-awareness and self-direction while expanding the student's awareness of occupations, clusters of related occupations, and
the changing employment market. Other recommendations included assisting the learner in formulating appropriate attitudes about
the personal and social significance of work, providing opportunity
for the learner to gain an entry-level marketable job skill prior to
leaving secondary school, acquainting each learner with the importance of continuing education as a means of advancement in employ-

ment careers, and gaining the knowledge, experience, and skills necessary to begin implementing career objectives.

Parallel to the ideas of Gibbons, the Commission recommended nonwork experiential learning activities in both the school and the community. These activities might be for a brief or an extended period of time and include projects such as participating in a political campaign, conducting a traffic survey, building a stereo system, landscaping a home, or carrying out a health information program for teenagers.

TWO PATTERNS FOR PROVIDING EXPERIENCE-BASED CAREER EDUCATION

The idea of experience-based career education (EBCE) was initiated formally in 1971 by the United States Office of Education. After a series of feasibility studies, four regional educational laboratories[1] were selected to develop the concept into operational alternatives for high school students. The four laboratories were the Appalachian Educational Laboratory, Far West Laboratory, Northwest Regional Educational Laboratory, and Research for Better Schools.

The four laboratories applied different strategies in developing their programs; however, each program is designed to achieve three common goals (National Institute of Education, 1976). First, each program is intended to provide personalized learning experiences to the students. Second, the focus of student learning activities is in the community. Third, each program includes procedures and materials for integrating academic learning with work experiences.

There are two other very important features of all four programs. One is that they require an educational program, called a learning plan, to be worked out by each student and approved by the staff. The other is that parental participation in the individual educational programming process is required.

The four programs vary in their relationships with the established local high school program. The two that are described are at op-

---

[1]Regional educational laboratories were started in 1966 for the purpose of improving education in a geographical region of the United States. They were funded by the federal government.

posite ends of this relationship. The program developed by Research for Better Schools functions as part of the local school program but has career exploration and career preparation activities that reach into the community and the world of work. The Northwest Regional Educational Laboratory (NWREL) program can function either independently of a school or in cooperation with a school. The NWREL program is presented first.

Alternative Educational Options

The experience-based career education program (EBCE) of the Northwest Regional Educational Laboratory (NWREL) can be offered as part of a school's regular program or as an alternative high school program. Thus, the school can be governed in the usual way by a local school board, with the assistance of an EBCE advisory group, or by its own board of directors as an alternative school. Under either option, the daily schedules of the EBCE students are based primarily on their planned experiences in the community.

Curriculum Design and Modes of Learning

The NWREL/EBCE curriculum is divided into three content areas—Life Skills, Basic Skills, and Career Development. The five Life Skills categories are: Creative development, critical thinking, personal/social development, science, and functional citizenship. The Basic Skills content concentrates on the reading, mathematics, writing, listening, and speaking skills needed to perform tasks involved in the program and also in later adulthood. Career Development focuses on identifying career interests, understanding the world of work, gaining knowledge about careers, and developing employability skills.

Academic content is delivered primarily through actual community experiences, and student projects are the principal program strategy for delivering that content. In addition, however, students can include regular high school classes in their learning plans if these are appropriate to the individual student's needs and goals. Similarly, students can enroll in selected classes at community colleges in the area.

Students gain practice in basic skills and critical thinking as they complete project activities in specific curriculum content areas. Through the process of career exploration, students gain job investigation and assessment skills. Work experiences at successively higher learning levels give students "hands-on" practice in the skills, knowledge, and attitudes required for specific jobs.

Development of the Student Learning Plan and Certification of Learning

Learning plans are worked out periodically by the staff and the student through a cycle of assessment, prescription, evaluation, and integration of experiences. The cycle begins with initial assessment of the student's needs and interests. Each student then develops learning goals with the staff and is helped to design a plan that prescribes learning strategies to meet personal and program goals. As a student progresses in the program, each completed activity is evaluated by the student, staff, and appropriate community resource people. This evaluation yields the assessment information on which successive learning activities are based. Students develop their own timelines for completing activities and then meet regularly with staff to report on their progress and/or renegotiate timelines as needed.

Grades are not assigned and student work is not broken into standard courses and units of credit; instead, students are required to complete their work at performance levels appropriate to their abilities and goals. Evaluation criteria for each learning activity are negotiated between the student and staff, and each completed learning experience is then evaluated and certified according to those criteria by the appropriate persons—including staff, parents, and community resources.

When students complete the program, they receive a certification portfolio that contains information for the parents, high school placement officials, potential employers, and college registrars. Graduating students also receive a standard high school diploma. Transfer procedures have been developed between the program and the parent school so that EBCE students can re-enter the regular high school program.

Career Planning and Decision Making

Career planning and decision making skills are fostered in many ways, such as through formal career interest assessment procedures, maintaining a student journal, and participating in world-of-work seminars, career exploration activities, and work experiences. All adults involved in the program participate in ongoing career counseling to help students improve their information gathering and problem solving skills and add to their store of career information. Career exploration is especially important in helping students gain career decision making skills. The exploration activities involve students in three- to five-day investigations of occupations in the community and help them practice assessment techniques they can use in career planning throughout their lives. The work experiences encourage the students to manage their own learning and to perceive the relationships among personal goals, career options, and specific knowledge and skills.

Community Participation

Business and labor people from the community, students, parents, and school district representatives all share in program planning and policy making. Citizens in the community help to generate and maintain public support for the program. The community provides the learning sites that are used by students to meet personal and program objectives. Working adults at these sites serve as 'instructors' for the students. They help students learn, counsel them, provide help on special problems, and give feedback to staff on student performance.

Parent Relations

Parental permission is required for students to enter EBCE. The staff interacts with parents several times before permission is sought to ensure that they, as well as the student, understand what the program can offer and will require. Throughout the year, staff and parent communication is immediate and ongoing. Parents are regularly apprised of student learning plans and progress through a combination of written reports, personal telephone calls, and periodic conferences.

Integration with the Regular School Program

The experience-based career education program (EBCE) of Research for Better Schools (RBS) is integrated with the regular school schedule. When students are at the school site, the same rules and procedures regarding course work and extracurricular activities apply to them as to other students.

Curricular Design and Modes of Learning

Each student's curriculum involves career exploration, career specialization, and career guidance in addition to regular high school course work. Three distinct modes of learning are utilized—the classroom, individual and group sessions at school outside the classroom, and activities in the community, including work.

Career exploration is built into mini-courses of 12 weeks duration. These courses are planned and conducted at community sites and include individual and group activities. Each mini-course is developed for a career cluster, not for a specific job. It is offered either as an elective or as a substitute for required social studies courses.

Career specialization provides students with individual project opportunities, including work in the community. A project may follow from a career exploration activity, a special interest of the student, or an interest related to a subject field. All projects mix career and academic learning for credit toward high school graduation and involve student input in project planning and hands-on student experience in the community.

Career guidance uses both structured and informal group guidance techniques to develop students' decision making and problem solving skills with respect to career planning. Initial sessions (usually one hour per week) are designed around a structured career clarification curriculum.

An academic resource center provides students with individually tailored instruction in English and mathematics, complementing and preparing the student to participate in career exploration mini-courses and career specialization projects. Remediation of special student needs is also provided. Students take regular high school courses in all subject fields other than English and math.

**Development of the Student's Learning Plan and
Certification of Learning**

School staff, functioning as counselors, help students plan their
EBCE program. Regarding career exploration, the student makes
a first, second, and third choice of career clusters to explore during
the school year. A program is then arranged so that the student can
explore the three clusters, spending an average of 12 weeks on each
one. Students interested in career specialization first negotiate with
a coordinator to determine what they are prepared to do. They then
find the resource site to carry out their proposed project, including
work. Students have the primary responsibility for identifying a
specialization with some help from the school coordinator.

Credit for the mini-courses and projects is determined at the discre-
tion of the school administration. Department heads and other staff
certify course content students have learned in the field.

Career Planning and Decision Making

Direct instruction and informal instruction are provided in career
planning and decision making regarding a career. Direct instruction
focused on career clarification is designed to develop student
understanding of the techniques and the information required for
career planning and decision making. Informal instruction is carried out in the exploration and specialization activities and is followed
up with group guidance seminars and individual guidance.

Community Participation

Community participation is required for four tasks:

Leadership in developing public support for the program and
initially recruiting participants.

Leadership in defining and designing career exploration and
career specialization opportunities and revising them as
necessary.

Filling instructional roles for career exploration and career
specialization courses (program staff retain supervisory roles).

Helping the schools organize and develop an administrative mechanism for fostering ongoing community participation and assuring effective participation by community personnel.

Group orientation and training of community participants takes place before students begin their field programs. Training sessions are conducted by school staff in a series of seminars focusing on program goals and objectives, site analysis, implementation, learning activity development, program maintenance, and evaluation. School staff continue to meet regularly with their community counterparts until the latter gain experience in dealing with students. Contact is then maintained on a less regular basis throughout the school year.

Parent Relations

Parents are actively involved in many facets of the program. Parental signatures are required before students become eligible for enrollment. The EBCE staff interacts regularly with parents to solicit parent input and to assess student progress. An EBCE parent advisory group helps and encourages students in many ways. For example, it articulates program concerns to the school administration, helps students bridge the gap between learning in school and learning in the community, recruits community participants, and organizes social activities for students.

LOCALLY DEVELOPED PROGRAMS OF CAREER EDUCATION

In the previous part of this chapter we explored two patterns of federally supported experience-based career education that were disseminated throughout the country. Noteworthy features of four locally developed programs are highlighted in the remainder of this chapter.

Career Awareness and Exploration in a Middle School

Webster Transitional School is a suburban middle school in Cedarburg, Wisconsin. It enrolls students in Grades 6, 7, and 8. The academic teachers and students are organized into instruction and advisory units while the other teachers are organized into allied arts specialist teams. Each academic instruction and advisory unit has a team of three or four teachers and 75 to 100 students. The teachers of the academic team and two or three specialist teachers serve as advisors to the students of the unit.

The academic teams meet with their groups of students for 4 1/2 hours daily. This block of time is used for teaching language arts, reading, mathematics, science, and social studies. Many career awareness activities are integrated with instruction in these academic areas. For example, the students and teachers discuss careers associated with each of the academic subject fields. Community resource persons are invited to these classes to discuss the kind of work they do. The students also take field trips to different places of work and recreation in the community.

Students take two classes daily in industrial arts, home economics, art, or music. In these courses, the students learn about careers related to these fields and to perform work activities that many persons normally perform in their homes. One especially interesting experiential learning activity is carried out each year. All the students enrolled in the home economics, art, and industrial arts classes mass produce very attractive items that are sold at Christmas time. The proceeds are managed by the students and used to support student activities, such as transportation and admissions to special events.

Two other interesting experiential activities are living at the school camp for three days and two nights, and taking care of an outdoor classroom of three acres that is part of the school site. The students helped to plant the outdoor classroom with native Wisconsin shrubs, trees, and grasses and are continuously landscaping it. During the school year students learn not only information about the flora of Wisconsin, but also how to take care of it.

Many mini-courses are offered each semester that are experiential in orientation and that indirectly may be related to careers. Pet grooming, taxidermy, gardening, crotcheting, skiing—any kind of activity of interest to students of this age may be developed into a mini-course.

Career awareness and exploration are given formal attention during the second semester of Grade 8 as part of the activities of the teacher-advisor program. A published booklet, *Vocational Interest Experience and Skill Assessment* (American College Testing Program, 1976) is used. The use of this material aids the students in identifying new recreational and vocational interests, relating their experiences to broad families of occupations, and assessing their own emerging skills that might be related to different job clusters and job families.

It should be clear that the main aim of the career awareness and exploration activities of Webster Transitional School is to broaden the avocational and vocational interests of the student. Toward the end of Grade 9 of Cedarburg High School a systematic effort is made through individual conferences and by other means to help the student decide more definitely about a career.

Cooperative Work Experience in a Junior High School

A Junior High Cooperative Work Experience Program is carried out in all of the junior high schools of Denver, Colorado. It involves the school, the business community, the home, and the student. It began in the Denver Public Schools in cooperation with the Colorado State Board for Community Colleges and Occupational Education in September, 1970.

Students who wish to enroll in the program are referred by the principal, social worker, counselor, other teachers, or parents to the Cooperative Work Experience teacher/coordinator in each junior high school. The teacher/coordinator selects 15 to 20 students for the class. The students must be at least 14 years of age and in the 9th grade.

Students enrolled in Cooperative Work Experience attend classes during the first three periods of each school day and all have the same teacher for at least two of the three class periods. Each student has an English class, a math class, and a work related class. If scheduling is possible, a team teacher will teach the mathematics or English class if the teacher/coordinator is not certified in both areas. The student typically works 15 hours per week for pay.

Cooperative Work Experience teacher/coordinators are vocationally certified to teach the work related course and are state certified to teach mathematics or English. Instruction at school is based on the needs of the individual student since most of the class is composed of students who have low motivation for academic course work and vary in academic ability and interests. Many of these students need work to help support themselves and their families. Teacher/coordinators are responsible for placing students in jobs that comply with all federal and state child labor regulations. They are required to visit each student at work no less than once every two weeks to monitor student progress. An advisory board composed of local business people assists in keeping teacher/coordinators informed about the employment needs of the community.

The students receive credit for both their classwork and their on-the-job experience. In certain sections of Denver, students may continue with Cooperative Work Experience in high school (10th grade) and enter the Cooperative Occupational Education Program in the 11th and 12th grades.

Eighty-one students were enrolled in the Cooperative Work Experience Program in its first year, 1970. In 1978-79, 263 students were enrolled in 14 different junior high schools in Denver. The earnings of the 263 students amounted to approximately $337,000 during the year. The amount of school absenteeism of the same students was lower in Grade 9 than it had been in Grade 8. The mean reading achievement on a standardized educational achievement test increased during Grade 9 by 1.7 grade equivalent and the mean mathematics achievement by 1.6 grade equivalent.

Cooperative Work Experience in a Small Comprehensive High School

Hood River Valley High School of Hood River, Oregon, enrolls students in Grades 10, 11, and 12. It is the only high school of the district. Hood River Valley High School includes work experience in its career exploration and career preparation programs.

The work experience program for career preparation is limited to students who choose either the job-entry option or the option of preparing to enroll in a community or technical college. The work experience for these students must be directly related to the career for which they have chosen to prepare. For example, the student in distributive education must work in marketing, sales, and similar jobs. A student may earn up to 4 credits toward high school graduation through work experience. To earn credit, the student must work at least 15 hours per week and must also perform the duties of the job and carry out relationships with the employer such that both the employer and the supervisor evaluate the student as having attained the objectives of the particular work experience.

As part of career exploration, any student, including those who plan to go to college, may earn up to 1 credit through work experience. The work need not be directly related to the career interests of the student.

A selection procedure has been developed to ensure that the student who participates in career exploration work will profit from it in terms of its educational values. The applicant is interviewed by the school principal, one of the school counselors, and the program coordinator. Three learning units dealing with orientation to careers and work are required before starting any work (they are also required for the cooperative work experience). To obtain credit for the work experience the student must be on the job a specified number of hours per week and must also be rated as having attained the educational objectives of the particular experience by the employer and the high school coordinator.

Career Specialty Programs in a Metropolitan High School

In each of the 15 high schools of Milwaukee there are one, two, or three career specialty programs. The specialties include career clusters such as chemical technology; theater; music; dance; marketing; small business management; energy and environment; broadcasting; journalism; community human services; agribusiness and natural resources; and law, law enforcement, and protective services.

Washington High School of Milwaukee has a career specialty program in computer data processing. Special features of the program include its own computer system, a curriculum developed with the guidance of Milwaukee area educational and business leaders, specially trained staff, extended school-day hours, a summer program, and a laboratory featuring the latest equipment.

The computer data-processing specialty is open to all students of Milwaukee who will be sophomores, juniors, or seniors in September of the new school year. Students may choose to attend Washington High School on a full-day or a half-day basis. Most students spend a half day at Washington and the other half at the student's home school. When a student attends both a home high school and Washington, free bus transportation is provided. About 20 percent of the total students enrolled at Washington are in the computer specialty; the others are in the traditional high school arrangement.

Students who elect the computer data-processing specialty have goals such as these:

> To enroll in a technical school or four-year college and prepare for a career in computer data processing.

> To enroll in a technical school or four-year college and prepare for a career which uses computer data processing.

> To be employed upon graduation in computer data processing work.

> To be employed upon graduation in a career which uses computer data processing.

> To evaluate computer data processing as a career.

> To become acquainted with computer concepts.

Students enrolled in a career specialty program in a Milwaukee high school must take at least eight required units in English, social studies, math, science, and physical education; four units of electives; and six units in the career specialty. The students who enroll in a career specialty program take only the usual course offerings when in Grade 9. In Grade 10 they take one course in the career specialty and four to five courses in other areas. Juniors and seniors take one to three career specialty courses. Many seniors work for pay in a job related to the specialty.

Many patterns of individual educational programs are made possible to Milwaukee students by having the different career specialty programs and the options of job entry, technical school, and college preparatory options within each specialty. Differences among students in their career interests and goals and in their aptitudes can be taken into account. Furthermore, it is possible to arrange an individual instructional program in each required and elective course of each career specialty that takes into account the student's aptitudes, interests, and learning styles. In Washington's computer specialty courses, there are many opportunities for experiential learning during both the junior and senior year. In their senior year, all the students in the job-entry option work for pay and course credit while many of those choosing the technical college or the four-year college do also. The kinds of students enrolled in the specialty and the variations in their individual educational problems during the first semester of the senior year may be inferred from the information which follows for three seniors.

Sarah, a senior, is 17, slim, 5 feet, 5 inches tall, and weighs 121 pounds. Her health status is good and she has no disability or other condition that would affect her educational program. She has an outgoing personality. Her school attendance is regular and she is not late to class.

Sarah is enrolled in the morning at Washington High School and in the afternoon at her home school. She is working part time in a computer-related job. Her career goal is to become a data-processing engineer after completing a college degree. There is a possibility she might go to a technical college instead. Her main hobbies are listening to music and watching and participating in sports.

Sarah completed the following courses in the first semester and was enrolled in the others in the second semester:

First Semester	Second Semester
Computer Applications 1	Computer Applications 2
Advanced Mathematics 2	Advanced Mathematics 2
U.S. History	U.S. History Seminar
Journalism	Advanced Computer Programming
French 2	French 2
Physics 1	Physics 1

Denise, a senior, is 18, 5 feet, 3 inches tall, and weighs 117 pounds. Her health is very good and she has no disability of any kind.

She attends school regularly and is not tardy. Denise works half time as a data control clerk in a major industry of Milwaukee. She plans to continue in this position upon high school graduation. She characterizes herself as having very favorable attitudes toward peers, teachers, classes, and toward the non-academic aspects of going to school. She indicates that she feels very good about herself.

In the first semester of her senior year Denise completed the following courses and was enrolled in the others in the second semester:

First Semester	Second Semester
Computer Applications 1	Computer Applications 2
Science Fiction	Ceramics
Advanced Computer Programming	Sociology
Data Entry Internship (carried out in connection with her work)	Computer Applications (on-the-job training)

Henry, a senior, is 18, with brown hair and eyes; weighs 135 pounds, and is 5 feet, 11 inches. His health status is good and he has no disabilities. He regards his main strengths as mathematics, logical thinking, and computer programming. He is rarely absent from school, but occasionally is tardy. On a recent ACT test he scored at the 86 percentile on national norms. His career interest is to become a systems analyst after college graduation. His hobbies include data processing, woodworking, and mechanical activities. He is employed part time for pay in the computer center of a major telephone company.

In the first semester of his senior year, Henry took the following courses and was enrolled in the others in the second semester:

First Semester	Second Semester
Computer Applications 1	Computer Applications 2
Advanced Mathematics 2	Advanced Mathematics 2
Physics	Physics
Computer Applications (on-the-job training)	Computer Applications (on-the-job training)

Many of the first students who completed this program as seniors in the spring of 1979 were employed shortly thereafter in accordance with their goals. Others entered technical colleges or four-year colleges. One senior won the computer programming contest sponsored by the Wisconsin Association for Educational Data Systems. He then enrolled in the Massachusetts Institute of Technology in the fall of 1979. Thus, it appeared that this particular specialty was achieving success in helping students to prepare for job entry upon graduation or to prepare for technical college or four-year college education.

References

American College Testing Program. *Vocational interest experience and skill assessment*. Iowa City, IA: American College Testing Program, 1976.

Brown, B. F., et al. *The reform of secondary education*. New York: McGraw-Hill Book Company, 1973.

Gibbons, M. *The new secondary education*. Bloomington, IN: Phi Delta Kappa, 1976.

Martin, J. H., et al. *The education of adolescents* (National Panel on High School and Adolescent Education). Washington, D.C.: U. S. Department of Health, Education, and Welfare, 1976.

National Institute of Education. *A comparison of four experience-based career education programs: What they offer, how they differ*. Washington, D.C.: Education and Work Program, U. S. Department of Health, Education, and Welfare, 1976.

Newcomer, L. B. et al. *The RISE report* (California Commission for Reform of Intermediate and Secondary Education). Sacramento, CA: California State Department of Education, 1975.

Suggestions for Further Reading

Bottoms, G., & Copa, P. A perspective on vocational education today. *Phi Delta Kappan*, 1983, *64*(5), 348-354.
The authors detail the nature of vocational education today and explain its crucial role in solving the problems confronting the workplace. The number of persons enrolled in vocational education programs increased from 5,430,000 in 1965 to 13,726,790 in 1980.

Feller, R. J., Miller-Tiedeman, A., & Tiedeman, D. V.   Career
    education and the states. *Journal of Career Education*, 1982,
    9, 85-91.
The authors discuss the importance of career education and describe
its present state throughout the nation.

Gibbons, M.   *The new secondary education* (A Phi Delta Kappa
    Task Force Report). Bloomington, IN: Phi Delta Kappa, 1976.
Experiential learning and productive activity are emphasized as greatly needed approaches to the improvement of learning in secondary
schools.

Jenks, C. L., & Murphy, C. J.   *Overview to experience-based learn-
    ing and the facilitative role of the teacher* (Book I). San Fran-
    cisco: Far West Regional Educational Laboratory for Educa-
    tional Research and Development, 1979.
This book provides the introduction to a set of staff development
materials consisting of four booklets, a *Coordinator's Handbook*,
and a 45-minute videotape. The materials are designed for use in
either preservice or inservice staff development programs. The
materials are designed to increase teachers' understanding of experiential learning and to aid the teacher in planning experiential
learning activities with students, monitoring student progress, and
evaluating student progress.

McClure, L., Cook, S. C., & Thompson, V.   *Experience-based
    learning: How to make the community your classroom.*
    Portland, OR: Northwest Regional Educational Laboratory,
    1978.
The focus of this entire book is experience-based learning. It is written
for teachers and other local school personnel.

National Institute of Education.   *A comparison of four experience-
    based career education programs: What they offer, how they
    differ.* Washington, D.C.: Education and Work Program, U.
    S. Department of Health, Education, and Welfare, 1976.
In this pamphlet, the experience-based career education programs
developed by four educational laboratories are described: Appalachia
Educational Laboratory, Charleston, West Virginia; Far West
Laboratory, San Francisco, California; Northwest Regional Educa-

tion Laboratory, Portland, Oregon; and Research for Better Schools, Philadelphia, Pennsylvania.

Silberman, H. F. (Ed.). *Education and work* (Eighty-first yearbook of the Society for the Study of Education. Part II). Chicago: University of Chicago Press, 1982.
Various writers review problems and concerns regarding vocational education. Lois-ellen Datta presents an interesting account of employment-related basic skills.

CHAPTER 6

STUDENT DECISION-MAKING ARRANGEMENTS

Herbert J. Klausmeier

Learning to make wise decisions and to accept responsibility for the decisions that are made follows a developmental sequence, just as does learning mathematical or writing skills. Many opportunities are potentially available for students to make individual decisions and group decisions regarding both their instructional programs and their educational programs. The decisions that individual students and groups of students make regarding their own education are of such importance that a separate component of the design for the improvement of secondary education is devoted to it.

The purpose of this chapter is to clarify the comprehensive and enabling objectives of the improvement design that pertain to student decision making.

Comprehensive Objective:

Students progressively assume more initiative for planning, implementing, and evaluating their programs and activities with a lesser amount of adult direction and control.

Illustrative Enabling Objectives:

Students in their classes and in meetings with their advisors are taught:

Decision-making skills that help them to make educational decisions as individuals.

Concepts and skills that enable them to participate in shared decision making with other students, the school staff, and parents.

The individual student exercises increasing initiative for making decisions, accepting the related consequences of the decisions, and evaluating decisions regarding:

The student's instructional program in each course.

The student's individual educational program for the semester.

The student's individual educational program for the school year.

Students as members of groups take increasing initiative for making decisions, accepting the responsibility for the decisions, and for evaluating the decisions regarding:

The objectives and activities in the course in which the group is enrolled.

The extracurricular activity in which the group participates.

The governance of the group.

Students are encouraged to serve:

As officers and to participate as members of student-governing groups.

As student representatives on the school's standing and ad hoc committees, councils, and task forces.

RATIONALE FOR INCREASING STUDENT DECISION MAKING

The National Panel on High School and Adolescent Education (Martin et al., 1976) concluded that adolescents are more mature in many ways than society perceives them to be. However, secondary schools have a history of relating to adolescents as if they are too immature to learn to make wise decisions about their own educational needs and how to achieve them. This condition persists, according to Martin et al., because the schools are seen as custodial institutions and adolescents are viewed as persons to be kept off the streets and out of the labor market. Also, academic excellence and obedience are valued more highly than is learning to become independent.

Many different means and opportunities for encouraging more independence in educational decision making by the high school student have been proposed. For example:

A wide variety of paths leading to completion of requirements for graduation from high school should be made available to all students. Individual students must be encouraged to assume major responsibility for the determination of their educational goals, the development of the learning activities needed to achieve those goals, and the appraisal of their progress. (Brown et al., 1973, p. 73)

Even more independence in decision-making responsibility is implied in the following proposal:

Regular training and experience in selecting, designing, implementing, and managing their own learning will enable students to become independent and will prepare them for a lifetime of self-education. (Gibbons, 1976, p. 61)

According to Gibbons, carrying out this recommendation involves students in choosing, planning, and organizing educational activities in a manner similar to that which teachers employ in developing and teaching a course.

The California Commission on the Reform of Intermediate and Secondary Education (Newcomer et al., 1975) proposed that learners should be able to choose from a number of options and should have the opportunity of learning according to their preferred learning styles. These recommendations are as follows:

School systems should make available to all learners a wide variety of choices or options in programs and curriculum content. Such options should enable the learner to meet personalized educational objectives in varied ways according to one's learning style. A system of alternatives or options might feature schools-within-a-school, work-study programs, regional occupational training programs, special interest schools or centers, and departmentalized traditional programs. . . .

School systems should provide multiple options in formats for learning. Multiple learning formats should allow the learner to take advantage of such opportunities as learning independently, learning in groups of varying size and composition, and learning in different locations outside the traditional school setting. (Newcomer et al., 1975)

Implementing the preceding proposals could have either a very positive or a very negative effect on student conduct and discipline at school and also in the community. To achieve a positive effect the large majority of the students, not merely an academically-oriented minority of them, must learn to make wise decisions and assume responsibility for implementing the decisions. This requires experience in making more comprehensive decisions and also adult guidance and assistance at the time of making a critical life decision, such as identifying a long-term educational goal and selecting a path at or away from the school site to achieve it. Instruction that follows a developmental progression and practice in decision making aid students in becoming more independent and wise decision makers.

A DEVELOPMENTAL PROGRESSION IN STUDENT DECISION MAKING

Gaining competence in educational decision making follows a developmental sequence. The developmental sequence has three important dimensions. The first dimension deals with the decision maker, that is, whether only the individual student, a group of students, or a group of students and adults make the decision. The second is the scope of the decision, that is, the proportion of the total educational program that is affected by the decision. The proportion can range from small to large, for example, the learning activities during a class period to the total educational program that is affected by the decision. The third dimension involves the effects of the decision, that is, the number of persons in the school setting who are affected by the decision. This can range from only one student to the entire student body and faculty of the school.

The progression calls for starting with an individual student's decisions that affect only part of that student's instructional program and progressively extending the scope of the decisions to include the total educational program for a semester and eventually the total high school program. Applied to group decision making, the implication is that the group is small initially and its decisions govern only a small proportion of the total activities of the group. Progressively, the group moves toward making decisions that affect a larger part of the group's activities and also a larger number of individuals. Eventually, representative students serve on school committees and councils with teachers and other staff members and participate in formulating policies that affect the entire student body and faculty of the school.

Another point is in order regarding the developmental progression. The processes involved in all three decision areas—individual student, groups of students, and groups of students and adults—require adult guidance. In addition, each area of decision making should be used to teacher students decision-making skills. The examples that follow of early student decision making are drawn primarily from Steuben Middle School of Milwaukee, WI, and Wy' East Junior High School of Hood River Valley, OR; while the examples of later decision making come from Cedarburg High School, Cedarburg, WI, and Irvine High School of Irvine, CA.

Individual Decision Making

One beginning point for individual students to make decisions with less direction from the teacher is in connection with their instructional programs in each course. For example, middle school students choose some of the activities in which they engage and the materials they study. Furthermore, rapid learners choose projects for enrichment or acceleration when they have completed the minimum requirements. The student typically chooses from alternatives made available by the teacher. The student does not have unlimited freedom. At the same time, the teacher does not always assign or prescribe.

Making decisions about activities in each course gives the student experience for making the more comprehensive decisions that are involved later in planning a total educational program of courses and other educational activities each semester. At successively higher grade levels, the student has more opportunity for choosing among required courses and deciding on electives and cocurricular activities. Whether to take a job outside school is also an important decision. Many high school students are able to make wise educational decisions about their semester programs, especially when one or more conferences that include the student, the advisor, and the student's parents are used for this purpose. Most students want support or reinforcement for their decisions, especially during the early high school years. As the student progresses through high school, less guidance and support are needed from the advisor and the parents.

In Grade 8, 9, or 10, students typically must make a tentative decision regarding a broad field career that they will prepare for during their high school years. Although this is an investigatory decision and can be changed from year to year, it affects the student's entire high school program and may influence post-high school life and other activities. Counselors and parents assist the student in making these decisions, usually in conferences involving the student, the parents, and a counselor.

All of these opportunities for decision making by the student provide opportunities for teaching decision-making skills. Later in this chapter, models of decision making and methods for teaching the skills are described.

Shared Decision Making and Planning by Student Groups

The developmental progression for groups is similar to that for individuals; there is, however, the additional dimension of the number of individuals affected by the decisions. A further consideration is that shared decision making involves not only individual decision-making skills, it also requires being sensitive to and respecting the values and desires of the other members of the group.

The progression here starts with small groups making decisions about course activities. For example, a class of 25 to 30 students is organized into four to six groups to identify and carry out activities in accordance with their aptitudes for learning the particular subject matter, their interests, or their learning styles. Such groups may be formed so as to be either heterogeneous or homogeneous with respect to any variable, such as aptitude for learning the particular subject matter.

The next step in the developmental progression is for the entire group of students enrolled in a course to make a decision regarding any course element, such as a project. In this case, all are involved in the project, and the decision affects all the students enrolled in the course.

In many high schools, students are given more group decision-making responsibility in their extracurricular activities than in their credit courses. As a matter of fact, a primary aim of many extracurricular activities is to provide experiential learning in democratic group processes. In some clubs and other extracurricular activities, students take much initiative for planning and carrying out their plans. Often the teacher advisor provides informal instruction in decision-making skills.

The student council is the traditional means of giving students responsibility for making decisions that affect the entire student body of the school. The history of the student council in achieving this goal is one of mixed success. In many cases, the student council has not dealt with significant issues and problems, or when it has, many of its decisions have either been vetoed or not implemented.

Irvine High School of Irvine, California, has solved this problem by organizing the entire student body and staff of the high school into smaller high schools of about 600 students. There is a student council for each smaller unit. Each student council makes many decisions that affect the students of its unit. The means of assuring that the views of each student council are heard is through the school's instructional improvement council. This council, consisting of students, faculty, and parents, has a student representative from each council. One role of the student representatives is to make sure that the students' views from each council are reflected in the decisions made by the instructional improvement council.

The instructional improvement council formulates school policies regarding the curriculum, instruction, evaluation, and student conduct. It also appoints ad hoc task forces for hiring new faculty members, planning major school events, making changes in the curriculum, strengthening the teacher-advisor system, and influencing other important areas of school life. At least one student is included as a member of each task force.

Shared Decision Making by Groups of Students and Staff

This kind of decision making starts at the classroom level. For example, the entire class or a representative group of students share decision making with the teacher regarding some element of a course, such as content, activities, instructional materials, evaluation tools, grading, or student conduct. At the subschool level students provide input regarding departmental or interdepartmental matters, or issues pertaining to a particular grade of school. At the school level, a committee or council of students and faculty deals with policies and programs affecting the entire student body and faculty.

Students Assuming the Consequences of Their Decisions

Schools that deliberately foster student decision making either have written policies or arrive at oral agreements which indicate the areas in which students will participate. Agreement is also reached concerning students assuming responsibility for the decisions that they make. This applies to the decisions made by students as individuals and as members of student groups. These agreements are reached at the classroom level by the students and the teacher and at the school level by a representative group of students and the faculty.

Provisions are also made for dealing with failure either to make a sensible decision or to assume the responsibility for acting in accordance with it. As we are aware, students have many rights that are now assured by the courts. It is important for the school staff, the students, and the parents to understand these rights. It is equally important to agree upon procedures to follow when a student or a group of students violates the rights of others, including a member of the school staff or another student.

MODELS TO GUIDE DECISION MAKING

Each of us engages in much decision making, but most of us have not considered the thought processes through which we arrive at decisions, nor have we considered how we might teach young people decison-making skills. On the other hand, scholars in the field of problem solving have provided us with good ideas about teaching and learning decision-making skills. We shall consider ideas pertaining to convergent problem solving, divergent problem solving, and decision-making counseling.

Convergent Problem Solving

Some scholars regard the process of arriving at a correct or useful decision as a problem-solving activity. Two of the early problem-solving models originated in the 1930's. Rossman (1931) identified six stages or phases in the problem-solving sequence as follows:

> A need or difficulty is experienced, the problem is formulated, information is gathered regarding the problem, a problem solution is formulated, the solution is tested, and the solution that appears to be best is accepted or put into practice. (Rossman, 1931)

Dewey (1933) identified five phases in problem solving which he treated as the reflective thinking process. He specified the phases thus:

> Experiencing a difficulty, locating and defining the problem, suggesting possible hypotheses, mental elaboration, and testing hypotheses. (Dewey, 1933, p. 107)

In these problem-solving models, decision making occurs mainly at the time of testing the hypotheses or problem solutions and accepting one as being correct or more useful than another. However, there is also some decision making involved at the other stages, starting with the formulation of the problem.

Another approach to aid individuals in solving problems includes six main steps (Klausmeier & Goodwin, 1975).

> *Identify solvable problems.* To teach problem-solving skills in the school setting, it is imperative to aid the student to identify real problems that are solvable, rather than problems that exist only at the verbal level and do not lead to meaningful action by the student.

> *Help students state and delimit the problem.* This calls for putting the problem in written form or stating it precisely in oral form so that another person understands it. One of the principal difficulties that students experience in gathering infor-

mation and finding solutions is that the problem is not formulated clearly or it is too comprehensive.

Help students find information. Students usually do not have the necessary information to solve their problems and they often do not know the sources and methods for getting information. Identifying and using sources of information is an important skill.

Help students process information. Students, like adults, have difficulty in recognizing whether information is accurate or inaccurate, complete or incomplete. Furthermore, they are not skilled in analyzing, synthesizing, and evaluating information. Most students will not learn to perform these intellectual skills well without instruction.

Encourage the stating and testing of hypotheses. Hypotheses formulated by students about school-related problems vary in complexity. For example, the hypotheses might involve which of a few activities or instructional materials might be most useful. More complex hypotheses might be formulated in connection with deciding whether to prepare for a job upon high school graduation, prepare for technical school and then take a job, or prepare to enter a four-year college and then possibly graduate school to enter a profession. In the simplest to the most complex situation, it is well to recognize what is involved on the part of the learner to generate hypotheses and, as appropriate, to talk through with the student the several hypotheses that may be formed.

Encourage independent discovery and evaluation. In many situations, students will look to the teacher for approval or acceptance of a course of action that has been decided upon. Many students who decide to prepare for a job upon high school graduation, rather than to prepare for entering a technical college or a four-year college, have serious doubts about the wisdom of the decision. They will want support and approval from parents, the teacher advisor, or both as they continue to act upon the decision during their high school years. It is important to recognize differences among students and differences in the importance of the decisions which they make. Support and reinforcement are needed in many cases. The goal, however, is to encourage students to take increasing initiative and responsibility for discovering workable solutions and for evaluating those solutions.

Divergent Problem Solving

Problem-solving strategies have been formulated for aiding persons to generate novel or creative solutions. For example, Osborn (1963) identified 10 steps for teaching creative problem solving: (1) think of all phases of the problem, (2) select the subproblems to be attacked, (3) think of the information that might help, (4) select the most likely sources of data, (5) dream up all possible ideas to solve the problem, (6) select the ideas to solve the problem, (7) think of all possible ways to test, (8) select the soundest ways to test, (9) imagine all possible contingencies, and (10) decide on the final answer.

Davis (1973) views the teaching of creative problem solving to students as having three main components: attitudes, basic abilities, and techniques. Davis and Houtman (1968) formulated and tested a strategy for creative problem solving in school settings that incorporates Davis' components, and some of Osborn's 10 steps. It has four main phases or steps: (1) understanding the problem and stating it generally, (2) finding main types of solutions, (3) finding specific ideas for each main solution, and (4) choosing the best ideas.

Students getting money to buy things they want may be used to illustrate the four steps. After the students experience a need for getting money to buy things, the next phase is to identify as many plausible means of getting it as possible, for example, by earning, borrowing, selling, or renting something. Next, many specific ideas related to each of these four means are generated, such as raking leaves, baby sitting, borrowing from sisters, selling out-grown clothing, or renting the watch dog. Then the individuals evaluate which ideas may be best and make their choices of how to proceed. If the choice or choices work in practice, the problem is solved. If not, the student goes back to review and reconsider the problem and its possible solutions.

Simberg (1971) has identified perceptual and emotional "blocks" to creative problem solving. As teachers, we should try to conduct instruction to prevent students from developing the blocks. In addition, the student who is experiencing the block should be helped to overcome it.

A. Perceptual blocks
   1. Difficulty in isolating the problem.
   2. Difficulty caused by narrowing the problem too much.
   3. Inability to define terms.
   4. Failure to use all of the senses in observing.
   5. Difficulty in seeing remote relationships.
   6. Not investigating what at first appears to be obvious.
   7. Failure to distinguish between cause and effect.

B. Emotional blocks
   1. Fear of making a mistake or making a fool of yourself.
   2. Grabbing the first idea that comes along.
   3. Rigidity of thinking (difficulty in changing set).
   4. Overmotivation to succeed quickly.
   5. Pathological desire for security.
   6. Fear of supervisors and distrust of colleagues and subordinates.
   7. Lack of drive in carrying a problem through to completion and test.
   8. Lack of drive in putting a solution to work.

You may wish to treat the preceding "blocks" as a self-checklist. If you view some of them as applicable to yourself, consider dealing with them through applying Osborn's or Davis's approach to creative problem solving.

Models Used in Decision-Making Counseling

Counselors typically do not have time to carry out a large number of conferences with each student. Accordingly, a procedure is needed that enables the counselor and the student to reach important decisions quickly. This requires the counselor to take considerable initiative in the decision-making process. Wallace, Horan, Baker, and Hudson (1975) formulated a model of decision-making counseling. It is designed to aid the counselor and the student in arriving at a decision quickly and also to aid the student in learning to make decisions independently. The 10 steps of the model follow and are illustrated with the student making a vocational decision. The model is presented here for consideration not only by guidance counselors but also by teacher advisors when working with their advisees in individual conferences (see Chapter 10 for information regarding teachers serving as advisors). In fact, teachers might apply the model to student decision making in classroom settings.

Define the problem as one of choice. During an initial interview or two, the problem is defined in discussions between the counselor and the student. The student comes up with a clear statement of the problem or the counselor does. In the latter case, the student indicates the problem as being defined by agreeing that it is as the counselor has stated.

Explain the decision-making paradigm. The decision-making paradigm is directly related to the area of the decision making. Horan illustrates explaining the paradigm to the student as follows:

> Arriving at a good vocational decision means that we have to look at all the alternatives, then weigh them in the light of information about you and the advantages and disadvantages of each course of action. I can't make the decision for you but together we can arrive at, and implement one. (p. 171)

Identify possible alternatives. The counselor first asks the student to identify alternatives. If this can be done during the interview, the student compiles a list and expresses it either orally or in written form. In situations where the student cannot compile a list during the interview, the assignment may be given to do this between interviews. The counselor also may identify additional alternatives if those identified by the student appear to be inadequate to the counselor or the student.

Gather relevant information from the student. The counselor invites the student to present any relevant information that the student has. If it appears that the information is not complete, the student may be assigned this activity between interviews. In situations where the student cannot gather complete information or does not have sufficient information, the student, the counselor, or both gather information during the interview or between interviews.

Present relevant information to the student. Here the counselor assembles all of the relevant information that is considered necessary for considering the various alternatives that have been identified. In the case of making a choice about career preparation, the counselor assembles information that the student does not have, including test scores and information about academic performance, vocational experience, and interests. Step 5 continues with the student until the student indicates that all of the information is understood.

Request that the student identify advantages and disadvantages for each alternative. This step is carried out during the interview as the counselor and student discuss the information related to the alternatives, between interviews, or both. Depending upon the nature of the decision, the student in oral or written form lists the advantages and the disadvantages pertaining to each alternative.

Present any additional advantages and disadvantages to the student. This step is carried out only if the student appears not to have identified some of the important advantages or disadvantages of one or more of the alternatives. The advantages or disadvantages of any one or more of the alternatives may be considered inadequate by either the counselor or the student. This step is regarded as successful when a list of advantages and disadvantages acceptable to both the counselor and the student has been compiled.

Request that the student select the most promising alternative. During the counselor-student discussion, or as an assignment between interviews, the student evaluates the alternatives and either selects one or rank orders the alternatives from the most to the least preferred.

Verbally cue and reinforce the student for gathering additional information about the most promising alternative. The counselor verbally reinforces the student for gathering information, for identifying the advantages and disadvantages of the alternatives, and for evaluating and ranking the alternatives. This is done as a means of strengthening the paradigm which has been employed by the counselor and the student. The objective is for the student to learn to use the paradigm independently.

Help the student implement the alternative. This follows immediately after the student has selected the alternative to implement. As part of this step, a tentative course of action is selected and tried out. If, subsequently, the student or the counselor finds that the decision is not satisfactory, they go back to either Step 3 or Step 6.

The preceding model can be applied to decisions that students might make in any of the areas discussed earlier in this chapter. It can also be applied to decisions made in a series of interviews with a teacher advisor or counselor. For example, in deciding which of several activities in a course to pursue, the student who understands the decision-making paradigm and who also is provided sufficient information about the alternatives that are possible could probably make a wise decision without much assistance from the teacher.

TEACHING STUDENTS DECISION-MAKING SKILLS

Until recently, few schools have attempted to teach decision-making skills formally. However, materials and methods have not become available for teaching decision-making strategies in career education programs.

Representative of this trend is the Career-Decision-Making Program developed by the Appalachia Educational Laboratory. The program includes several printed items about careers, a text for students dealing with career decision making, audiovisual materials, and a teacher's edition (Appalachia Educational Laboratory, 1978). These materials may be used as part of a course, in the period set aside for the teacher-advisor group, in a separate semester course, or in other ways. The program has the goal of helping students gain greater understanding of themselves and the world of work by facilitating the development of decision-making skills.

A unit, or module, on decision making appears early in the program. In it, a five-step decision-making strategy is introduced and taught to the students. The students then use the strategy in the remaining 13 units of the program. Although the strategy is to be used in making decisions about careers, students could probably learn it and apply it, with teacher guidance, to any area of educational or personal decision making. The five steps of the process follow with an accompanying example to clarify each step.

STEP ONE: Clarify the situation.

The purpose of this step is to make sure you understand the situation. You can do this by defining your goals and values as they relate to the situation. State as well as you can the outcome you want. This may be the problem you want solved. It may be a change you desire. What solution would be ideal? How much time do you have to decide?

Example

Bob is about to finish his junior year of high school and wants a job for the summer. Any money he makes is his to do with as he pleases.

STEP TWO: Search for Alternatives

Look for ways to achieve the outcome you want. What did you do in similar situations in the past? What have other people done when they have had a problem like this? What can you read that might help you discover solutions? Find as many alternatives as you can. The more alternatives you have, the more likely you are to find an acceptable solution.

Example

Bob needs to find out about possible jobs. First, he thinks he might like to join several friends who plan to work part-time for the recreation department. Next, he considers the job he had the previous summer. He worked for his father as a plumber's helper. And he remembers that Ms. Jackson, a teacher, is looking for volunteers to build several playgrounds in areas where they are needed. This would be a full-time summer job. Bob is not completely happy with the three alternatives so he decides to move on to Step Three.

STEP THREE: Identify the Criteria

List the standards an alternative should meet to satisfy you. To do this, refer to the outcomes or ideal solutions you stated in Step One. List the standards that must be met for the solution to be acceptable. Then list the standards you would like to be met. The following questions may help you identify criteria.

What goals must the solution meet?
What values are involved?
Is there enough time to resolve the situation?
How much money or other resources do I have to work with?
Who could help me?
What parts of my life do I not want changed by this decision?

Example

Bob needs to determine the important factors in this situation so that he can evaluate the alternatives. He needs to decide what standards an alternative must meet to be acceptable. The factors will influence his decision. An important factor is that he would like to make enough money to buy a car by the end of the summer. Another is that he would like to get work experience that will help him decide on an occupation. A third factor is that he prefers a job where he can be more of less on his own.

STEP FOUR: Evaluate the Alternatives and Make Decision

Judge each of the alternatives from Step Two by checking it against your criteria (Step Three). Rate the desirability, probability, and risk of each alternative as high, medium, or low. The desirability is how much you want this outcome. The probability is the likelihood the alternative would bring the outcome you desire. The risk is the possible loss to you, if you choose the alternative. If you are not happy with any of the alternatives, try to find new ones or revise the old ones. You may also need to change your criteria. Then select the best alternative. Review it closely to make sure your choice meets your goal.

Example

Bob begins Step Four by examining each alternative—each job —carefully. This method helps him get rid of the alternatives he does not want. It also prevents him from overlooking the alternatives he does want. He starts with the first job, "recreation worker." He quickly decides that this job does not meet the standards or criteria he has established. He cannot make a lot of money on this job and he does not have a special interest in recreation. Next, he considers the job "plumber's helper." He remembers that it paid well. But he has already worked on this job and is not interested in becoming a plumber. The third job is "volunteer worker." This alternative would provide useful work experience but no pay.

Bob is not happy with the jobs he has examined. He decides to call his uncle to check if he knows of any other possible jobs. Bob learns that his uncle has been looking for a van driver's helper for the summer. His uncle is having a hard time finding the right person. He is looking form someone older than Bob. However, Bob can have the job if it is all right with his parents. Bob talks to his parents and they give him their permission. This alternative does not pay quite as much as the plumbing job, but the work experience will be valuable. The experience will help him clarify his interest in driving trucks. Bob looks over his list of alternatives and compares them in light of the factors that are important to him. He decides that the best alternative is to work for his uncle as a van driver's helper.

STEP FIVE: Develop a Plan of Action and Follow Through

Make a plan to carry out your decision. As you plan and take action, you may get new information. As this occurs, review your plan to make sure you are moving toward your goal. If not, you may need to change your plan or develop a new one.

Example

Even though Bob has made his decision, he has not completed the decision-making strategy. For the decision to be effective, he must develop a plan of action. First, he calls his uncle and tells him that he would like to have the job. Then, he needs to set up his work schedule, transportation to and from the transfer company, and so on. He will also continue looking for other alternatives in case he does not get this job. (Appalachia Educational Laboratory, 1978, pp. 42-45)

A final point should be made regarding investigatory decisions and final decisions. An investigatory decision is one that is made, acted upon, but then can be changed with a minimum amount of penalty for changing. Thus, a Grade 9 student makes an investigatory decision about a career field and, with an advisor, plans a high school program of course work and other activities. The student should be able to change the career choice at any time with a minimum amount of penalty. In general, formal and informal instruction in decision making in secondary school should recognize the importance of investigatory decisions.

A NOTE ON STUDENT DECISION MAKING AND DISCIPLINE

Many teachers properly hesitate to share decision making with students for fear that they will lose control of the class and that discipline problems will ensue. This will occur if the teacher has not yet established respect and authority as the classroom leader and if the students have not had successful prior experience in shared decision making with teachers. Despite this, we recognize that many students, upon becoming adults, will remain essentially childlike in their decision-making skills if the school does not provide formal or informal instruction in decision making. Our purpose here is to highlight crucial knowledge regarding classroom management and discipline. This is done to assure teachers that in many situations it is possible to have an excellent learning environment and also to share decision making with well behaved students.

Effective classroom management has been studied systematically only in recent times. Kounin (1970) started the modern era of research on it. He identified a number of classroom management competencies associated with high work involvement by students and freedom from deviant disruptive and withdrawal behaviors.

One competency is characterized as "with-it-ness." Teachers "with it" are alert to student deviant behavior and stop it before it spreads to others or gets serious. A second competency is attending to more than one activity at a time. While working with an individual student or a small group, the teacher also notices what is going on throughout the room. A third competency is referred to as smoothness and momentum. The teacher keeps the lesson moving at a fast pace and shifts from one activity to another easily without interrupting the lesson or breaking into student activities. Similarly, irrelevant questions or events are not allowed to divert seat work or a teacher presentation. Group alerting is a fourth teacher behavior that gets good results. Students are kept attentive and on their toes by questioning, choosing students to recite, signaling for quiet, and similar techniques.

Stoops and Stoops (1981) provide excellent ideas regarding both classroom management and discipline as follows:

> On the first day, cooperatively develop classroom standards.
>
> Incorporate school and district policies in the classroom list.
>
> Establish consequences for good and poor behavior.
>
> Expect good behavior from your students, and they will try to live up to your expectations.
>
> Plan and motivate interesting, meaningful lessons. Show your own enthusiasm for lesson activities.
>
> Prevent negative behavior by continuous emphasis upon positive achievement.
>
> Develop student self-discipline as rapidly as possible. Lead each student to make his or her own decisions rather than to rely on yours.
>
> If behavior problems cannot be solved in the classroom, seek the help of counselors and administrators.
>
> Reinforce good behavior by rewarding students in public. Correct or punish in private.
>
> Work closely with parents. Encourage them to send students to you with positive attitudes toward classroom learning.

Avoid useless rules, snap judgments, and loss of composure. Be consistent, fair, and firm.

Refrain from threats or promises that you may not be able to carry out.

Recognize that children have limited attention spans and assign alternate activities.

Discipline yourself in manners, voice, disposition, honesty, punctuality, consistency, fairness, and love for your students, so that your own example inspires behavior at its best. (p. 58)

I analyze discipline more fully in another book (Klausmeier, 1985, in press). In it, I have indicated categories of discipline problems, causes of discipline problems, and preventive and corrective procedures. The five main categories of discipline problems are related to physical aggression, attention seeking, resisting authority, making negative criticisms, and socializing with peers. Factors contributing to discipline problems include the family situation, the peer group, television viewing, the school climate, teacher behaviors, and the unique characteristics of the individual student. It should be clear that the individual teacher cannot control or correct all of the causes. However, given the same students, some teachers develop and maintain a far better learning environment than others. Similarly, administrators, teachers, and parents work far more effectively in some schools than in others to establish a good school climate. In this regard, the Commission on Excellence in Education (1983) recommended that the burden on teachers for maintaining discipline should be reduced through two procedures. One procedure involves the development of firm and fair codes of student conduct that are enforced consistently. The other is to establish alternative classrooms, programs, and schools to meet the needs of continually disruptive students.

Most schools can establish a good school climate and in this kind of climate most teachers are able to establish a good learning environment, free of disruptive discipline problems. For this to occur, it is imperative to establish an orderly learning environment at the beginning of the course. A synthesis of the suggestions of Kohut and Range (1979) and Swick (1980) with respect to getting a class off to a good start follow:

Learn school policies. Know what the school expects from both the teacher and students concerning discipline.

Establish a few classroom rules or guidelines. These should be fair, reasonable, and their rationale should be explained to the students. Don't have a long list of do's and don't's.

Discuss expectations. Explain the purposes and goals of the class and the obligations of both the students and the teacher to make the learning experience successful.

Learn names. Learn the names of the students as quickly as possible. Initially, a seating chart may be necessary. Calling a student by name early in the year gives the student a sense of well-being that he or she is more than just a student in your class. Furthermore, students will perceive that you are well-organized and in control.

Overplan lessons. For the first few weeks overplanning lessons will impress upon students that the entire class period will be used constructively. Students' expectations concerning how you value the time spent with them, as well as your control of the learning situation, are often established very early. By your model students will determine the values and expectations you desire.

Set a positive example. Teachers who are cynical, not motivated, and not organized are asking for behavior problems. The teacher who is well organized, listens to students, and portrays interest and concern in active learning has fewer behavior problems that less involved teachers.

Invite students to succeed. Give students verbal and nonverbal attention. When students who are becoming behavior problems begin to receive positive messages from the teacher on a continuous basis their behavior problems diminish. This is a practice which is easier said than done. However, the cycle of negative messages-negative behavior-negative messages should be replaced with a positive approach if the teacher wants to see positive behavior.

Be firm and consistent. This does not mean being harsh with students. Firm and consistent teachers can also be friendly, caring, loving, supportive and warm with students. Misbehavior in students is usually not a negative reaction to the teacher personally, but is caused by many other factors, including the students' perception of the role of "teacher." Firmness and consistency in discipline provides an environment where all students can expect fairness and also have a feeling of security concerning behavior expectations.

Restore order when a problem occurs. When serious misconduct occurs in class the other students will judge the teacher by the way the misbehavior is handled. The restoration of classroom order is the first priority. Minor problems may be handled by ignoring them or by simply stating to the student what the misbehavior was and reminding the student of the preferred behavior, for example, "Lisa, stop writing notes and get to work on our assignment."

Avoid emotional outbursts. Avoid arguing with the student in front of the class, making the punishment personal, being sarcastic, or making threats that cannot be fulfilled. If the situation is tense the use of humor can often be the best course of action to defuse the situation. Relax the other students and thwart an offending student's challenge to your authority. At times, removal of a student from the classroom may be the best method of restoring classroom order. Other students feel more comfortable when they know the teacher is in control of the class.

Handle your own problems whenever possible. Students behave better in classrooms where they know the teacher really is in control and does not always search for the principal to handle problems. Although some situations may require outside help, try to handle misbehavior yourself whenever possible.

Help students understand the negative consequences of their misbehavior. The sooner students perceive their behavior is hurting themselves and their classmates, the greater are the chances that the misbehavior will diminish. Help students understand that positive individual behavior is much more conducive to making the whole class successful than misbehavior.

Schedule conferences when necessary. If initial efforts to control student behavior fail, an individual teacher-pupil conference allows the teacher to get to know the student better, to identify possible causes of the misbehavior, and to plan solutions to the problem. Parents can provide the teacher with information that can be useful in understanding the student's problem. Parents can also suggest what actions might be most effective and also speak to their child about the classroom problem. When parents and teachers are communicating with each other, behavior problems are more likely to be solved than if this contact does not exist. Prior to scheduling or speaking with parents it is often useful to get the input of other teachers, guidance counselors, the school psychologist, and the principal concerning their experiences with the particular student and the parents.

A final suggestion is for the teacher to model enthusiasm and self-disciplined behavior continually. Much learning occurs through observing a model. Students can learn self-control and socially-constructive attitudes and conduct if they have appropriate models. The teacher who is respected by the students and whose own behavior is in control can be sure that students will also learn self-control. The students will assume increasing responsibility for the decisions that they make regarding their learning activities and their conduct.

References

Appalachia Educational Laboratory, Inc. *Exploring career decision-making* (teacher edition). Bloomington, IL: McKnight Publishing Co., 1978.

Brown, B. F. et al. *The reform of secondary education*. New York: McGraw-Hill Book Co., 1973.

Davis, G. A. *Psychology of problem solving: Theory and practice*. New York: Basic Books, 1973.

Davis, G. A., & Houtman, S. E. *Thinking creatively: A guide to training imagination*. Madison: Wisconsin Research and Development Center for Cognitive Learning, 1968.

Dewey, J. *How we think*. New York: Heath, 1933.

Gibbons, M. *The new secondary education* (Phi Delta Kappa Task Force Report). Bloomington, IN: Phi Delta Kappa, Inc., 1976.

Klausmeier, H. J. *Educational psychology* (5th ed.). New York: Harper & Row (1985, in press).

Klausmeier, H. J., & Goodwin, W. *Learning and human abilities: Educational psychology* (4th ed.). New York: Harper & Row, 1975.

Kohut, S., Jr., & Range, D. G. *Classroom discipline: Case studies and viewpoints*. Washington, D.C.: National Education Association, 1979.

Kounin, J. S. *Discipline and group management in classrooms*. New York: Holt, Rinehart & Winston, 1970.

Martin, J. H., et al. *The education of adolescents* (The Final Report and Recommendations of the National Panel on High School and Adolescent Education). Washington, D.C.: U.S. Government Printing Office, 1976.

National Commission on Excellence in Education. A nation at risk: The imperative for educational reform. *The Chronicle of Higher Education*, 1983, *26*(10), 11-16.

Newcomer, L. B. et al. *The RISE Report* (Report of the California Commission for Reform of Intermediate and Secondary Education). Sacramento, CA: California State Department of Education, 1975.

Osborn, A. F. *Applied imagination* (3rd ed.). New York: Scribners, 1963.

Rossman, J. *The psychology of the inventor.* Washington, D.C.: Inventors, 1931.

Simberg, A. L. Obstacles to creative thinking. In G. A. Davis & J. A. Scott (Eds.), *Training creative thinking.* New York: Holt, Rinehart, & Winston, 1971.

Stoops, E., & King-Stoops, J. Discipline suggestions for classroom teachers. *Phi Delta Kappan*, 1981, *63*(1), 58.

Swick, K. J. *Disruptive student behavior in the classroom.* Washington, D.C.: National Education Association, 1980.

Wallace, W. G., Horan, J. J., Baker, S. B., & Hudson, G. R. Incremental effects of modeling and performance feedback in teaching decision-making counseling. *Journal of Counseling Psychology*, 1975, *22*, 570-572.

Suggestions for Further Reading

Appalachia Educational Laboratory, Inc. *Exploring career decision-making* (teacher edition). Bloomington, IL: McKnight Publishing Co., 1978.

This teacher edition accompanies a textbook for students, called *Exploring Career Decision-Making.* The second of the 15 units is designed to teach students a decision-making strategy that is applicable not only to career decision making but to decision making generally. In the teacher edition, the teacher is given specific and concrete instructions as to how to use the textbook, filmstrips, and other materials to aid the students in learning the strategy.

Doremus, R. R. What ever happened to . . . Northwest High School? *Phi Delta Kappan*, 1982, *63*(8), 558-559.

An excellent account of a high school that unwisely gave naive inexperienced students too much freedom for making all kinds of decisions about their education. The school had swung about half way back by 1981 after a plan was worked out and implemented to permit students to exercise some freedom regarding courses to be taken, leaving the campus, missing classes, etc., only after they had demonstrated a high level of mature decision making, including keeping their parents informed.

Etzioni, A.   The role of self-discipline. *Phi Delta Kappan*, 1982, *64*(3), 184-187.
Etzioni relates discipline to character development. Students learn self-discipline, including the making of wise decisions, in carefully structured situations, not in authoritarian or permissive situations.

Horan, J. J.   *Counseling for effective decision making: A cognitive-behavioral perspective.* North Scituate, MA: Duxbury Press, 1979.
Excellent, readable summary and synthesis of the problem-solving models of decision making, and also the decision-making models used in counseling.

Lasley, T. J., & Wayson, W. W.   Characteristics of schools with good discipline. *Educational Leadership*, 1982, *40*(3), 28-31.
A concise account of the symptoms of discipline problems, e.g., disrespect for people; causes of the problems, e.g., lack of student involvement, wishy-washy leadership; and preventive and corrective activities, e.g., written rules and clearly specified consequences for breaking them strictly enforced, staff cooperation.

Schuerger, J. M., & Watterson, D. G.   *Using tests and other information in counseling: A decision model for practitioners.* Champaign, IL: Institute for Personality and Ability Testing, 1977.
Presents a model of decision making for use in counseling and a good discussion of how to interpret test results in assessing a student's learning characteristics.

CHAPTER 7

EVALUATION AND IMPROVEMENT STRATEGIES

Herbert J. Klausmeier

Much time, effort, and money are given to testing and evaluating. Teachers regularly assign letter grades to students on the basis of written tests, performance tests, work samples, or observations. Over two-thirds of the states have minimum competency testing. A vast amount of standardized achievement testing is done in local schools today and even more is likely to occur in the future. In this regard, the National Commission on Excellence in Education (1983) recommended that standardized tests of achievement

> should be administered at major transition points from one level of schooling to another and particularly from high school to college or work. The purposes of these tests would be to: (a) certify the student's credentials; (b) identify the need for remedial intervention; and (c) identify the opportunity for advanced or accelerated work. The tests should be administered as part of a nationwide (but not federal) system of state and local standardized tests. This system should include other diagnostic procedures that assist teachers and students to evaluate student progress. (p. 14).

If this recommendation is accepted, students will very likely be tested in each grade until they have scored at a desired minimum level in each subject field included in the testing program.

Even though much time and effort are given to testing, there is strong resistance on the part of educators to use the results of testing and evaluation to improve instruction, the curriculum, or any other element of the school's educative process. Yet, the information regarding student achievement and other outcomes that schools collect could be used in identifying areas of needed improvement and in ascertaining the extent to which planned improvements have been successful. Evaluative information must be used in implementing each of the three improvement strategies incorporated in the design for improving secondary education: individual educational programming, individual instructional programming, and goal setting for groups of students. The first two strategies were explained in Chapters 2 and 3. The goal-setting strategy is discussed later in this chapter.

The purpose of this chapter is to clarify the comprehensive and enabling objectives of the improvement design that pertain to evaluation and improvement strategies.

Comprehensive Objective:

The individual student's progress toward attaining his/her course objectives, the student's instructional program in each course, the student's total educational program, and the school's total educational program are evaluated systematically and the results of the evaluation are used in improving the educative processes of the school.

Illustrative Enabling Objectives:

Appropriate measurement and evaluation techniques are used:

To evaluate each student's progress toward attaining his/her learning goals in each course.

To evaluate each student's instructional program in each course.

To evaluate each student's educational program each semester in terms of the student's attainment of his/her goals, and in terms of the appropriateness and value of the program for the student.

To evaluate each student's total educational program for the complete school level, i.e., middle school, high school.

To evaluate elements of the school's total educational program.

The results of the evaluation of each student's educational program each semester are used, primarily *by teachers and students*:

To set a goal for improving the student's program the next semester.

The results of the evaluation of the school's total educational program are used *by teachers and other school staff*:

To set goals annually for composite groups of students to attain, such as those of a particular grade in school or those taught by a teaching team.

To evaluate each group's attainment of the goals.

The results of all evaluation activities are used *by teachers and other school staff*:

To improve the curriculum, instruction, and other elements of the school's educational program.

To improve the school's advising, organizational, and administrative structures and processes.

Before proceeding to the discussion of measurement and evaluation, we should be aware that in many schools today teachers assign grades to students, but the school does not use the grades to improve the educative processes of the school. Similarly, standardized mental ability tests and achievement tests are administered, but these results typically are not used in the guidance or instruction of the individual student or in improving the curriculum or instruction in any subject field. However, as we shall see in Chapter 13, schools that used the results of their testing program to improve the education of their students made remarkable progress in doing so. Clearly, schools can use test results and other evaluative information to improve education without any threat to teachers, administrators, students, or parents.

MEASUREMENT DEVICES AND PROCEDURES

Measurement is necessary in evaluation, but measuring is not the same as evaluating. Educational measurement, often performed with the use of tests or questionnaires, is the process of assigning a numeral or a letter grade to a student's performance. For example, we measure a student's achievement in algebra by administering a test. We measure a student's attitude toward algebra by administering a questionnaire.

Evaluation calls for establishing criteria and relating the results of measurement to the criteria. Thus, after measuring a student's achievement in a course during a semester, criteria are needed to relate the actual achievement to a desired criterion of achievement. For example, did the student's achievement meet a specified criterion of mastery? Did it reach a level lower than mastery that was appropriate for the student in terms of the student's ability or career goals?

We shall deal with criteria in later sections of this chapter. At this point an overview of various kinds of frequently used published and locally constructed measurement devices are related to various purposes of securing the measurements.

Table 7.1 shows commonly used measurement devices and the purpose for which each may be used. The five main purposes are to get an estimate of the student's capability, or aptitude, for learning different subject matters, the student's entering achievement level in a course and the level upon completing it, the student's progress during the course, the student's learning styles and learning strategies, and the student's affective characteristics. It is assumed that the reader is familiar with these purposes. However, a brief review of the uses of intellectual ability, aptitude, achievement, norm-referenced, and criterion-referenced tests may be helpful.

General intellectual ability is also referred to as general intelligence, academic ability, or mental ability. A *general intellectual ability test* is designed to measure the capability for successfully performing tasks that involve the use of language, mathematics, and abstract reasoning. An *aptitude test* is designed for measuring the ability that is required for successfully performing tasks related to a specific area, such as algebra, French, engineering, music, or clerical skills. An *educational achievement test* is designed to measure what the individual has learned in a particular subject field such as reading, mathematics, chemistry, German, or U. S. history.

Although general intellectual ability tests are very widely used, not all persons accept the idea that intelligence is unitary. Thurstone (1938) defined intelligence as consisting of several primary intellectual abilities, including number, word meaning, and spatial. Tests based on this idea are sometimes used in career counseling. Guilford (1967) identified 120 specific intellectual abilities, including 20 related to creative thinking. Creative thinking tests based on Guilford's ideas are sometimes used in schools to aid in identifying potentially creative students.

One main use of mental ability tests of any kind is to secure an

Table 7.1   Frequently Used Measurement Devices and Their Purposes

Measurement Device or Procedure	Capability for learning subject matter	Achievement level at beginning or end of course	Progress during course	Learning style, learning strategy, etc.	Interests, attitudes, self-concept, etc.
Standardized norm-referenced intellectual ability or other aptitude test	X				
Standardized norm-referenced educational achievement test	X	X			
Published criterion-referenced test	X	X	X		
Locally constructed criterion-referenced test	X	X	X		
Teacher-made paper-and-pencil test, teacher-developed test of performance, or teacher rating of work sample	X	X	X		
Teacher observation	X	X	X	X	X
Published inventory or questionnaire				X	X
Locally constructed inventory or questionnaire				X	X

estimate of how well the student should be able to learn particular subject matters. Thus, the student who scores well above average on a general intellectual, or mental, ability test is expected to achieve above average in courses in English, mathematics, reading, science, and social studies. Similarly, the student who scores high on a music or art aptitude test is expected to achieve higher than one who scores low. However, since the correlation between ability and achievement is less than perfect, we do not expect to find a perfect correspondence between a student's measured ability and the same student's achievement. Moreover, many factors other than ability, such as prior achievement, motivation, effort, learning style, and learning strategy, also influence a student's achievement in any course.

Although there is not a perfect correspondence between an individual's measured ability and achievement, the average mental ability of a group of students, such as those enrolled in Grade 7 or Grade 10, is a good predictor of the average achievement of the group in the academic subjects. For example, we found that even a difference as small as two to five points in mental ability between two Grade 7 classes of a middle school and Grade 9 classes of a high school was accompanied with different mean achievement levels in the academic subjects—English, mathematics, reading, science, social studies (Klausmeier, Serlin, & Zindler, 1983). Moreover, to increase the academic achievement of the students of a grade in any academic subject, one appropriate technique is to identify the students who are achieving farthest below mental ability and work with them to increase their effort and to improve their learning strategies and study habits.

Let us now examine norm-referenced and criterion-referenced achievement tests. A standardized norm-referenced achievement test is one in which the meaning of a raw score made by any student is interpreted in relation to other students' scores on the same test. For example, a student's raw score of 25 on a standardized test does not provide meaningful information. However, when it is found on a table of norms to be equivalent to the 50th percentile rank, we recognize that this student's achievement level is equal to the median of the national sample. Standardized educational achievement tests have accompanying manuals that provide tables for converting any raw score to a percentile rank, grade equivalent, standard score, or some other kind of derived score. The derived scores are based on the scores of the national sample of students who were involved in the standardization of the test. This national sample is the norming group.

Standardized achievement tests indicate to a school how its student are achieving in relation to the national sample. They are also useful for measuring changes in student achievement across longer time periods, such as a semester or year. A standardized test is a valid measure of the achievement of the students of a particular school to the extent that the items of the test measure the objectives of the school's educational program. Accordingly, schools should examine the items of a test to assure that the items measure the results of their educational program before adopting the test.

Criterion-referenced tests may be published or locally constructed. The first step in constructing a criterion-referenced test is to specify the educational objectives. Then, a short test is developed for measuring student achievement of each objective, or a set of closely related objectives. A criterion, such as 85% correct, is specified as indicating mastery of the objectives. Thus, a criterion-referenced test yields scores that are interpreted in terms of the student's achievement of the educational task to a desired criterion. Each student's score is interpreted in relation to each particular task or set of objectives, not in relation to other students' scores as in the case with norm-referenced tests.

Criterion-referenced testing is being used increasingly in connection with student achievement of minimum competencies. The minimum competencies are stated as instructional objectives, and instruction is directed specifically to enable students to achieve the objectives. Criterion-referenced testing in one or more subject fields, and particularly mathematics, reading, and spelling, is also employed in schools that follow a pattern of performance-based education. The tests are used to measure the entering achievement level of the students, to place each student properly, to monitor progress thereafter, and to measure final attainment of the objectives. The strength of criterion-referenced tests is their close relationship to the school's educational objectives. A weakness is that the results cannot be related to the achievements of students in other schools of the state or nation.

EVALUATION AND INDIVIDUAL INSTRUCTIONAL PROGRAMMING

The instructional programming strategy was explained in Chapter 3. When implementing it, the teacher not only carries out instruction but also monitors each student's progress and evaluates each student's instructional program. Thus, gathering and using evaluative information is an integral part of the instructional programming strategy.

The time and related purposes of gathering and interpreting evaluation information when implementing individual instructional programming are as follows:

Time 1:   Prior to starting a course and each unit within the course.

Purpose: To plan an appropriate instructional program for each student enrolled in the course.

Time 2:   During the course and each unit of the course.

Purpose: To provide feedback information to the student to facilitate learning, and to the teacher to facilitate instruction.

Time 3:   At the end of the course and each unit within the course.

Purpose: To determine whether the student has attained his or her learning goals.
          To decide the student's next activities.
          To evaluate the student's instructional program.
          To evaluate the effectiveness of the instruction of all the students.
          To improve instruction in the course.

Three kinds of information regarding the student are especially important in working out an instructional plan with the student at the beginning of a course. One is the capability of the student for learning the particular subject matter. This capability may be estimated on the basis of prior grades, criterion-referenced test results, or the results of standardized tests of achievement and mental ability. A second is the student's subject field interests and, at the high school level, career goals. Typically, students readily communicate this kind of information to the teacher. A third kind of information is the student's learning styles. A checklist of learning styles that might be administered to the student was given in Chapter 3. Other information that is also useful was indicated in Figure 2.1. Typically, all of this information is gained from records before the course starts or it is gotten during the first day or two of class.

Monitoring the student's progress may be based on teacher observation of the student's performance, teacher-constructed criterion-referenced tests, work samples, and other means of gathering information. The main purpose of monitoring is to assure that the student gets information that is needed to correct errors and inadequacies.

Evaluation of the student's achievement at the end of a unit or course involves, first, comparing the student's achievements with the criterion that has been established for goal attainment. The usual criterion is either mastery of objectives or attainment to a level judged to be appropriate for the particular student. The same kinds of devices that are used to measure progress are also used to measure achievement at the end of an instructional sequence. In addition, standardized achievement tests are often administered at one-year or two-year intervals. These results are useful in assessing the student's achievement over longer time periods.

Another important aspect of the evaluation process is judging the value and appropriateness of the instructional program for the student in terms of the student's aptitudes, interests, learning styles, and other characteristics. This can be accomplished during a class period, for example, on the day that grades are reported. Individual conferences are sometimes necessary with the student who has not achieved as well as expected.

Figure 7.1 is a student questionnaire related to reading. Its purpose is to secure the student's opinions regarding the appropriateness and value of the reading course. A questionnaire of this kind may be prepared for any course and administered to a group of students in a few minutes, or it may be used in a conference with the student. The questions can be adapted to each teacher's preferences. (The parenthetical information is not part of the questionnaire. It indicates what the item is intended to measure.)

In many situations the teacher does not have time to evaluate each student's instructional program at the end of a course, much less at the end of each unit. However, carefully evaluating the completed programs of a male and female low achiever, a male and a female middle achiever, and a male and female high achiever provides very useful information to the teacher regarding the value and appropriateness of the instructional programs of all the students who took the course.

EVALUATION AND INDIVIDUAL EDUCATIONAL PROGRAMMING

The individual educational programming strategy was explained in Chapter 2. Gathering and using evaluative information is an im-

Figure 7.1   Student Course Survey

Directions: Below you will find questions about your reading class.
Place a check next to the group of words that describes how you feel
about it.

1. In reading (motivation)

_____ I did as well as I possibly could have.
_____ I did about as well as I could have.
_____ I didn't do as well as I could have.
_____ I didn't do nearly as well as I could have.

2. Reading was (aptitude for learning to read)

_____ very hard for me.
_____ hard for me.
_____ easy for me.
_____ very easy for me.

3. Reading was (interest)

_____ very interesting to me.
_____ interesting to me.
_____ uninteresting to me.
_____ very uninteresting to me.

4. In reading I would rather have spent more time (learning style)

_____ learning by myself.
_____ learning with another student.
_____ learning with a small group of students.
_____ learning with the whole class.
_____ everything was about right.

5. I think what I learned in reading will be (value)

_____ very useful to me.
_____ useful to me.
_____ not useful to me.

---

portant part of the strategy. The timing and purposes of evaluation
related to implementing the individual educational programming
strategy may be summarized as follows:

Time 1:   Prior to the assignment of the student to particular
          courses or to activities and objectives within each
          course.
Purpose: To plan an appropriate total educational program
          for and with each individual student each semester.

Time 2:   During the semester and year (at least twice per semester).

Purpose: To provide feedback to the student so that the student can take appropriate actions relative to each course.

To monitor the student's progress in all courses and activities, to identify possible difficulties the student may be experiencing and their causes, and to take appropriate actions with the student and/or to make changes in the program.

Time 3:   At the end of each semester.

Purpose: To determine the extent to which the student has achieved his/her learning goals in each course.

To determine how effective the various elements of the total program were for the student in terms of the criteria that were established.

To provide the information for planning the next educational program (of the student who continues in the same school).

To identify areas of possible improvement of specific courses and other curricular elements.

The main steps in implementing individual educational programming follow, and the kind of evaluative information that is used at each step is indicated.

In a conference with each continuing student and each incoming student and with the student's parents, develop an educational plan with the student for the semester. As was explained in Chapter 2, a tentative educational plan is worked out prior to the start of the semester and the final plan is completed at the beginning of the semester. The plan includes a list of the courses, extracurricular activities, study periods, and other educational activities in which the student will engage in the school and community. Changes as necessary are made in the plan throughout the semester to provide the best program possible for the student.

As part of the planning process, the student sets one or more goals in each course. With guidance of the advisor, the student sets his/her goals in terms such as the number of objectives to be attained, the number of units to be completed, the letter grade to be earned, or the percent correct to be attained on a locally constructed test or the percentile to be obtained on a standardized educational achievement test.

The kinds of information needed about the student and about the possible courses, extracurricular activities, study periods, and other opportunities available to the student were given in Chapter 2. Among the most important kinds of information are the student's capability for learning different subject matters, subject matter and career interests, and learning styles.

Monitor the student's progress related to each element of his or her program. Three important points to consider regarding the monitoring process are the involvement of the student, the frequency of the monitoring, and the fact that all elements of the student's educational program require monitoring. The student participates directly in the monitoring. Individual conferences are held in which the student and the advisor supply the information necessary to assess the student's progress. Problems related to any element of the educational program are identified and resolved.

Each school determines the frequency of the monitoring conferences. One or two conferences each semester coming between the planning conference early in the semester and a conference at the end of the semester are sufficient for most students. A conference immediately after each grading period works well. The end-of-semester conference and the first planning conference for the ensuing semester are often combined.

Since the monitoring process involves all elements of the student's program, it also involves courses taught by various teachers. In team teaching situations, a team meeting may be used to deal with problems that a student is experiencing in the various courses taught by the team members. In other situations, other arrangements are worked out that include the teacher advisor, the teacher of the course where a difficulty is being experienced, and the student. The counselor or curriculum coordinator may provide assistance in scheduling these conferences and also in conducting them.

The information supplied by the teacher of each course when reporting grades may be adequate for monitoring the progress of students who achieve reasonably well in relation to expectancy. On the other hand, both the student and the teacher are invited to provide the advisor information as soon as a student experiences difficulty in any course or any other educational activity. Similarly, parents are invited to indicate when their child is experiencing problems, and the parents are informed by the advisor of the situation as soon as it becomes known to the advisor.

Evaluate the student's semester program in terms of the extent to which the student attained his/her goals and in terms of the appropriateness and value of the program to the student. Evaluating the student's attainment of his or her goals in each course starts with the statement of the goals included in the student's educational plan. Then, evaluative information regarding the student's achievements in each course and other educational activity is compiled. Most of this information is supplied by the teachers in their report forms to the parents. In an individual conference, the student and the advisor compare the two and judge the achievement as above, at, or below each goal that was set.

To evaluate the appropriateness of the program for the student, one consideration is how well the student achieved in relation to the student's aptitude for learning the particular subject matter. Other considerations are how well the course activities and materials related to the student's general interests (and career interests if applicable), the student's learning styles, and motivational characteristics. The value criterion involves whether the student, the advisor, and parents regard each part of the program, and the program in its totality, as worthwhile at the present time, in the future, or both.

Figure 7.2 is a form that the student completes to provide the advisor with an estimate of the appropriateness and value of his or her completed program. The advisee completes it either prior to a conference with the advisor or during the conference. In the conference, the advisor and student discuss the student's achievements and activities in each course. They conclude the conference with a discussion of the ratings. It may be observed that the items of the checklist are intended to serve as a starting point for discussing the appropriateness and the value of the course to the student from the student's viewpoint.

As the students gain experience in educational planning and evaluation, they take greater initiative in all aspects of the planning-monitoring-evaluation sequence. At Cedarburg High School, for example, many students lead the conferences. As was indicated in Chapter 6, students not only should participate in decision making regarding their educational programs but also should learn decision-making strategies and skills through working with the advisor. Engag-

Figure 7.2   Student Opinion of a Completed Educational Program

Directions: Think about all the courses and your other educational activities for last semester. Then check each item. You, your advisor, and your parents will discuss your opinions in a conference. No other persons will see them.

1. The amount of effort for me to attain my course goals was (check one):

_____ far too much.
_____ too much.
_____ about right.
_____ too little.
_____ far too little.

Comments regarding specific courses:

2. The value of my courses to me was (check one):

_____ very high.
_____ high.
_____ moderate.
_____ low.
_____ very low.

Comments regarding specific courses:

3. My interest in the content and activities of my courses was (check one):

_____ very high.
_____ high.
_____ moderate.
_____ low.
_____ very low.

Comments regarding specific courses.

4. Consider the total number of courses, their value and difficulty, and your interest in them. In terms of furthering your educational development, you regard them in their totality as:

_____ aiding you to make excellent progress in your educational development.
_____ aiding you to make above average progress in your educational development.
_____ aiding you to make average progress in your educational development.
_____ contributing to below average progress in your educational development.
_____ contributing to very little progress in your educational development.

Comments regarding specific courses:

Figure 7.2 (continued)

---

5. Consider not only activities and relationships among the students
   in your classes but also in your extra-curricular activities. In
   terms of your relations with other students, these activities:

   _____ aided you in maintaining or developing excellent relations
           with other students.
   _____ aided you in maintaining or developing good relations with
           other students.
   _____ neither aided nor interfered in any way with your relation-
           ships.
   _____ contributed to less desirable relationships with other
           students.

   Comments regarding specific courses:

6. High school is designed to help students accept the responsibilities
   of adulthood when they graduate. Consider all of your school experiences this past semester. You regard them as:

   _____ providing excellent support for assuming, or preparing to
           assume, more adult responsibilities.
   _____ providing some support for assuming, or preparing to assume,
           more adult responsibilities.
   _____ having neither supported nor interfered with your assuming
           or preparing to assume more adult responsibilities.
   _____ having interfered somewhat with your assuming or preparing
           to assume more adult responsibilities.
   _____ having interfered greatly with your assuming or preparing
           to assume more adult responsibilities.

   Comments regarding specific courses:

---

ing in planning their program, monitoring their own progress, and
evaluating their educational program provides students an unusual
opportunity for learning decision-making skills, for making wise decisions, and for learning to assume the consequences for decisions that
are made.

Annually determine the percentage of students who attain their goals and whose programs were appropriate for them. This step is not a direct part of the planning-monitoring-evaluation sequence. However, it provides very useful information for evaluating the school's total educational program. But more important, when it is carried out systematically from one year to the next, changes to bring about improvements for individual students can be planned and the effectiveness of the planned improvements can be determined.

Before leaving the individual educational programming strategy, we may examine how the profile of a student's achievement and mental ability may be helpful in implementing the strategy. Test publishers provide a computer printout that gives extensive information regarding each student's achievements in all the areas tested, including mental ability if it is included in the testing program. The grade equivalents and IQ scores follow for three students who were tested in the spring of Grade 7 are shown in Table 7.2.

Table 7.2   IQ Scores and Achievement in Grade Equivalents for Three Grade 7 Students

Student	Total Rdg	Language	Spelling	Math Comp	Math Concepts	Math PS	Total Math	Science	Soc St	IQ
A	8.4	6.2	8.1	5.7	8.1	6.3	6.7	9.9	8.3	100
B	8.4	9.3	9.1	8.3	7.3	8.5	8.0	8.3	8.3	107
C	9.9	8.7	6.7	5.5	6.5	6.0	6.0	9.9	7.1	117

We observe that all three students have some low scores and that, relative to mental ability, Student A is achieving much higher than Student C except in total reading and language. This information is useful to the teachers and advisor in estimating how well each student has learned thus far and also in planning an educational program with the student for the following semester. Other information, of course, including grades in these areas and other teacher judgments should be used. Provided that the grades and teacher judgments support the test results, Student C should be encouraged to set achievement goals in spelling and in all four math areas commensurate with the achievement in total reading and science and with the relatively high IQ score. Moreover, if the entire Grade 7 class is achieving relatively low in mathematics in comparison with the other subject fields as these three students are, the curriculum and instructional arrangements in mathematics should be improved.

The profiles for three Grade 9 students that follow have similar implications for evaluating prior achievement and for individual goal setting. The achievement test scores are indicated in percentiles in Table 7.3.

Table 7.3   IQ Scores and Achievement in Percentiles for Three Grade 9 Students

Student	Total Rdg	Eng Usage	Spell-ing	Total Lang Arts	Total Math	Soc St	Science	Use of Sources	IQ Score
A	19	36	10	21	81	18	8	5	126
B	79	56	40	49	55	88	80	80	108
C	81	79	52	68	41	84	90	44	99

EVALUATION AND GOAL SETTING FOR GROUPS OF STUDENTS

In the preceding section we examined the use of evaluative information in implementing the individual educational programming strategy. A different strategy is necessary for improving elements of the school's total educational program, such as achievement in a subject field, attendance, or attitudes toward school. The goal-setting strategy that follows is for use in improving elements of the school's educational program. The goals are set for composite groups of students, such as the composite group enrolled in each grade, rather than for the individual students of the grade. This goal-setting strategy has been alluded to, but it has not been explained in earlier chapters. However, it was employed by the schools that participated in the cooperative research that is reported in Chapter 13.

Goal-Setting Strategy

1. During a planning period, identify the purposes of gathering the evaluative information, the areas to be

evaluated, the composite student groups to be included, the information gathering tools and procedures, the means of analyzing and summarizing the information, the kinds of evaluation judgments to be made, and the kinds of actions to be taken based on the judgments.

2. Gather, process, summarize, and interpret the information regarding each area of interest for each composite student group. This first year is the baseline year. For example, the Grade 9, Grade 10, Grade 11, and Grade 12 groups of the first year are the baseline grade groups for each later year. The outcomes for the grade groups of each later year can be compared with those of the groups of the baseline year.

3. Based upon the interpretation of the data, set goals in the areas of interest for each continuing group of students and for the incoming group.

4. Develop an improvement plan that includes the activities for achieving the goals.

5. Carry out the activities and monitor progress toward achieving the goals.

6. Gather, process, and summarize the information during the next year.

7. Determine the extent to which the goals for each composite group of students were attained.

8. Evaluate the improvement activities that were carried out in terms of their effectiveness.

9. Summarize and synthesize the evaluative results for all the composite groups and all the areas involved.

10. Continue the cycle of evaluation, goal setting, planning, monitoring progress, and evaluation each year, making refinements in the goal-setting strategy and related practices as appropriate.

The preceding strategy is applicable to any area of interest, such as improving student achievement in one or more subject fields at each grade level, reducing the percentage of students of each grade who do not meet the minimum competency criteria, increasing average daily attendance, and decreasing the dropout rate. We shall first examine applications of the strategy to raising student achievement in academic subject fields.

Use of Standardized Achievement and Mental Ability Tests

In the next pages, two different means of summarizing standardized test information are described, one at Steuben Middle School and the other at Hood River Valley High School. In these two schools the goal setting was not implemented until after the second year of data collection. The kinds of improvement activities carried out and the results of implementing the goal-setting strategy in these schools are given in Chapter 13.

Steuben Middle School

Information follows to show the standardized test information that was gathered at Steuben Middle School and how it was analyzed. This is followed with an interpretation of the test results and an indication of the kind of goals that may be set based on the test results.

Composite Student Groups. Grade 7 and Grade 8.

Metropolitan Achievement Test Scores. Word knowledge, reading, total reading, language, spelling, math computation, math concepts, math problem solving, total math. The test battery was administered in the spring to the students of Grade 7 and Grade 8.

Otis-Lennon Mental Ability Test. This test was administered when the students were in Grade 5. (It was school district policy not to administer an ability test after Grade 5.)

Analysis of the Achievement and Mental Ability Test Results. The scores of the Grade 7 and Grade 8 students on each standardized achievement test and the ability test were ranked from lowest to highest (10 rankings were made, 1 for each test). Next, a score equivalent to the 10th, 25th, 50th, 75th, and 90th percentile was computed for the Grade 7 and Grade 8 students of Steuben. Then, the national percentile rank corresponding to each of the five preceding local percentile scores for each test was derived, using appropriate test manuals. This information was summarized in tables for the Grade 7 and the Grade 8 students.

This approach enables a school to compare five levels of mental ability with five levels of achievement in each subject field corresponding to the five percentile ranks, i.e., 90th, 75th, etc. It does not permit comparing the mental ability and the achievements of the same students since the scores are ranked for each one of the

10 sets of test scores. Accordingly, in a Grade 8 class of 300 students, only part of the same 30 students may be at or below the 10th percentile rank in any two or more of the 10 areas tested. Similarly, only part of the 150 students may be at or above the 50th percentile rank in any two or more of the 10 areas tested. A main benefit of this approach is that, regardless of the particular students who may be involved, comparisons at each percentile rank can be made across the different test scores.

Table 7.4 gives the results of the mental ability test and the standardized tests in total reading, spelling, and total mathematics for Grade 7 and Grade 8 for the baseline year. We may examine this table, which gives only part of the large amount of available data, to illustrate the key questions raised by the Steuben staff and also the related answers for the first, or baseline, year.

1. Are the national mental ability percentiles for the two grades the same? The national mental ability percentiles for Grade 7 and Grade 8 are about the same. The largest difference is between Grade 7 (82) and Grade 8 (75) for the local 90th percentile.

2. How do the local mental ability percentiles and the national mental ability percentiles compare? The differences between the local mental ability percentiles and the equivalent national mental ability percentiles are quite large for both Grade 7 and Grade 8 except for the local 10th and 25th percentiles. For example, Steuben's Grade

Table 7.4   National Percentile Ranks on Standardized Tests for Grades 7 and 8

Local %ile	Mental Ability Grades		Total Reading Grades		Spelling Grades		Total Math Grades	
	7	8	7	8	7	8	7	8
	(National %iles)		(National %iles)		(National %iles)		(National %iles)	
90	82	75	74	72	78	79	73	74
75	59	58	56	50	60	54	48	57
50	33	36	31	27	40	28	26	29
25	19	20	12	12	21	15	13	16
10	10	10	4	3	12	7	6	7

7 50th percentile is equivalent to the national 33rd percentile, and its Grade 8 50th percentile is equivalent to the national 36th percentile. This indicates that the mental ability of the Steuben students is considerably below that of the national student population. The related inference is that the students should not be expected to achieve as high as the national population.

3. Are the achievements of Grade 7 and Grade 8, taking into account the mental ability levels, the same, higher, or lower? The achievement percentiles of Grade 7 are lower than the mental ability percentiles in reading and math but higher in spelling, except for the 90th percentile. The achievement percentiles of Grade 8 are lower than the mental ability percentiles in all 15 instances, but not as much lower as Grade 7 in mathematics. Thus, the pattern is different for math than for reading and spelling.

4. Are the amount and the direction of the differences between the mental ability percentiles and the achievement percentiles different for the high and the low local percentiles? The differences between the national achievement percentiles and the mental ability percentiles are about the same for the different percentile ranks. This suggests that the educational program of the school is about equally effective for the students of all five ability levels.

Based on the preceding interpretations, a reasonable goal for Grade 7 for the ensuing year is to maintain the present level of achievement in spelling and to raise the achievement in reading and mathematics. A realistic goal for Grade 8 is to raise the achievement in reading, spelling, and mathematics. The goal might be stated more precisely "to raise the achievement level in each subject to the mental ability level." However, when a school has no prior experience in goal setting, it is probably wise to take a more cautious approach.

We note that the Grade 7 achievement in spelling was above mental ability. How much might students be expected to achieve above mental ability? There is no definitive answer to this question. It is raised here to emphasize that the goal-setting strategy does not imply that the achievement level should not exceed the mental ability level. On the contrary, goals should be set to raise achievement above the mental ability level until the amount of effort required to get a small increase does not appear to warrant the time and effort that is expended.

Hood River Valley High School

Results from a standardized achievement test battery and an academic aptitude test were used in goal setting at Hood River Valley High School. However, the analysis of the data was slightly different from that of Steuben Middle School.

General Aptitude Test Battery. Administered to the students when in Grade 9 of the junior high school and to the students who entered Hood River Valley High School without GATB scores.

Analysis. Obtain the G score from the test publisher's computer printout for the students of each Grade 10, 11, and 12. Divide the students of each grade into quarters based on their G scores. Compute the mean G score of each quarter of each grade. Change the mean G score to the equivalent percentile rank using the test manual table(s).

Stanford Test of Academic Skills. Reading, English, and mathematics. Administered to all students of Grades 10, 11, and 12 in May.

Analysis. Enter the standard achievement test scores of each student of each quarter of academic aptitude. Do this for each grade for reading, English, and mathematics. Compute the mean achievement for each quarter and convert the mean to a percentile rank using the appropriate test manual table(s). This permits comparison of the mean percentile rank in achievement of each quarter with their mean mental ability percentile rank.

Table 7.5 gives the percentile ranks for Grade 10 that are equivalent to the means of each quarter in mental ability, reading, English, and mathematics. Three observations are readily made. First, all four quarters are achieving above their academic aptitude levels in reading and below in English and mathematics. Second, achievement is considerably lower in English than in mathematics or reading. Third, the second and third quarters are achieving relatively lower in all three subjects than the highest quarter (Quarter 4) and the lowest quarter (Quarter 1).

These test results imply that improvement in English should be given high priority. Also, ways should be sought to get higher achievement by the students in the middle range of academic aptitude.

Goals based on these interpretations may be stated as follows: Maintain the high level of reading achievement of all four quarters;

Table 7.5   National Percentile Ranks for Quarters of a Grade
10 Class in Mental Ability and Their Equivalent National Percentile Ranks in Reading, English, and
Mathematics

	Quarter 4	Quarter 3	Quarter 2	Quarter 1
	National %ile	National %ile	National %ile	National %ile
GATB	93	77	60	30
Reading	94	80	72	46
English	78	54	42	28
Mathematics	89	66	48	29

raise the achievement in English and mathematics of all four quarters
and especially of the second and third quarters. Another way of
stating the goals in English and mathematics is to raise the achievement level of each quarter in these areas, either to its mental ability
level or to its reading achievement level. As was indicated earlier,
goals should be set to raise achievement above the mental ability level
until the payoff in terms of time and effort appears to be
unwarranted.

Before proceeding, we should be aware that goal setting can be
based on the results of achievement testing without the use of mental ability scores. The main reason for using available mental ability
scores is, first, to get an estimate of the ability of the group and,
second, to estimate whether the educative processes is equally effective for students of different levels of ability, such as four quarters
of a class.

The simplest, but an effective, way of using standardized achievement test results in goal setting involves use of the data provided
by the test publisher in the computer printout. For example, as shown
in Figure 7.6, the average grade equivalent in each area tested was
provided for the students of Grade 7 who took the test in the spring
of Grade 7. (It was also provided for each Grade 7 classroom group).

We see that this Grade 7 class had an average grade equivalent
(GE) of 8.0 or higher in four areas and below 8.0 in five areas. (At
the end of Grade 7 an average GE of 8.0 is expected of students
whose average mental ability is roughly 100.) An appropriate goal
to set for the ensuing year is to maintain or raise the mean achieve-

Table 7.6   Mean (Average) Achievement of a Grade 7 Class in
             Grade Equuivalents

	Total Rdg	Lan- guage	Spell- ing	Math Comp	Math Concepts	Math PS	Total Math	Science	Soc St
Grade Equivalent	8.0	8.4	8.1	7.7	6.9	7.5	7.3	8.1	7.7

ment in reading, language, spelling, and science and to raise it in
the four math areas and social studies. If a school cannot plan and
carry out improvement activities in all areas, high priority should
be given to mathematics. (The mean mental ability of this class was
106.)

Similar information for a Grade 10 class of a senior high school
follows in Table 7.7; however, the test was administered in the fall.

Table 7.7   Mean (Average) Achievement of a Grade l0 Class in
             Grade Equivalents

	Total Rdg	Eng Usage	Spell- ing	Total Lang	Total Math	Soc St	Science	Use of Sources
Grade Equivalent	15.5	16.0	15.6	16.0	14.5	15.2	16.4	16.1

The average grade equivalents of this Grade 10 class range from
4.5 to 6.4 above the actual grade in which the students are enrolled.
The levels of achievement are consistent, ranging from 15.2 to 16.4,
in all areas except mathematics. Without information regarding mental ability, an appropriate goal is to maintain the high level of achievement in all areas and to raise it in mathematics. (The mean mental
ability of this Grade 10 class was 117, equivalent to a national percentile rank of 87.)

Use of Other Measures of Achievement and Aptitude

Locally constructed achievement tests, locally constructed and
published criterion-referenced tests, locally constructed and criterion-

referenced performance tests, and teacher ratings of students' performances and work samples are used to measure student achievement. The scores or ratings from any of these devices may be averaged and used in implementing the goal-setting strategy. Grade point average in the subject field may also be employed. As we are aware, grade point average in a subject field along with the mean, or average, standardized test score in the same subject field are two widely used indicators of the level of achievement of the students of each grade. However, we typically desire more than the grade point average when evaluating student achievement because teachers do not base their grades uniformly on how well the students achieve.

Aptitude for learning particular subject matter is usually measured by some type of aptitude test rather than by some form of teacher rating. A mental ability score is a good predictor of achievement in the academic subject fields, but not in other areas such as the applied and fine arts and physical education. Moreover, it is not a good predictor of creativity and of various other thinking skills. Other published tests are available to measure creativity and aptitudes for learning specific subject matters. Teachers' ratings of each student's capability, or aptitude, for learning particular subject matters is not typically used in secondary schools. This is because each teacher has many different students for only one semester or a year and cannot reliably estimate the aptitudes of all the students. Moreover, to secure ratings from each teacher in a large school and then arrive at an average rating in each subject field is time consuming.

Inasmuch as the use of standardized achievement test results in goal setting was illustrated in the prior sections, it may be appropriate to show how grade point average and the results of criterion-referenced tests may be used. Their use will be described without reference to mental ability test results.

To employ grade point average, the grades received by all the students of a particular grade in the subject fields of interest are averaged for a grading period, a semester, or a year. These grade point averages are examined and a goal is set to maintain or to raise the average in each subject field. When computer processing is available in the school, the averages can be computed in a few hours, and the printouts can become available to the interested staff in a very short period of time. The difficulty in using only grade point average is that any given average may not reflect an equal level of achievement across subject fields. For example, a 2.0 in mathematics may not indicate the same level of achievement as a 2.0 in English. Moreover, teachers are able to raise or lower the grade assigned to the same level of achievement whereas this cannot be done on either a standardized or a criterion-referenced test.

One way of using the results of criterion-referenced testing in goal setting is to start by computing the percentage of the students who master each test in each grade. These percentages are then examined and a goal is set either to increase the percentage mastering the test, or in a parallel fashion, to decrease the percentage not mastering it. To illustrate, Webster Transitional School of Cedarburg, Wisconsin, employed criterion-referenced tests in connection with its goal setting. Every student at Webster is expected to master the following objective when in Grade 6, Grade 7, or Grade 8: "Given a multiplication problem involving two fractions, the learner will identify the product." A nine-item test was used to measure each student's achievement of this objective. The test was used as a pretest in the first week of school in Grade 6 and as a posttest in the spring in Grades 6, 7, and 8. The percentage of students who mastered the posttest in each grade was computed, and a goal was set to increase the percentage of Grade 6, Grade 7, and Grade 8 students who mastered it the following year.

We should note that mastery of this and all the other mathematics objectives is considered as the minimum competency level in mathematics for completing Grade 8 at Webster Transitional School. Although this is the case, a student who does not master all the objectives is not retained in Grade 8. A strong effort is made, however, to get all students to the minimum competency level. Summer school attendance, homework during the week, and Saturday homework are encouraged by low-achieving students of Grades 6 and 7 as well as Grade 8.

EVALUATION AND GOAL SETTING RELATED TO OTHER STUDENT OUTCOMES

We have seen that different kinds of information may be used as a basis for setting goals related to student achievement. Goals can also be set related to other student outcomes in the cognitive domain and to outcomes in the affective and behavioral domains.

Other outcomes in the cognitive domain include divergent and convergent thinking skills that are not associated with achievement in any particular subject field. Based on the Bloom taxonomy (1956), the convergent thinking skills include application, analysis, synthesis, and evaluation. Guilford's structure of intellect (1967) indicates that originality, flexibility, and elaboration are essential for creative production. Strategies of learning is another important set of outcomes. Some form of test or rating is typically employed to secure information regarding those outcomes, and the usual goal is for the student of each grade to become more competent in the skills or strategies.

The affective domain includes interests, attitudes toward various aspects of schooling, and self-concepts. The Instructional Objectives Exchange (1972a) has prepared objectives and related tests to measure students' attitudes toward teachers, school subjects, learning, the social structure and climate of the school, and peers. The Instructional Objectives Exchange has also developed objectives and constructed tests pertaining to four dimensions of the self-concept: family self-esteem derived from family interactions, peer self-esteem associated with peer relations, academic self-esteem derived from success and failure in scholastic endeavors, and general self- esteem that is a comprehensive estimate of how the self is regarded (Instructional Objectives Exchange, 1972b). An inventory or rating scale is employed in measuring these outcomes. The usual goal is to maintain or to develop more positive attitudes and self-concepts.

The behavioral domain includes outcomes such as attendance, tardiness, discipline referrals, suspensions, and drop-outs. Many schools keep records of these student behaviors. The usual goal set in connection with these behaviors is to maintain or increase attendance and to reduce the incidence of tardiness and other undesired behaviors.

References

Bloom, B. S. (Ed.). *Taxonomy of educational objectives. Handbook I: Cognitive domain.* New York: McKay, 1956.

Guilford, J. P. *The nature of human intelligence.* New York: McGraw- Hill, 1967.

Instructional Objectives Exchange. *Attitude toward school K-12* (Rev. ed.). Los Angeles, CA: Instructional Objectives Exchange, 1972a.

Instructional Objectives Exchange. *Measures of self-concept K-12* (Rev. ed.). Los Angeles, CA: Instructional Objectives Exchange, 1972b.

Klausmeier, H. J., Serlin, R. C., & Zindler, M. C. *Improvement of secondary education through research: Five longitudinal case studies* (Program Report No. 83-12). Madison: Wisconsin Center for Education Research, 1983.

National Commission on Excellence in Education. A nation at risk: The imperative for educational reform. *The Chronicle of Higher Education*, 1983, *26*(10), 11-16.

Thurstone, L. L. Primary mental abilities. *Psychometric Monographs,* 1938, *1*.

Suggestions for Further Reading

Anderson, L. W., & Anderson, J. C. Affective assessment is necessary and possible. *Educational Leadership*, 1982, *39*(7), 524-525.

Published tests that measure motivation, self-concept, attitudes, and other affective variables are listed and the reasons for testing in the affective domain are explained.

Bloom, B. S., Hastings, J. T., & Madaus, G. F. *Handbook on formative and summative evaluation of student learning*. New York: McGraw- Hill, 1971.

This practical handbook provides many examples of excellent test items for measuring knowledge and comprehension, Chapter 7; application and analysis, Chapter 8; synthesis and evaluation, Chapter 9; and affective outcomes, Chapter 10. Chapters 13 through 23 provide models and examples of test items for different school levels and various subject fields: Chapters 13 and 14, preschool; Chapter 15, language arts, Chapter 16, social studies; Chapter 17, art; Chapter 18, science; Chapter 19, mathematics; Chapter 20, literature; Chapter 21, writing; Chapter 22, second languages; and Chapter 23; industrial arts.

Brooks, D. M., & Van Cleaf, D. W. *Pupil evaluation in the classroom: An all level guide to practice*. Lanham, MD: University Press of America,

Provides strategies for evaluating academic achievement and social behavior. It is written specifically for teachers rather than test specialists.

Ebel, R. L. Three radical proposals for strengthening education. *Phi Delta Kappan*, 1982, *63*(6), 375-378.
As a means of strengthening education, Ebel proposes that (a) no instructional program should be continued in the absence of evidence of its effectiveness, (b) school systems should publish the results of assessments of student achievement annually, and (c) each teacher should submit evidence periodically of the achievement of his or her students.

Gronlund, N. E. *Measurement and evaluation in teaching* (4th ed.). New York: Macmillan, 1981.
Chapters 5 through 10 of this practical book deal with the construction of classroom tests, including objective, interpretive, and essay. Observational techniques are explained in Chapter 16 and peer appraisal and self-report inventories in Chapter 17.

Hopkins, K. D., & Stanley, J. C. *Educational and psychological measurement* (6th ed.). Englewood Cliffs, NJ: Prentice-Hall, 1981.
Most of this book is devoted to constructing tests. Chapter 7 deals with achievement tests; Chapter 8 essay tests; Chapter 9 objective tests; and Chapter 10 affective and noncognitive objectives. Chapter 13 explains standardized tests for measuring scholastic aptitude; Chapter 14 educational achievement; and Chapter 15 interests, personality, and social areas.

Jaeger, R. M., & Tittle, C. K. (Eds.). *Minimum competency achievement testing: Motives, models, measures, and consequences*. Berkeley, CA: McCutchan, 1980.
This book contains case studies of state and school district programs and also essays on competency testing. The possible effects of minimum competency testing on teachers, students generally, and handicapped students are outlined in Part III of the book.

Joint Committee on Standards for Educational Evaluation. *Standards for evaluations of educational programs, projects, and materials.* New York: McGraw-Hill, 1981.
Standards are presented for conducting evaluations and for analyzing information and reporting conclusions.

PART III: ADMINISTRATIVE— ORGANIZATIONAL—ADVISING ARRANGEMENTS

CHAPTER 8

ADMINISTRATIVE ARRANGEMENTS AND PROCESSES

James M. Lipham

What administrative arrangements and processes foster improvement of the secondary school? How can the secondary school be structured to enhance schoolwide planning and shared decision making? What kinds of administrative arrangements have secondary schools utilized successfully in carrying out their improvement efforts? Answers to these questions are of great importance since the administrative arrangements and processes impact directly on the educational program of the total school. Hence, this chapter addresses and explains the processes essential for achieving the following comprehensive and enabling objectives of Component 6 of the design for improvement—Administrative Arrangements:

Comprehensive Objective:

The school's administrative arrangements provide for cooperative planning and sharing decision making by the persons responsible for implementing the plans and decisions that are made, mainly administrators, counselors, teachers, and students.

Illustrative Enabling Objectives

The school:

Is organized into administrative units, each of which has no more than 500 students.

Has one or more committees, composed of representatives of the administrative team, counselors, teachers, students, and parents that make decisions and formulate plans regarding the school's curriculum, instruction, advising, evaluation, organization, and staffing.

An *Educational Improvement Committee*, or other committee or council that has representatives of the administrative team, curriculum coordinators, counselors, and teachers:

Plans the school's educational improvement activities with input from the total faculty.

Students, parents, and citizens:

Participate in meetings of the *Educational Improvement Committee* when matters of concern to them are on the agenda.

Serve as regular members of the *Educational Improvement Committee.*

One or more district committees, composed of the district administrator, representative principals, curriculum coordinators, counselors, teachers, students, parents, and citizens:

Coordinate the improvement activities of the district, taking into account district policies and state requirements.

Secure district and other specialists for consultation regarding improvement activities.

The principal provides leadership and, with appropriate involvement of members of the *Educational Improvement Committee* and the school staff:

Establishes policies and procedures that facilitate the school's educational improvement efforts.

Coordinates the use of facilities, materials, equipment, supplies, and other resources.

Provides time, space, and other physical arrangements that are needed for teaching teams, school committees, and other groups to meet and conduct their business during the school day.

Establishes effective two-way communication among administrators, other staff, teachers, and students; and between the school and parents and citizens of the community.

Participates as a member of district committees.

Transmits information to and from district committees.

Attempts to have implemented the decisions made by district committees.

The first part of this chapter examines the administrative arrangements and processes essential for implementing planned educational improvement. Next, the structures and processes necessary for improving educational decision making are explored. Then, diagrams and descriptions are presented of four different administrative arrangements that have been utilized to improve secondary schooling. The chapter concludes by considering some substantive issues to be resolved if the administrative arrangements and processes in secondary schools are to be improved in the years ahead.

IMPLEMENTING EDUCATIONAL IMPROVEMENT

Certain administrative structures, processes, and behaviors are crucial to the successful implementation of a planned educational improvement. Recent studies conducted in secondary schools that were engaged in implementing one or more components of the Wisconsin design have shown that:

1. The nature and quality of the leadership behaviors provided by administrators, counselors, department chairpersons, and teachers that are appropriate to the various phases of the implementation process help to bring about educational improvement (Brittenham, 1980). Moreover, continuity in leadership positions on the part of administrators is essential. Those schools experiencing greatest difficulty in implementing educational improvement had a high rate of turnover in administrators (Gaddis, 1978).

2. Strong commitment to educational improvement, coupled with a combination of decentralized management decision making and centralized curriculum development, greatly supports the changeover to the individual instructional programming strategy (Neiner, 1978).

3. Special project and grant funds from outside sources are helpful but not essential to implementing educational improvement (Daresh, 1978). Instead, educational leaders utilize local resources, capitalizing on such historical circumstances as school consolidations and building construction or remodeling to implement change.

4. Planning for improvement includes clear specification of the objectives of the change, an accurate assessment of the present system, a specific allocation of the resources needed, appropriate administrative arrangements to implement the improvement process, a continuing process of curricular development, an adequate staff development program, a realistic time frame which specifies short- and long-range goals, an identification of appropriate strategies to be used, and a comprehensive evaluation process (Neiner, 1978; Watkins, 1978).

5. Some additional resources are helpful during the initial phase of the change process for intensive staff and curricular development activities. Continuing inservice is essential, particularly for new and incoming teachers, to help them acquire the skills necessary to function effectively as teachers and as advisors (Lehr, 1979).

6. The following elements are necessary for effecting educational improvement: a shared decision-making structure, the creation of a warm and personalized learning environment, an advising system for students, curricular development, and use of one or more of the improvement strategies (Artis, 1980). The specific administrative arrangements for shared decision making can vary widely from school to school. Some of the schools examined failed at the outset clearly to specify staff and student behavioral expectations and to provide the structures necessary for staff and students to fulfill their new role expectations, but subsequent steps were taken to correct this mistake (Zimman, 1980). In their approach to advising, all teachers and other staff members viewed student advising as an integral aspect of their expanded roles (Brittenham, 1980). In their approach to curriculum and instruction, giving students credit on the basis

of objectives accomplished—not on the amount of time spent in a course—was an integral aspect of the improvement process (Rankin, 1981).

Appropriate leadership and decision making behaviors are essential during each phase of the implementation process (Lipham, Dunstan, & Rankin, 1981). Although principals have great responsibility for constructive change throughout the implementation process, they must not just stay "one step ahead of the group," but must adapt leadership and decision-making modes to unfolding events. Early in the implementation process, during the awareness-assessment phase, the principal serves as initiator, stimulator, communicator, and influencer, so that the perspectives of the staff and others can be broadened (Dunstan, 1981). The principal must have an articulated philosophy of education and must communicate to the staff and others the anticipated outcomes of the improvements (Watkins, 1978). Working with key teachers who have both expertise and interest, the principal must coordinate awareness activities that will move the principal's vision of planned change to a schoolwide plan for improvement. This plan should be based on a needs assessment, an exploration of issues and attitudes, and the sharing of information about means of meeting the needs of the organization and the individuals within it. The principal must encourage widespread participation during this phase, must emphasize the possible new goals, and must support the staff as they participate with the principal in goal setting and planning.

In the commitment phase, the principal is instrumental in shaping the decision to adopt by stimulating the enthusiasm of the staff; by securing the district's commitment of human and material resources; and by appropriately involving parents, citizens, and others in assessing the need for change and the potential benefits of the proposed program. Apparently, a few principals still tend to think that they can "go it alone," and do not adequately inform the staff about the magnitude of the change being attempted or listen sufficiently to suggestions from the staff about possible problems that might be created by the proposed improvement. Still others tend to stress the autonomy of "me and my staff," and fail to obtain the necessary support of school district officials, the board of education, parents, and citizens. During the commitment phase, leadership behavior high in goal emphasis and high in supportiveness must be provided.

Local schools do not engage in major change in isolation. Principals and staff members in effective schools reach out to the larger educational environment for ideas and resources for improvement. Initially, these leaders depend heavily on national professional associations and publications, colleges and universities, and research and development centers for innovative ideas and approaches. Subsequently, they depend on leagues of similar schools, state and intermediate educational agencies, and individual educational consultants to refine their implementation activities (Daresh, 1978). Administrators and teachers accept as authentic "that which works" in other schools (Klausmeier, 1978).

It also must be recognized that implementation of a major improvement effort requires substantial time. Many innovative educational programs falter and fail because they are so rushed (Neiner, 1978). Ample time must be provided for the modification of existing roles or the creation of new roles, and for these altered expectations to become internalized, if the change is to be effective (Brittenham, 1980). Most major educational improvements require several years—not months.

As the start-up phase begins, the primary role of the principal and other leaders shifts from that of initiator to that of coordinator. Leadership behavior high in work facilitation and supportiveness becomes paramount. Staff members struggling with anticipated and unanticipated problems related to implementing an improvement need both organizational and psychological support.

As implementation of the innovation proceeds, instrumental leadership is required to monitor progress, to reinforce effective practices, to correct inadequacies, and to resolve difficulties. In this regard, the failure of some principals to be able to shift to instrumental leadership behavior at this juncture can be quite dysfunctional. As staff members become busily engaged in their roles or activities they do not wish to continue high engagement in participative decision making—or as one teacher put it, "redeciding decisions." Instead, the need exists to have the previously made decisions clarified, codified, and enforced—otherwise, the staff experiences early "burnout."

Subsequently, during the refinement and institutional phases, the school develops its own improvement capability and moves toward making it permanent and enduring. It continues to refine its needs analysis procedures, its refinement strategies, and its organizational structures and processes. Roles and relationships become clarified, expanded, and stabilized. As the staff engages in the improvement activities they continuously require new knowledge and also more sophisticated skills. In these phases it becomes important for the principal and other leaders to recycle and return to a participative leadership style.

Thus, those who would be leaders in secondary schools, whether principals, counselors, chairpersons, or teachers, must not only engage in certain essential leadership and decision-making behaviors, but must also vary them according to the different phases of carrying out planned change. In this regard, the leadership behavior of both principals and staff change markedly from the beginning phases of an improvement program to the institutionalization of an enduring refinement capability in the school. In developing this capability, appropriate involvement in decision making is essential.

IMPROVING EDUCATIONAL DECISION MAKING

To improve the quality of educational decisions, attention must be paid to "what" a decision concerns, "who" is involved in making it, and "how" the decision is made (Lipham, 1974). The "what" of decision making concerns the basic functions of curriculum and instruction, staff personel, student personnel, finance and business management, and school-community relations. The "who" can range from the board of education to students, through various combinations of administrators, supervisors, specialists, teachers, parents, and citizens. "How" decisions are made can range from a rational, stepwise process to a highly political, personalized one that even in successful schools almost defies description (Holmquist, 1976; Kawleski, 1977; Moyle, 1977; Speed, 1979; Watkins, 1978).

Regarding "what" an educational decision is concerned with, the implementation of a major educational improvement ultimately concerns all of the content areas. For example, a major curricular change affects the human input mix of staff, students, parents, and citizens, as well as the material input mix of facilities, equipment, supplies, and instructional materials. This dynamic interaction often raises philosophical and policy issues for which widespread participation in the decision-making process is essential (Brittenham, 1980; Zimman, 1980). These issues become differentiated, delegated, and dealt with according to their relevance at each level of the school organization. Hence, it is essential that a clear philosophy of educational decision making be articulated and that appropriate administrative arrangements and decision-making structures be established if the school is to be successful (Watkins, 1978; Wright, 1976).

The issue of "who" should be involved in decision making is often determined by the substance of the decision to be made. This content can deal with decisions that are routine, negotiated, or heuristic. Both the frequency (how often) and extent (at what level) of involvement in decision making also must be considered. Excessive involvement causes frustration ("Why doesn't the principal just decide and leave us alone?"), whereas underinvolvement creates hard feelings ("Why wasn't I consulted?"). Thus, one always strives for a condition of equilibrium and involves others appropriately, depending on their interest, expertise, and representation of their constituencies.

Whether decision involvement is mandatory, permissive, or prohibited also must be considered (Dunstan, 1981). Mandatory issues include those that call for widespread staff participation in decision making, such as determining objectives, establishing policies, and evaluating instruction; permissive issues are those that may or may not call for total participation, such as the selection of equipment, textbooks, and teaching materials; and prohibited issues include those that do not call for staff participation, such as the assignment of staff or the evaluation of individual teachers. Thus, in seeking a balance between authoritative and participative modes, effective administrators and the faculty agree at the outset on the appropriate level for staff participation in decision making.

Recent research regarding staff involvement in decision making shows that teachers generally feel quite deprived from making schoolwide and districtwide decisions (Flannery, 1980; Speed, 1979; Warner, 1981). Special care should be taken, therefore, to include teachers in the following decisions from which they feel particularly deprived: determining the administrative and organizational structure of the school, determining procedures to be used for teacher evaluation, selecting departmental chairpersons or team leaders, evaluating subject departments or teams, hiring new faculty members, setting and revising school goals, and establishing schoolwide policies (Thierbach, 1980).

Regarding "how" decisions are made, essentially the process includes a unique combination of rational, logical stages or phases, as well as political and personal influences that result in a particular course of action being taken. This process occurs primarily in structured and ad hoc committee settings, using small group procedures with a search for consensus (Watkins, 1978). When viewed as a rational process, the stages of decision making typically include identifying the issue or problem, defining the problem, suggesting alternative solutions, weighing alternatives, making the decision choice, implementing the decision made, and evaluating outcomes of the decision (Lipham, 1974). In practice, however, the decision-making process does not proceed so rationally and systematically, but in three broad phases, "before the decision," "the moment of decision," and "after the decision" (Dunstan, 1981).

The "before-the-decision" phase includes many interactive activities and behaviors that typically include a high degree of posing alternative solutions as a means for defining and redefining the problem or issue at hand (Rankin, 1981). That is, instead of each alternative being rationally considered in terms of its positive and negative values and outcomes, various alternatives are weighed, one against another, as to their desirability or acceptability. Then, it is not at all unusual for the "most satisfactory" alternative to be selected as the appropriate decision to be made.

Although the "moment of choice" typically is viewed as the crucial stage in the decision-making process, in actuality it is anticlimactic. Frequently, it is difficult to determine when major educational decisions actually are made. Even in formally structured committees, majority votes are seldom taken, and, when they are, the outcome usually can be predicted. Instead, vocal consensus ("Let's do it that way"), silent affirmation ("Does anyone object?"), or actual exhaustion ("Do whatever you wish") seem to be the rule (Holmquist, 1976; Moyle, 1977). In fact, the tendency exists, even in successful secondary schools, to talk about issues until the time runs out—sometimes shifting the decision-making process from the participative to the authoritative mode (Artis, 1980; Brittenham, 1980; Zimman, 1980).

"After-the-decision" behaviors and activities differ substantially from the previous two phases. Here, commitment, interest, and expertise predominate, so that the "doers" take over where the "talkers" leave off. After the decision choice is made, particular individuals become the "driving forces" for putting the decision into action (Kawleski, 1977). Thus, the decision-making process is qualitatively and quantitatively different "before the decision" and "after the decision." "Before-the-decision" behaviors include a high degree of input and involvement using group processes; "after-the-decision" behaviors include a high degree of individual effort and initiative (Lipham and Rankin, 1982).

In summary, the decision-making process can be improved when the school is appropriately structured to enhance staff involvement in making major educational decisions.

ALTERNATIVE ADMINISTRATIVE ARRANGEMENTS

In this section we describe administrative arrangements which provide for cooperative planning and shared decision making in implementing educational improvement. These structures were developed in four secondary schools—three senior high schools and a middle school representing a wide range in size, location, and clienteles served— that were engaged in implementing components of the Wisconsin design. Each example includes a brief description of the school followed by an analysis of the administrative arrangements utilized. Here, the focus is on schoolwide decision making, whereas in the following chapter the emphasis is on decision making at the teaching and advising level.

East High School, Denver, Colorado

East High School in Denver, Colorado, is a comprehensive school enrolling approximately 1,300 students in Grades 10, 11 and 12. Approximately 70 percent of the students enter college after graduation. The school, located adjacent to a city park, is housed in an impressive multistory building of classic school architecture characteristic of the late twenties; it has been modernized through the years. The professional staff is comprised of the principal, three assistant principals, five guidance counselors, and approximately 150 staff members, both certificated and classified.

As shown in Figure 8.1, the administrative structure of the school follows a somewhat traditional departmental pattern, yet several provisions have been made for the teaching staff to participate in schoolwide decision making and the related planning of improvement programs. Here, it can be seen that the administrative team consists of the principal and assistant principals for instruction, student personnel, and administrative services. The assistant principal for instruction is responsible for coordinating the entire instructional program of the school. The areas of responsibility include curriculum development, implementation, and evaluation; educational equipment, supplies, and materials; staff selection, placement, supervision, and evaluation; and relations between the school and the community. The assistant principal for student personnel is responsible for the coordination and supervision of student testing and diagnosis; counseling; psychological, health, and social services; placement; and follow-up of graduates. The assistant principal for administrative services is responsible for managing the daily operations of the school, including building maintenance and security, student conduct and discipline, and co-curricular programs and activities. Together with the principal, the assistant principals constitute the administrative team which meets frequently—formally once a week and informally as necessary—to share in making immediate and long-range decisions.

The faculty, as in most secondary schools, is organized into academic departments consisting of the several subject fields. In this arrangement, counseling, the media center, and other service units are also considered as departments. Department chairpersons are elected for three-year terms. The faculty of each department is responsible for planning, offering, and evaluating the courses or services rendered.

A key prerequisite to effective representation of the staff in this administrative arrangement is that provisions must be made for establishing a viable schoolwide shared decision-making structure to deal with policy, program, and process issues of vital concern throughout the school. At Denver East, staff members participate in decision making through a representative schoolwide Curriculum Council which consists of the chairpersons of each academic and service department, plus the coordinators of special programs, such as in reading. The Council is chaired by the assistant principal for instruction and meets monthly during the school day. The Curriculum Council is a very important group which sets curriculum policy and objectives; determines curricular patterns, offerings, and requirements; and approves all courses required for graduation. It also oversees all of the individualized educational programs which include work study, reading and mathematics proficiency, advanced college placement, executive internship, and the senior seminar (an alternative interdisciplinary program which emphasizes experiential learning in real-life situations).

The work of the Curriculum Council is also accomplished through the use of subcommittees, task forces, and other representative staff, student, parent, and community groups that deal with particular issues of schoolwide and districtwide importance. In addition to using these structures for formal communication, the staff, students, and others engage frequently in informal two-way communication which enhances opportunities for shared decision making throughout the school.

To emphasize curriculum and instruction, many schools that are structured like Denver East assign assistant principals on the basis of their interests, preparation and expertise to responsibilities for the instructional leadership of several academic departments. Thus, the span of control of the administrative staff is reduced so that both immediate and sustained attention can be paid to instructional planning, implementation, and evaluation in the several subjects. In such schools, the assistant principals also are contributing members of the schoolwide curriculum improvement committee or council.

An example of the administrative arrangements for shared decision making in a school which is structured into broad fields, rather than academic departments, is now presented.

Hood River Valley High School, Hood River, Oregon

As described earlier, Hood River Valley High School is a comprehensive school enrolling approximately 750 students in Grades 10, 11, and 12. Approximately 50 percent of the students enter college after graduation. The school is housed on a campus plan. Classrooms in the main building, most of which are of open-space design, surround the school's resource center and offices. The staff

Figure 8.1 The Administrative Structure of East High School, Denver, Colorado

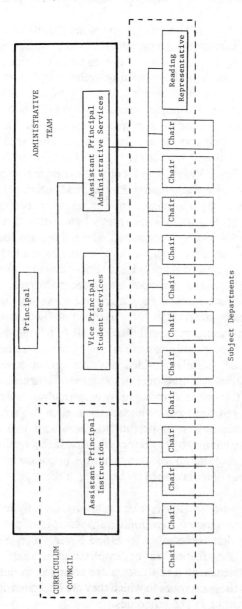

consists of the principal, two associate principals, three guidance counselors, and approximately 60 certificated and classified staff members.

As in East Denver High School, the administrative team at Hood River Valley consists of the principal and associate principals who meet frequently to provide leadership to the total educational program (See Figure 8.2). They monitor courses and units of instruction to ensure that the school's philosophy of individual rate and continuous progress is implemented. Two other structures, in addition to the administrative team allow for meaningful and effective schoolwide participation in decision making. They are the Cabinet and the Curriculum Committee.

At Hood River Valley, the faculty is organized into six broad fields—science and mathematics, humanities, vocational education, physical education, counseling, and the resource center. Fields are served by coordinators. Within three of the fields there are team leaders. A team leader is appointed where there are four or more teachers in a curricular area, such as science or mathematics. The major body for shared schoolwide decision making is the Cabinet, which consists of the principal, associate principals, field coordinators, and team leaders. The Cabinet meets weekly during school and is chaired by the principal. It has policy-making, coordination, and decision-making responsibilities in all functional areas.

Since the educational program of the school is career-oriented, objective-based, flexibly-provided, and competency-based (allowing for the continuous progress of each student) the instructional involvement of the Cabinet is augmented by a curriculum review committee consisting of representative teachers of each subject. The work of this committee is so important to the school that it is called "Vital." Also chaired by the principal, Vital meets regularly during school to review and approve any changes in course offerings and units of instruction developed by teachers in the several subjects or broad fields.

Although other small secondary schools currently may lack the sophistication in their instructional purposes, plans, programs, and processes as that represented by Hood River Valley Senior High School, the key feature to be emphasized is that all the administrators, teachers, and students are arranged so that they provide input to those decisions in which they are interested and in which they have a stake in the outcomes.

Figure 8.2   The Administrative Structure of Hood River Valley
Senior High School, Hood River, Oregon

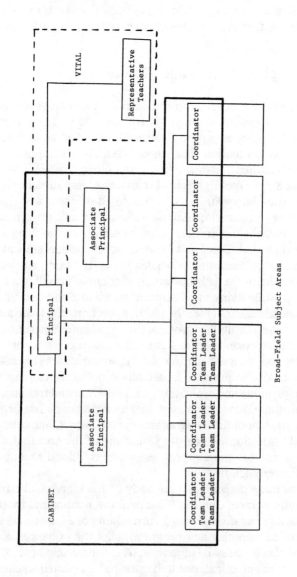

Such involvement also is possible in large, comprehensive secondary schools which are structured quite differently from either subject department or broad field arrangements, and it is to a different example, that of the subschool structure, that we now turn.

Irvine High School, Irvine, California

Irvine High School is a comprehensive school enrolling over 1,800 students in Grades 9 through 12. It is located in a suburban area south of Los Angeles. Approximately 60 percent of the students enter college after graduation. The school is built on a campus plan with separate buildings for instructional and other activities. As shown in Figure 8.3, Irvine High School is organized into subschools. Each of these subschools, or units, is composed of about 600 students, 30 teachers, a counselor, and an assistant or unit principal.

At Irvine, the administrative, counseling, and teaching staff is organized into subschool units, each of which includes students from all grade levels. Each unit is headed by an assistant principal who is responsible for the daily operations of the unit, including the supervision and evaluation of staff, student attendance and discipline, and unit management activities. In addition, unit principals are assigned leadership responsibilities for specific academic departments and schoolwide service functions, such as guidance, student health, athletics, and bilingual education. Unit principals are responsible to the principal who provides leadership in policy development, curriculum planning and evaluation, staff selection and training, needs assessment and long-range planning, and extraorganizational relations of the school with the community, the district, and other agencies and institutions. Under the leadership of the principal, the administrators work cooperatively as a team to fulfill the requisite administrative functions.

The primary decision-making body of the school is the Instructional Improvement Council. It has major responsibilities for stating, formulating, and disseminating curriculum policy, assessing educational needs, adopting new programs, allocating finances, and setting schoolwide goals and objectives. The membership of the Council consists of the principal, one unit principal, an elected teacher from each unit plus two teachers elected at large, a student and a parent from each unit, and one member of the classified staff elected at

Figure 8.3   The Administrative Structure of Irvine High School, Irvine, California

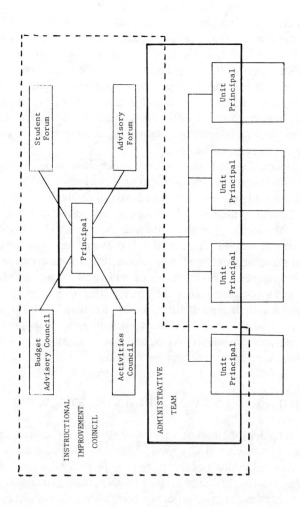

large. The Council meets weekly during school and is chaired by the principal.

The Council receives, reviews, and acts on reports and recommendations from all standing and ad hoc committees. These include the Budget Advisory Council which has primary responsibility for preparing the total school budget, the Activities Council which is responsible for planning and managing the student activities program, the Student Forum which deals with problems and issues of concern to the student body, and the School Advisory Forum which presents parents' opinions and concerns and also serves as a sounding board for school problems and proposals. Thus, at Irvine, teachers, counselors, students, and parents continually share in the decision-making process with administrators. The faculty engages in a great deal of cooperative planning; they also share in carrying out their job responsibilities.

The instructional program at Irvine includes a wide variety of in-school and community-based learning experiences. All courses are objective based and have assigned levels of difficulty. Within each course, students may earn from one to five credits, based on the number of specific objectives attained. A wide variety of grouping arrangements and learning activities is provided, appropriate to each student's learning style and other characteristics. Instruction suited to each student's educational needs and career goals is facilitated by the subschool administrative arrangement which helps create a personalized environment for teaching, learning, and advising.

Such conditions are also characteristic of schools that are structured into interdisciplinary units, and it is to an example of this administrative arrangement that we now turn.

Steuben Middle School, Milwaukee, Wisconsin

Steuben Middle School in Milwaukee, Wisconsin, enrolls approximately 850 students in Grades 6, 7, and 8. The school is housed in a traditional multistory structure built in 1929. The professional staff is comprised of the principal, two assistant principals, a curriculum coordinator, two guidance counselors, and approximately 80 certificated and classified staff.

As shown in Figure 8.4, Steuben Middle School is organized into seven Instruction and Advisory units, each of which consists of ap-

Figure 8.4   The Administrative Structure of Steuben Middle
School, Milwaukee, Wisconsin

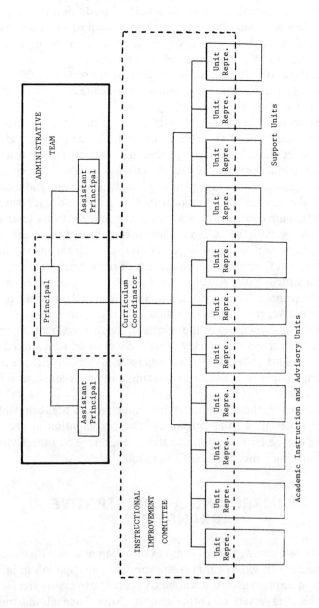

proximately 120 students, four teachers, and an aide. Unit teachers are responsible for the students' instruction in English, reading, mathematics, science, and social studies. In addition to the seven Instruction and Advisory units, there are support units consisting of specialist teachers in physical education, industrial arts, home economics, art, and music, as well as teachers of special and exceptional education. The specialist teachers do not serve as student advisors, but they consult frequently with academic unit teachers regarding student programs and progress.

The administrative team consists of the principal and two assistant principals who share responsibilities for student personnel services, scheduling, and data processing, and together with the guidance counselors and faculty are responsible for student conduct and discipline. Curriculum planning, implementation, and evaluation in the academic and support units is under the leadership of the curriculum coordinator who assists the administrative team and is responsible with the faculty for instruction throughout the school.

The major decision-making body of the school is the Instructional Improvement Committee which consists of representatives from each of the Instruction and Advisory units and the support units, together with the principal, the curriculum coordinator, the teacher union representative, the lead teacher aide, and a student representative. Under the chairmanship of the principal, the Instructional Improvement Committee meets weekly during school to set educational objectives and make decisions regarding issues of schoolwide concern. It is responsible for decisions regarding all improvement activities of the school.

In summary, the administrative arrangement of Steuben Middle School is designed to assure widespread participation in decision making on the part of administrators, teachers, and others vitally concerned with the success of the school.

IMPROVING ADMINISTRATIVE ARRANGEMENTS

We have examined four examples of different administrative arrangements utilized to enhance appropriate participation in bringing about improvements in secondary schools of varying size, location, clienteles served, and other characteristics. Each administrative arrangement has evolved in response to the need to increase involvement in and enhance the quality of schoolwide planning and decision making.

Here, we consider briefly two questions that must be answered by the staff of any secondary school in improving its administrative arrangements and processes:

1. What are the role expectations and relationships among the administrative team in the local school?

2. What formal structures are necessary to enhance schoolwide decision making and cooperative planning?

The Administrative Team

Much attention has been paid in recent years to the management team concept whereby those responsible for the administration of the school work cooperatively to fulfill organizational and individual goals (ASCD,1978; Wagstaff, 1973). Undoubtedly, the quality of the leadership of the principal is a key factor to the success of the school (Lipham, 1981; Lipham and Daresh, 1979; Lipham & Rankin, 1982). The administrative structure, therefore, should provide the principal with opportunities to meet and confer both formally and informally with other members of the administrative team and with the staff to plan, implement, monitor, and evaluate the progress of program improvements throughout the school.

Generally, two approaches have been followed in establishing an effective administrative team: the specialist approach and the generalist approach. In the specialist approach, such as in Denver East High School and Steuben Middle School, assistant or associate principals have specified duties and are responsible primarily for supervision in such areas as instruction, student personnel, or administrative services. In the generalist approach, such as in Hood River Valley and Irvine High Schools, the duties of assistant or associate principals range across all of the functional or decisional content areas. In either case, it is essential that under the leadership of the principal, the administrative team functions as a vital, cohesive decision-making group.

The Schoolwide Decision-Making Body

Whether called an Instructional Improvement Committee, Curriculum Council, or Cabinet, successful secondary schools have established formal arrangements for insuring that those affected by a decision have representative involvement in planning, implementing, and evaluating educational decisions. As with the administrative team, the schoolwide decision-making body functions under the leadership of the principal who is responsible for chairing meetings, preparing agendas and minutes, and coordinating the implementation and evaluation of decisions made. Typically, schedules are arranged so that the group meets at least weekly, usually during school time.

In establishing a schoolwide decision-making body, the staff must pay attention to many issues. Is there a basic commitment of administrators and teachers to the philosophy of shared decision making? This element is essential. How large should the group be? In some schools the group is so large that active participation in meetings is curtailed. Who should serve—administrators, department heads, unit leaders, counselors, teachers, parents, students, others? Increasingly, there is a tendency to bring parents and students into the decision-making process. What is the scope of responsibility— for only some functions, such as curriculum, or for the total program of the school? To what extent should teachers participate in cooperative planning and decision making regarding schoolwide concerns without having a reduction in teaching load or receiving additional pay for the additional work? Decisions must be made regarding these and other issues if appropriate administrative arrangements are to be established to improve schoolwide decision making.

The administrative arrangements at the schoolwide level are appropriate only insofar as they contribute to effective teaching and advising at the instructional level. Recently, several alternatives to the traditional departmentalized organization for instruction have been explored, including the broad field, subschool, and interdisciplinary forms of organization for instruction and advising. These arrangements will be described in greater detail in the next chapter which deals with organizational arrangements for instruction and student advising.

SUMMARY

In this chapter we stressed that the administrative arrangements and processes of the school must facilitate implementing educational improvement and involving the staff appropriately in decision making. Research and practice regarding these processes in secondary schools engaged in implementing various components of the Wisconsin design were examined and explored as a basis for establishing appropriate administrative arrangements to improve secondary schooling.

Next, we described and depicted alternative administrative arrangements for schoolwide planning and decision making used in four secondary schools of different size, grade levels, and other characteristics. The chapter concluded by considering the importance of the administrative team and the schoolwide decision-making body as mechanisms for improving the administration and operation of secondary schools.

References

Artis, J. B. *An ethnographic case study of the administrative organization, processes, and behavior in a selected senior high school.* Madison: Wisconsin Research and Development Center for Individualized Schooling, 1980.

Association for Supervision and Curriculum Development. Administrative team concept can assure better focus on instructional improvements. *News Exchange*, January 1978, *20*(1), 1, 12.

Brittenham, L. R. *An ethnographic case study of the administrative organization, processes, and behavior in an innovative senior high school.* Madison: Wisconsin Research and Development Center for Individualized Schooling, 1980.

Daresh, J. C. *Facilitative environments in senior high schools that individualize instruction.* Madison: Wisconsin Research and Development Center for Individualized Schooling, 1978.

Dunstan, J. F. *An ethnographic study of the decision-making process and leadership behavior at the schoolwide level in selected secondary schools.* Madison: Wisconsin Research and Development Center for Individualized Schooling, 1981.

Flannery, D. M. *Teacher decision involvement and job satisfaction in Wisconsin high schools.* Unpublished doctoral dissertation, University of Wisconsin-Madison, 1980.

Gaddis, M. T. *Organizational and personal constraints on the successful institutionalization of individually guided education.* Madison: Wisconsin Research and Development Center for Cognitive Learning, 1978.

Holmquist, A. M. *A definitional field study of decision making in IGE/MUS-E schools.* Madison: Wisconsin Research and Development Center for Cognitive Learning, 1976.

Kawleski, S. J. *Decision making of the instruction and research unit in IGE schools: functions, processes, and relationships.* Madison: Wisconsin Research and Development Center for Cognitive Learning, 1977.

Klausmeier, T. W. *Desirability and implementation of IGE/secondary schooling: Middle and junior high schools.* Madison: Wisconsin Research and Development Center for Individualized Schooling, 1978.

Lehr, J. B. *Staff development needs in middle and junior high schools that individualize instruction.* Madison: Wisconsin Research and Development Center for Individualized Schooling, 1979.

Lipham, J. M. Improving the decision-making skills of the principal. In J. A. Culbertson, C. Henson, & R. Morrison (Eds.). *Performance objectives for school principals.* Berkeley, CA: McCutchan, 1974.

Lipham, J. M. *Effective principal, effective school.* Reston, VA: National Association of Secondary School Principals, 1981.

Lipham, J. M., & Daresh, J. C. *Administrative and staff relationships in education: Research and practice in IGE schools.* Madison: Wisconsin Research and Development Center for Individualized Schooling, 1982.

Lipham, J. M., Dunstan, J. F., & Rankin, R. E. *The relationship of decision involvement and principal's leadership to teacher job satisfaction in selected secondary schools.* Madison: Wisconsin Research and Development Center for Individualized Schooling, 1981.

Lipham, J. M., & Rankin, R. E. *Change, leadership, and decision making in improving secondary schools.* Madison: Wisconsin Center for Education Research, 1982.

Moyle, C. R. J. *Decision making of the instructional improvement committee in IGE schools: Functions, processes, and relationships.* Madison: Wisconsin Research and Development Center for Cognitive Learning, 1977.

Neiner, G. A. *Analysis of planned change within comprehensive senior high schools that individualize instruction.* Madison: Wisconsin Research and Development Center for Individualized Schooling, 1978.

Rankin, R. E. *A qualitative study of the decision-making processes and leadership behavior at the teaching-advising level in selected secondary schools.* Madison: Wisconsin Research and Development Center for Individualized Schooling, 1981.

Speed, N. E. *Decision participation and staff satisfaction in middle and junior high schools that individualize instruction.* Madison: Wisconsin Research and Develoment Center for Individualized Schooling, 1979.

Thierbach, G. L. *Decision involvement and job satisfaction in middle and junior high schools.* Unpublished doctoral dissertation, University of Wisconsin-Madison, 1980.

Wagstaff, L. H. Unionized principals—You may be next. *NASSP Bulletin*, November 1973, *57*(376), 40-47.

Warner, W. M. *Decision involvement and job satisfaction in Wisconsin elementary schools.* Unpublished doctoral dissertation, University of Wisconsin-Madison, 1981.

Watkins, A. N. *Actual and ideal decision-making processes utilized in senior high schools that individualize instruction.* Madison: Wisconsin Research and Development Center for Individualized Schooling, 1978.

Wright, K. W. *Development of an instrument to measure real and ideal decision structure and involvement in IGE schools.* Unpublished doctoral dissertation, University of Wisconsin-Madison, 1976.

Zimman, R. N. *An ethnographic study of the administrative organization, processes, and behavior in a model comprehensive high school.* Madison: Wisconsin Research and Development Center for Individualized Schooling, 1980.

CHAPTER 9

ORGANIZATION FOR INSTRUCTION AND ADVISING

James M. Lipham

Whereas our concern in the preceding chapter was with schoolwide administrative arrangements, this chapter considers the organizational arrangements needed for effective instruction and student advising in secondary schools. Inasmuch as Chapter 10 focuses specifically on teacher-advisor programs, this chapter emphasizes the organization for instruction more than the organization for advising:

Comprehensive Objective:

The faculty and students are organized into small groups that permit instruction and advising to be personalized.

Illustrative Enabling Objectives Pertaining to Instruction:

A staff member of each instructional group:

Chairs the meetings of the group.

Serves on the school's *Educational Improvement Committee* and participates in the Committee's planning and other activities.

Transmits information, decisions, and plans from the teaching staff to the *Educational Improvement Committee.*

Transmits information, decisions, and plans to the teaching staff.

Related to instruction, *each group of teachers*, such as an interdisciplinary teaching team, cooperatively:

Develops the procedures for planning, monitoring, and evaluating each student's instructional program in each course taught by the group.

Plans and evaluates the group's instructional strategies.

Related to the group's instructional functions, *each teacher:*

Outlines the content of his or her courses.

Develops the learning guides that students use in the courses.

Plans the instructional methods that are employed in the courses, including the use of time, materials, and modes of instruction.

Participates in all aspects of the group's planning and evaluation activities.

Carries out his or her instructional activities in accordance with the group's plans.

The first half of this chapter is concerned with the organization for instruction wherein the processes dealing with staff personnel and instructional improvement are considered at the workflow or teaching level of the school. Then, four alternative organizational arrangements utilized in secondary schools engaged in implementing one or more components of the Wisconsin design are charted and described. The chapter concludes by considering some basic issues to be resolved in improving the arrangements for instruction and advising in secondary schools.

ORGANIZING THE STAFF FOR INSTRUCTION AND ADVISING

The improvement of teaching and advising is the foremost function of the school. An important factor in determining the success or failure of a school is the ability of the principal to organize the staff appropriately to engage in assessing educational needs, setting instructional objectives, improving teaching and learning activities, and evaluating educational outcomes (Lipham, 1981). Working with individuals and groups of teachers to align educational needs, objectives, curricula, and outcomes is a demanding job that requires the principal to have a broadly developed set of understandings, skills, and attitudes. There is a vast difference between "knowing about" the instructional program and being intimately involved in its design, development, implementation, evaluation, and refinement (Notar, 1980).

Studies show that principals of effective schools:

1. Are committed to instructional improvement (Georgiades, 1979; Trump, 1977; Wellisch et al, 1978).

2. Show thorough and intimate knowledge of classroom teaching activities (Austin, 1979; Venezky & Winfield, 1979).

3. Monitor the effective use of classroom time (Denham & Lieberman, 1980; Fisher et al, 1978).

4. Engage actively in instructional improvement (Cawelti, 1980; Georgiades, 1978; Goodlad, 1977; Huitt & Segars, 1980).

5. Have positive attitudes toward staff and students (Clark, Lotto, & McCarthy, 1980; Ianni & Reuss-Ianni, 1980; Olivero, 1980).

In organizing the staff for instruction and advising, the principal pays attention to the essential educational processes of setting goals, clarifying roles, providing leadership, improving decision making, and planning for and implementing change as they are operative at the technical level of the school organization. Here, the principal's active involvement in the staff personnel functions of recruitment, identification, assignment, orientation, supervision, development, and evaluation are crucial to program success. In many districts, en bloc staff allocations to buildings are the norm, hence the staffing decisions made by principals affect substantially the achievement of schoolwide objectives (Bossert et al, 1982; Morris et al, 1982).

Principals recognize that without capable teachers it is impossible to count on any other factors related to instructional effectiveness (Duke, 1982). They also know that careful attention to recruitment, identification, assignment, and orientation of staff at the outset is a wise investment of time, reducing considerably later remedial or "catch up" efforts (Brundage, 1980).

Regarding staff assignments, an equitable division of labor and of leadership responsibilities must be established. Kawleski (1977) discovered, for example, that most school staffs are better at cooperative planning than they are at cooperative teaching. When people work together closely day in and day out ways must be found to increase task interdependence as well as planning interdependence. An equitable division of work responsibilities must be reached, particularly among staff members within departments, broad fields, and Instruction and Advisory units, since the size of teaching-learning groups, instructional activities, numbers of advisees, and other load factors may vary considerably from time to time.

Regarding staff supervision, principals in successful schools devote sustained effort to the coordination and control of instruction and are skilled at the tasks involved (Maryland State Department of Education, 1978; New York Office of Education, 1974). They make themselves available to discuss teachers' problems and ideas (Chesler, Schmuck & Lippitt, 1975); they do direct observations of teachers' work and hold them accountable for fulfilling their duties (Leithwood et al, 1982); they discuss instructional issues and work problems with staff (Wellisch et al, 1978); and they are supportive of teachers' efforts to improve (California Department of Education, 1977). At the same time, principals recognize that teachers, especially in schools where they are teamed and work closely together, do not respond positively to close supervision (Schmuck, Charters & Carlson, 1981), but, instead, appreciate principals who consistently emphasize educational objectives and who offer support and resources for attaining those objectives (Center for Educational Policy and Management, 1982).

Although the form of organization for instruction sets general expectations for role performance, the informal interpersonal working relationships within the school and its subunits largely determine program success. The quality of these interactive interpersonal relationships is particularly important in schools engaged in educational programming for the individual student because the number of primary, continuing interactions within, between, and among groups of administrators, teachers, students, parents, and others is much greater than in the traditional school. Although it is hard to express the essence of the multitude of interactions involved in serving as a staff member in a teaching team, we wish to highlight the importance of interpersonal compatibility among team members. Interpersonal compatibility concerns the extent to which the needs, dispositions, abilities, and interests, as well as values, of the members of a primary work group are complementary. Decisions made regarding "who works with whom on what and for how long" are much more than organizational-structural; they are personal-individual, since it is the people who make any organization work.

Regarding interpersonal compatibility among teaching teams, studies (Evers, 1974; Gilberts, 1961) have shown that the personality variables involved in the selection and assignment of staff to teams or Instruction and Advisory units within the school may be much more significant than the role variables. Therefore, in designing an appropriate organization for instruction and advising, one must pay close attention to both the selection of staff members and their assignment to compatible work units. Many schools have found inservice activities in group dynamics, issue identification, sensitivity training, and strength bombardment to be helpful in increasing interpersonal skills and compatibility among the staff of the teaching units and the total school.

Adequate, appropriate, systematic staff development is absolutely essential for the school to be successful (Lehr, 1979; Lipham, 1981, & Davis, 1982). Such inservice training should help new staff members acquire the understandings, skills, and attitudes required to assimilate them successfully, rather than assuming that, as with "old timers," new staff members understand and are committed to program goals and objectives (Watkins, 1978). Effective inservice programs make provisions for meeting specific, identified training needs of staff; engaging the staff in active, rather than passive, learning activities; and providing the staff with appropriate immediate and long-term financial rewards for participation (Lehr, 1979; Davis, 1982). In sum, effective principals "put their money on preparing people" and effective schools result.

Rather than overemphasing formal, summative staff evaluation, effective principals often use informal, progress evaluation to improve staff performance, motivation, and morale. They know and understand the strengths and weaknesses of individual staff members and interact continually with them, suggesting activities and resources, critiquing progress toward goals, and commending performance (Brittenham, 1980; Zimman, 1980). And even though the formal reward system in schools is weak, effective principals find informal ways to acknowledge and recognize the earned achievements of staff members.

The organization for instruction and advising must also be represented appropriately in schoolwide decision making. Recognizing that teachers often feel deprived from making important educational decisions, effective principals establish formal schoolwide Instructional Improvement Committees or Councils that include representative teachers and others from each instructional unit or department (Lipham & Fruth, 1976). Such committees set schoolwide goals, policies, and objectives and foster the implementation and evaluation of all programs within the school. These representative committees enhance staff participation in decision making (Dunstan, 1981; Rankin, 1981). Teachers on such committees often become involved, not only as a result of their individual interest and expertise, but also because of the need to represent constituent interests (Brittenham, 1980; Zimman, 1980). Such decision involvement inspires commitment from staff members when they see their participation as being legitimate and the council or committee actually making important educational decisions (Artis, 1980). Often, such formal committees exert considerable impact on the effectiveness of the school—particularly if the principal and the staff are committed to a philosophy of shared decision making (Watkins, 1978). In such schools, staff involvement does not "water down" decisions; it renders them more potent (Kawleski, 1977; Moyle, 1977; Nerlinger, 1975). In addition, informal, ad hoc committees and task forces, with membership based on relevance, interest, and expertise, are particularly helpful for ensuring effective decision making by those close to the point of implementation (Dunstan, 1981; Rankin, 1981). Therefore, the output and productivity of both ad hoc and formal committees is often instrumental to the success of the school.

In addition to the formal and informal organizational structure, the organizational climate, "atmosphere," or "tone" of the school, in terms of human relationships, continually emerges as crucial to a school's success. Thus, the principal seeks to balance the emphasis on organizational goals and roles with an emphasis on individual interests and abilities, so that the climate of the total school and that of the units and classrooms within it is conducive to effective teaching and advising.

ALTERNATIVE ARRANGEMENTS FOR INSTRUCTION AND ADVISING

Teachers and students are organized in many different ways for instruction and for advising. Moreover, there is a considerable difference between middle schools and high schools because of the difference in the subject matter, or courses, required of all students. There are very few elective courses in the middle school but there are many, including the required subjects in the high school.

In middle schools that implement this component of the design, the academic teachers and students are typically organized into groups in such a way that the academic teachers both teach and advise their group of students. In many middle schools, the advising is quite informal, carried out during the block of time that the teachers have the students for instruction. In most high schools in which teachers serve as advisors, the instruction is not provided by a team even though the teacher advisors may be organized into interdisciplinary teams. As a matter of fact, there is very little team teaching in high schools involving three or more teachers after the last grade in which all students are required to take English, mathematics, science, and social studies. In some high schools this occurs in Grade 9 and in other schools in Grade 10.

There is considerable variability with respect to the instructional role of teams both at the middle school and high school levels. In some teams, the members merely meet together and keep one another informed of what they are teaching and how they evaluate. In other teams, the members confer with each other about the content to be taught, how it will be taught, the evaluation tools that will be used, and all other elements of the instructional process. Moreover, they reach consensus on these matters. Then they carry out the instruction according to the team's plan. In some schools when carrying out the instructional process, two or more of the teachers meet with a larger group of students, and each teacher contributes to the instruction. The most typical procedure is for each teacher to have a group of students for a specified time period and to teach these students according to the team's plan.

Another matter is quite critical with respect to teaming and instruction. In some schools each team is given considerable freedom in determining its own procedures related to planning, teaching, and evaluating. In other schools, all teams are encouraged to use identical procedures. Similarly, within teams the amount of freedom for individual teachers varies. In line with the philosophy of the design, the recommended practice is to encourage freedom rather than to demand conformity. This practice heightens teacher creativity, motivation, and morale. At the same time that freedom is encouraged, each teacher and each team is held accountable for productivity.

Regardless of the extent to which the team members plan or teach with considerable independence or in an integrated manner, teaming provides a powerful means of improving instruction. School administrative officials, curriculum coordinators, counselors, and others can meet and confer with the team, rather than with each individual teacher. The team members can come to understand their students better. The team can set goals for its students and can work together to achieve the goals. As will be indicated in Chapter 13, research shows that goal setting followed with planning to achieve the goals provides a realistic means of raising student achievement, improving student attitudes and self-concepts, increasing attendance, and attaining other desired outcomes.

Our purpose here is not to explain the individual educational programming strategy (Chapter 2), the individual instructional programming strategy (Chapter 3), the goal-setting strategy (Chapter 7), or the advising process (Chapter 10). Rather the focus is on the organizational structure that facilitates the implementation of the strategies and the advising process. We will now examine the organization for instruction and advising in four secondary schools—two middle schools and two senior high schools. Each example includes a description of the organizational arrangements utilized for teaching and student advising.

Steuben Middle School, Milwaukee, Wisconsin*

Steuben Middle School in Milwaukee, Wisconsin, enrolls approximately 850 students in grades 6, 7, and 8. As described previously and shown in Figure 8.4, Steuben Middle School is organized into seven Instruction and Advisory (I & A) units, each of which consists of approximately 120 students, four teachers, and an aide. These

---

*This description is based on: H. J. Klausmeier and J. C. Daresh, *A description of Steuben Middle School, 1977-78.* Madison: Wisconsin Research and Development Center for Individualized Schooling, 1979. Some changes may have occurred in this school's practices since 1977-78. The same is true of the other descriptions of school practices which follow.

teachers are responsible for the students' instruction in English, reading, mathematics, science, and social studies. In addition to the seven I & A units, there are two units consisting of specialist teachers who consult with the I & A unit teachers and teach the allied arts to all students. Another unit consists of teachers of special and exceptional education. They also consult with the teachers of the I & A units and teach small groups of exceptional students.

Instruction is planned by the teachers in each I & A unit working as a team. The teachers of each unit have a joint planning period each day; in addition, each teacher also has an individual daily preparation period. The team planning period is devoted to matters dealing with instructional strategies, materials, and student activities. In addition, meetings may be held with the principal, curriculum coordinator, counselors, resource personnel, or parents during the team planning period.

Although the instructional day is divided into seven modules of approximately 50 minutes, bell times are relevant only for specialist sections of the students' day. At other times, flexible scheduling by unit teachers is used so that activities which go beyond 50 minutes may be incorporated into the instructional plan. The staff of each I & A unit utilizes large group, class group, small group, student pairs, and individual arrangements, as appropriate. Each team exercises much initiative in determining its methods. In teams composed of teachers initially certificated as elementary teachers, the teachers tend to teach more than one subject and also to develop and implement a team plan of teaching and evaluating. In teams composed of teachers initially certificated as high school teachers the tendency is to teach one subject and to proceed with considerable independence of other team members.

The instructional materials used consist of a combination of commercially available items and materials developed by the Steuben teachers. The materials purchased or developed have the following characteristics:

1. Clearly stated instructional objectives,

2. Pretests and other evaluation procedures to ascertain each student's level of achievement related to the objectives,

3. A variety of possible learning activities by which students may attain the objectives,

4. Posttests or other evaluation procedures to ascertain each student's level of achievement related to the objectives,

5. Record keeping forms and procedures, and

6. Guidelines regarding the sequencing of instruction.

The progress of individual students is evaluated by the I & A unit staff so that students are able to progress appropriately from one unit of instruction to the next. Each unit staff member serves as a homeroom advisor to a group of students, keeping track of their educational progress and reporting to parents. The advising is relatively informal.

In summary, the organizational arrangement for instruction and student advising at Steuben Middle School provides flexibility to the staff of each I and A unit and maximizes the utilization of the specialized resources available in the school. Another middle school provides a more highly structured organizational arrangement for instruction and advising.

Webster Transitional School, Cedarburg, Wisconsin*

Located north of Milwaukee in Cedarburg, Wisconsin, Webster Transitional School is a middle school that enrolls about 700 students in Grades 6 through 8. The school is structured into eight academic I & A units, an allied arts team, and a support team. Each academic unit is composed of 75 to 100 students and a team of three to four teachers. Five of the academic units are composed of sixth and seventh graders, while three include only eighth graders. The teachers of each I & A unit are responsible for the instruction of their students in language arts, reading, mathematics, science, and social studies. The allied arts team is composed of 12 teachers; two each from industrial arts, home economics, and art; three from music; and three from physical education. The support team has eight members and includes the director of the instructional materials center, two guidance counselors, a reading consultant, and four special education teachers.

---

*This description is based on: H. J. Klausmeier and J. C. Daresh, *A description of Webster Transitional School, 1977-78. Madison: Wisconsin Research and Development Center for Individualized Schooling, 1979.*

Team teaching and student advising are enhanced by the physical design of the building. Each I & A unit is housed in a separate pod. The large open areas of the pods and movable furniture allow teachers to utilize different groupings for instruction, including large group, small group, and individual study. Instructional materials are either stored in the pod or are within easy access in either of two instructional material centers. The students of each unit have direct access to an IMC.

The primary functions of I & A teams are to plan instructional programs appropriate for each student, to teach, to evaluate, to advise students, and report to parents. Within each team, a specialist is identified for each subject. This specialist assumes responsibility for formulating the objectives of the particular subject for the students of the unit. This teacher is also a member of a subject team of the school and works on developing objectives and content in the subject on a schoolwide basis. For example, a teacher with expertise in language arts identifies the objectives in language arts for the students of the unit and plans the related teaching activities and evaluation procedures for the team. The specialist in each subject field may also teach the subject to all students of the unit without the assistance of other team members, or other team members may also teach the subject to some of the students in the unit.

Every teacher of each I & A unit teaches some of the students the basic skills which the team identifies as needed by the students. Each team sets a time when each teacher teaches a different skill in the same subject to students who have not yet mastered the skills. Decisions regarding the use of time, facilities, and materials are made by the team as a whole.

Grouping of students for instruction is a team task. The use of time and the arrangements of students into instructional groups and for individual study are flexible within each I & A unit. Flexible ways for using time include longer blocks per day in any subject or not having instruction in every subject every day.

The unit staff plans cooperatively as a team. There are no formally designated team leaders. Instead, members of each team share the responsibility for four positions that generally rotate monthly or quarterly: team leader, team recorder, representative to the Faculty Advisory Committee, and Student Council advisor for the pod. The person who serves as team leader establishes the agenda and chairs the formal weekly team meeting. During these meetings major instructional decisions are made for the unit, teaching assignments are made, evaluation results are discussed, and nonteaching tasks are shared.

Each teacher of an I & A unit serves as an advisor to some of the students of the unit. The teacher-advisor program at Webster will be described in detail in the next chapter. Members of the allied arts team and the support team join the academic teachers for advising. The teacher advisors meet with their advisees on Mondays and Thursdays. Whole group, small group, and individual activities during these sessions deal with goal setting, decision making, values clarification, career awareness, and other matters. Some advisors also meet with their groups or with individual students outside the regularly scheduled sessions to discuss educational progress and meet with the student's parents.

Having described the organization for instruction and advising in-middle schools, we now examine the arrangements used in senior high schools engaged in implementing one or more components of the Wisconsin design.

Hood River Valley High School, Hood River, Oregon*

Hood River Valley High School is a comprehensive school enrolling approximately 750 students in Grades 10, 11, and 12. The staff consists of a principal, two associate principals, three guidance counselors, and 45 teachers. As shown previously in Figure 8.2, the staff is organized into six broad fields: mathematics/science, physical education/driver education, vocational education, humanities, guidance, and the resource center. Within each broad field, if there are four or more teachers in the same subject, a team leader assists the coordinator.

Each staff member, including the associate principals, teachers, counselors, and classified staff is assigned a group of 15 to 20 students for advising. The advisor, called a guide, meets daily with

*This description is based on: H. J. Klausmeier and J. C. Daresh, *A description of Hood River Valley High School, 1977-78*. Madison: Wisconsin Research and Development Center for Individualized Schooling, 1979.

his or her students individually or as a group. The guide assists the students with scheduling courses and learning units, monitors academic progress, and serves as the contact person between the school and the home. As necessary, students may be referred by the guide to a guidance counselor. Each of three counselors coordinates the activities of one-third of the guides and their advisees and is also responsible for any additional counseling needed.

The curriculum of the school is organized into courses made up of learning units with performance objectives that are designed so that most students are able to complete them in three weeks. Students must master the objectives in order to receive credit toward high school graduation. Courses vary in length; the shortest course has a single learning unit and the longest course has ten learning units. Alternative learning activities for each unit include large group or small group work, the use of audiovisual materials, or selected independent study in the IMC.

The members of each academic team are responsible for planning the units of instruction which are then submitted to the schoolwide curriculum committee for approval. Team planning is also essential for sequencing the three-week units of instruction, sharing facilities and instructional materials, carrying out the instructional activities, and evaluating student progress. Within this organizational arrangement, the major expectations of teachers are as follows:

1. Teach five 55-minute class periods each day.

2. Meet with their guide groups for two 30-minute periods and three 10-minute periods each week.

3. Spend one 55-minute period each day preparing for teaching or related activities.

4. Take care of other obligations, such as staff meetings, and individual conferences with students, parents, and other teachers.

A different arrangement for instruction and student advising is used in a larger suburban senior high school.

Cedarburg High School, Cedarburg, Wisconsin*

Cedarburg High School enrolls 1,100 students in Grades 9 through 12. As shown in Figure 9.1, at Cedarburg a majority of the faculty teaches separate subjects of class-sized groups in the familiar departmental arrangement. The teachers and students of Grade 9, however, are organized into Instruction and Advisory (I & A) units. The departments and the I & A units are represented on the schoolwide Educational Improvement Committee.

The administrative staff of Cedarburg High consists of the principal and three assistant principals. Each administrator has designated responsibilities. Instruction throughout the school is coordinated by the Educational Improvement Committee which meets monthly and includes the assistant principals for instruction and for student services, and representatives of the departments and I & A units. Meetings of this group are devoted to reviewing schoolwide policy and stating schoolwide objectives.

Each I & A unit has 100 students and a team of four academic teachers. The students receive their instruction in English, mathematics, science, and social studies from a team of four teachers and an aide. Outside of these required subjects, students elect courses in the traditional subject departments.

The academic teachers in the Grade 9 teams serve as educational advisors to their students. Each other academic teacher serves as an advisor to about 25 students of Grade 10, 11, and 12.

The unit teachers, the aide, and the team leader meet each morning during a common team planning session. At this time, team members exchange information concerning individual students; work on curriculum; plan for activities, such as parent-student-teacher conferences; and devise ways of utilizing the five-hour block of instructional time allocated for the team each day. Decisions concerning the scheduling of specific classes for the block of time are made each day.

---

*This description is based on: J. C. Daresh and H. J. Klausmeier, *A description of Cedarburg High School, 1977-78*. Madison: Wisconsin Research and Development Center for Individualized Schooling, 1979, and other information regarding the school in the 1982-83 school year.

Figure 9.1 The Organization for Instruction and Advising at
Cedarburg High School, Cedarburg, Wisconsin

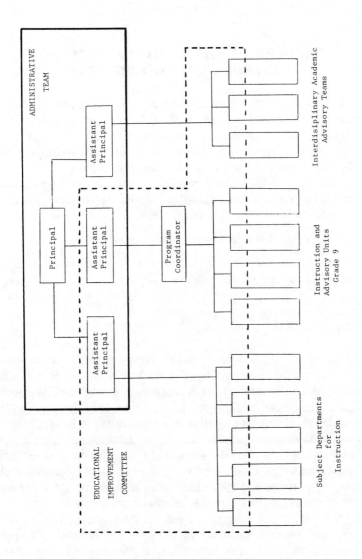

In summary, the organizational structure of Cedarburg High School includes departments, I & A units in Grade 9, and teacher advising in the other three grades.

IMPROVING THE ORGANIZATION FOR INSTRUCTION AND ADVISING

We have presented examples of four different organizational arrangements for instruction and advising in secondary schools of varying size, location, clienteles served, and other characteristics. Each has evolved in response to the need to enhance the instruction and advising of individual students in secondary schools.

Here, we consider briefly two issues that must be addressed by the staff of any secondary school in improving its organizational arrangements for instruction and for advising:

1. What is the educational philosophy of the school?

2. What is the nature of the curriculum and the total educational program of the school?

The Educational Philosophy of the School

The basic values held by administrators, teachers, students, parents, and others exert a powerful influence on the behavior and outcomes of the total school organization. Research (Klausmeier, 1978; Watkins, 1978; Dunstan, 1981; Rankin, 1981) has shown that in order for the implementation of improvement to be successful a reasonable degree of consensus must be established regarding the goals and objectives of the school. Moreover, agreement must be reached regarding which specific components of the design for improvement are viewed by the staff as philosophically desirable and operationally useful in specific school situations.

Undoubtedly, the educational values held by the staff result from a host of complex personal variables and situational influences through time, hence they seem almost impervious to change. Even so, school leaders must first give attention to assessing both the nature and extent of agreement on educational values and then engage in consensus building activities. Failure to do so prior to program implementation tears the school asunder. In some secondary schools, for example, staffs become polarized regarding the philosophy of decision-making involvement, the desirability of teachers also serving as advisors, the involvement of citizens and parents, or any of several other values issues. Hence, many exemplary schools engage in values clarification, consensus building, and other organizational and staff development activities prior to and during the implementation of a major change.

The Educational Program of The School

The organizational arrangements for teaching and advising must be designed to plan, manage, support, and evaluate the educational activities of the school. Hence, the organizational arrangements described in this chapter were those used in four schools wherein sustained attention was given to educational programming for the individual student, curriculum arrangements, experiential learning and career education, student participation in decision making, evaluation of student learning and educational program, or other components of the Wisconsin design.

In the previous chapter we indicated that different administrative arrangements are appropriate for schools of varying size, grade levels, and other characteristics. In this chapter we presented alternative forms of school organization to improve instruction, advising, or both. These include the departmental structure, the broad field structure, and the interdisciplinary structure. In many schools—particularly high schools—the departmental structure prevails for providing most of the instruction, yet these schools have also established special arrangements for formal student advising. These arrangements for the operation of teacher-advisor programs will be depicted and described in the next chapter. Analysis of the school's administrative arrangements, organization for instruction, and structures for student advising should be helpful to secondary school staffs engaged in planning and implementing educational improvement.

SUMMARY

In this chapter we examined different ways of how to organize the secondary school for effective teaching and student advising. First, we examined organizational relationships in terms of the staff personnel functions of orientation, assignment, supervision, interpersonal relations, inservice training, and evaluation. Then, detailed descriptions of the organizational arrangements for instruction and advising were presented for four secondary schools engaged in implementing one or more components of the Wisconsin design. The chapter concluded by stressing that agreement on educational philosophy and the nature of the educational program is essential for implementing a school improvement effort.

References

Artis, J. B. *An ethnographic case study of the administrative organization, processes, and behavior in a selected senior high school.* Madison: Wisconsin Research and Development Center for Individualized Schooling, 1980.

Austin, G. R. Exemplary schools and the search for effectiveness. *Educational Leadership*, 1979, *37*(l), 10-14.

Bossert, S. T., Dwyer, D. C., Rowan, B., & Lee, G. The instructional management role of the principal. *Educational Administration Quarterly*, 1982, *18*(3), 34-64.

Brittenhamn, L. R. *An ethnographic case study of the administrative organization, processes, and behavior in an innovative senior high school.* Madison: Wisconsin Research and Development Center for Individualized Schooling, 1980.

Brundage, D. (Ed.). *The journalism research fellows report: What makes an effective school.* Washington, D.C.: Institute for Educational Ledership, George Washington University, 1980.

California Department of Education, Office of Program Evaluation and Research. *School effectiveness study: The first year.* Sacramento, CA: California Department of Education, 1977.

Cawelti, G. Effective instructional leadership produces greater learning. *Thrust for Educational Leadership*, 1980, *9*(3), 8-9.

Center for Educational Policy and Management. The principal's role: How do we reconcile expectations with reality? *Perspectives*, 1982, 1-8.

Chesler, M., Schmuck, R. A., & Lippitt, R. The principal's role in facilitating innovation. In J. V. Baldridge & T. E. Deal (Eds.), *Managing change in educational organizations*. Berkeley, CA: McCutchan, 1975.

Clark, D., Lotto, L. S., & McCarthy, M. S. Factors associated with success in urban elementary schools. *Phi Delta Kappan*, 1980, *61*(7), 467-470.

Daresh, J. C. *Facilitative environments in senior high schools that individualize instruction*. Madison: Wisconsin Research and Development Center for Individualized Schooling, 1978.

Davis, H. A. *Incentives, involvement, and teacher satisfaction with staff development programs in Wisconsin secondary schools*. Unpublished doctoral dissertation, University of Wisconsin-Madison, 1982.

Denham, C., & Lieberman, A. (Eds.). *Time to learn*. Washington, D.C.: National Institute of Education, 1980.

Duke, D. L. Leadership functions and instructional effectiveness. *NASSP Bulletin*, 1982, *6*(458), 1-12.

Dunstan, J. F. *An ethnographic study of the decision-making process and leadership behavior at the schoolwide level in selected secondary schools*. Madison: Wisconsin Research and Development Center for Individualized Schooling, 1981.

Evers, N. A. *An analysis of the relationship between the effectiveness of the multiunit elementary school's instruction and research unit and interpersonal behaviors*. Madison: Wisconsin Research and Development Center for Cognitive Learning, 1974.

Fisher, C. W., Filby, N. W., Marliave, R., Cahen, L. S., Dishaw, M. M., Moore, J. E., & Berlinger, D. C. *Teaching behaviors, academic learning time and student achievement*. San Francisco, CA: Far West Laboratory for Educational Research and Development, 1978.

Georgiades, W. *How good is your school?* Reston, VA: National Association of Secondary School Principals, 1978.

Georgiades, W., et al. *Take five—A methodology for the humane school*. Los Angeles, CA: Parker, 1979.

Gilberts, R. D. *The interpersonal characteristics of teaching teams.* Unpublished doctoral dissertation, University of Wisconsin-Madison, 1961.

Goodlad, J. I.   Principals are the key to change. *AIGE Forum*, 1977, *2*(2), 74-78.

Huitt, W. & Segars, J.   *Characteristics of effective classrooms.* Philadelphia, PA: Research for Better Schools, 1980.

Ianni, F. A. J., & Reuss-Ianni, E.   Crime and social order in schools. *Education Digest*, 1980, *45*(9), 2-5.

Klausmeier, H. J., & Daresh, J. C.   *A description of Steuben Middle School, 1977-78.* Madison: Wisconsin Research and Development Center for Individualized Schooling, 1979.

Klausmeier, H. J., & Daresh, J. C. *A description of Hood River Valley High School, 1977-78.* Madison: Wisconsin Research and Development Center for Individualized Schooling, 1979.

Klausmeier, H. J., & Daresh, J. C.   *A description of Webster Transitional School, 1977-78.* Madison: Wisconsin Research and Development Center for Individualized Schooling, 1979.

Klausmeier, H. J., & Daresh, J. C.   *A description of Cedarburg High School, 1977-78.* Madison: Wisconsin Research and Development Center for Individualized Schooling, 1979.

Kawleski, S. J.   *Decision making of the instruction and research unit in IGE schools: Functions, processes, and relationships.* Madison: Wisconsin Research and Development Center for Cognitive Learning, 1977.

Lehr, J. B.   *Staff development needs in middle and junior high schools that individualize instruction.* Madison: Wisconsin Research and Development Center for Individualized Schooling, 1979.

Leithwood, K. A., & Montgomery, D. S.   The role of the elementary school principal in program improvement. *Review of Educational Research*, 1982, *52*(3), 309-339.

Lipham, J. M.   *Effective principal, effective school.* Reston, VA: National Association of Secondary School Principals, 1981.

Lipham, J. M., & Fruth, M. J.   *The principal and individually guided education.* Reading, MA: Addison-Wesley, 1976.

Maryland Department of Education.   *Process evaluating: A comprehensive study of authors.* Baltimore, MD: Maryland Department of Education, 1978.

Morris, V. C., Crowson, R. L., Hurwitz, E., Jr., & Porter-Gehrie, C. The urban principal: Middle manager in the educational bureaucracy. *Phi Delta Kappan*, 1982, *63*(10), 689-691.

Moyle, C. R. J. *Decision making of the instructional improvement committee in IGE schools: Functions, processes, and relationships.* Madison: Wisconsin Research and Development Center for Cognitive Learning, 1977.

Neiner, G. A. *Analysis of planned change within comprehensive senior high schools that individualize instruction.* Madison: Wisconsin Research and Development Center for Cognitive Learning, 1978.

Nerlinger, C. M. *Participative decision making in IGE/MUS-E schools.* Madison: Wisconsin Research and Development Center for Cognitive Learning, 1975.

New York Office of Education. *School factors influencing reading achievement: A case study of two inner-city schools.* Albany, NY: New York Office of Education, 1975.

Notar, E. E. *An investigation of instructional television and the administrator's relationship to level of use.* Unpublished doctoral dissertation, University of Wisconsin-Madison, 1980.

Olivero, J. L. *The principalship in California: The keeper of the dream.* Newport Beach, CA: Association of California School Administrators, 1980.

Rankin, R. E. *A qualitative study of the decision-making processes and leadership behavior at the teaching-advising level in selected secondary schools.* Madison: Wisconsin Research and Development Center for Individualized Schooling, 1981.

Schmuck, P. A., Charters, W. W., Jr., & Carlson, R. O. (Eds.). *Educational policy and management: Sex differentials.* New York: Academic Press, 1981.

Trump, J. L. *A school for everyone.* Reston, VA: National Association of Secondary School Principals, 1977.

Venezky, R. L., & Winfield, L. F. *Schools that succeed beyond expectations in teaching reading.* Newark, DE: University of Delaware Studies on Education, 1979.

Watkins, A. N. *Actual and ideal decision-making processes utilized in senior high schools that individualize instruction.* Madison: Wisconsin Research and Development Center for Individualized Schooling, 1978.

Wellisch, J. B., MacQueen, A. H., Carriere, R. A., & Duck, G. A.
  School management and organization in successful schools.
  Sociology of Education, 1978, *51*(3), 211-226.
Zimman, R. N. *An ethnographic study of the administrative
  organization, processes, and behavior of a model comprehensive high school*. Madison: Wisconsin Research and Development Center for Individualized Schooling, 1980.

CHAPTER 10

TEACHER-ADVISOR PROGRAMS

James M. Lipham and John C. Daresh

Increasingly, secondary schools are establishing teacher-advisor programs wherein teachers work closely with students as advisees. In such schools, teachers know and understand their advisees as individuals and care about their educational, personal, and social growth. Similarly, students and their parents have an adult within the school to whom they can readily turn for assistance.

The purpose of this chapter is to clarify the comprehensive and enabling objectives of Component 7 of the design for the renewal and improvement of secondary education that focuses on student advising:

Comprehensive Objective:

The faculty and students are organized into small groups that permit instruction and advising to be personalized.

Illustrative Enabling Objectives:

Related to advising, *each group of teachers*, such as an inter-disciplinary team, plans the group's advising activities related to:

Promoting the educational development of each student.

Increasing schoolwide communication.

Improving home-school-community relations.

Enhancing the personal and social development of each student.

Related to advising functions, individual staff members with assistance of a guidance counselor:

Serve as advisors to students.

Assume responsbility for planning, monitoring, and evaluating their advisee's educational programs and for attaining other objectives of the advising program.

In schools with teacher-advisor programs agreement usually has been reached on the following:

1. The school should attempt to meet the total needs of individual students—academic, personal, and social.

2. The need exists to bring about a continuous, trusting, and helping relationship between adolescents and adults so that secondary schools can become more personalized.

3. The need exists to improve and enhance relationships among teachers, students, and their parents.

4. The need exists to help students develop a greater sense of identity, purpose, and self-understanding.

Teacher-advisor programs may be arranged to fulfill one or all of the following functions: (a) promoting the educational development of the students, (b) increasing schoolwide communication, (c) improving home-school-community relations, and (d) enhancing the personal and social development of the students. Each of these functions is now examined.

PROMOTING EDUCATIONAL DEVELOPMENT

Although secondary schools have assumed responsibility for meeting many expectations, they are, first and foremost, academic institutions. In fact, through the years, the major task of the schools has been that of emphasizing intellectual achievement. The cornerstone of all activities that take place in the school is this educational purpose. Therefore, the central function of the teacher-advisor program is that of promoting the educational development of the students.

To understand what this function implies, we can contrast the role of the teacher in a typical secondary school with that wherein the teacher also serves as an advisor. Typically, a teacher is able to express concern for the academic performance of students only occasionally and informally. Rarely is the teacher able to do much more than ask the student how he or she "is doing" in other classes. Beyond this, the teacher finds it difficult to assist the student outside the teacher's regular classes. By contrast, the teacher as an advisor meets with a particular group of students regularly in group sessions and in individual conferences. Formal procedures are established which require the teacher to ascertain the extent to which advisees are making satisfactory progress in meeting course objectives, pursuing their interests, and making progress toward immediate and eventual goals. The important distinction between this approach and that of "How are you doing in your classes?" is that the concerns of the teacher, the student, and the student's parents or guardians are translated into a continuous, formalized monitoring process.

Providing continuous educational advisement includes three essential processes: planning the educational program with the advisee and his or her parents or guardians, monitoring the progress that each student is making toward short- and long-range goals, and evaluating the advisee's educational program at least once per year. The teacher-advisor should meet formally at least once each semester with each advisee and his or her parents to select a program of curricular experiences and extracurricular activities appropriate for meeting the advisee's educational and career goals. Not only must state and local requirements be met, but appropriate attention also must be paid to the wise choice of elective courses and activities appropriate for each student.

In addition to the choices across courses, choices must be made within courses. In some secondary schools, the educational program is structured to allow considerable flexibility for students to select different objectives within courses, different levels of difficulty, and different rates of time to achieve the objectives. In such schools, the teacher-advisor fulfills a monitoring role by meeting with advisees regularly to see that they are choosing appropriate objectives and units of instruction, engaging in the learning activities, and attaining the objectives. In short, the teacher-advisor monitors each advisee's educational progress. In so doing, the teacher-advisor not only works closely with the student and his or her parents but also interacts frequently with the advisee's other teachers.

INCREASING SCHOOLWIDE COMMUNICATION

Schoolwide communication is increased to the extent that teacher advisors work with other staff members in the school and the district to understand and meet the needs of their advisees. Thus, an effective teacher-advisor program increases communication within the school as well as between and among the schools of a district.

The teacher-advisor program helps to improve communication within the school in a number of ways. First, meetings between teacher advisors and their advisees are the ongoing vehicle for the transfer of schoolwide information and policies from the administration to students. In this way, the teacher-advisor program functions much like a traditional homeroom. Explanations of schoolwide policies and announcements concerning activities are given to advisees. In schools wherein teacher-advisor groups meet daily, these managerial matters usually occupy the first few minutes of the meetings.

Second, communication within the school is enhanced by the teacher-advisor program since each teacher advisor must understand the total educational program of the school if the basic function of educational advisement is to be fulfilled effectively. Such widespread knowledge of the total school's program on the part of teachers stands in sharp contrast to that in typical schools wherein, at best, teachers may be familiar only with offerings in their own departments, teams, or instructional units.

Communication also is increased within the school since the teacher advisor often acts as the liaison between the individual student and his or her other teachers. For example, students may discuss difficulties in any of their classes with their advisors. Likewise, other teachers are able to come to the advisor with concerns relating to a student's performance in their classes. The effect is that more people are discussing the educational progress of students.

Communication between or among the schools of a district also may be enhanced by a teacher-advisor program. Teacher advisors in secondary schools often serve as linkage agents with the other schools in the district. Senior high school advisors are able to become familiar with the programs in the feeder intermediate schools. Middle or junior high school advisors develop understanding of the programs in their feeder elementary schools and also in the high schools to which their advisees will go. For example, some school districts have deliberately established a policy wherein advisor groups move intact from one level of schooling to the next, thus providing students with a familiar group with which to identify in their new school. Thus, a smoother transition for students is provided as they proceed from one school to another. Moreover, teacher advisors in the receiving school are able to visit in advance with their advisees and their current teachers in the sending school. Information is shared regarding each advisee's previous progress, interests, and achievements to enhance suitable school placement. Thus, communication among schools is improved.

IMPROVING HOME-SCHOOL-COMMUNITY RELATIONS

In many secondary schools, communications between the school and the home generally take place only when issues of immediate interest arise. For example, most parents know or hear little about their child's progress in school other than through periodic grade reports. Other communications from the school are often negative and received only when the student is having either an academic or behavioral problem. By contrast, the teacher-advisor program serves to bridge the communication gap between the school and the home. Since one teacher is able to develop relationships with a particular group of students over time, the teacher advisor becomes the obvious contact person in relations with the home.

In schools with teacher-advisor programs most contacts between the school and the home involve the teacher advisor. Grade reports and other official communications may be sent not only from the principal's office, but also from the teacher-advisor. At Cedarburg High School, for example, written grade reports are prepared by advisors and sent often. Each teacher advisor, regardless of his or her subject area of specialization, is aware of the progress of students in all curricular areas. When parents wish to know how their child is doing in school, or even when they have no specific concerns about a particular subject, the teacher advisor is able to give a complete picture of the student's progress or lack of it.

Increasingly in secondary schools, teacher-student-parent conferences are being utilized, at least once each semester, as a formal means of reporting student progress to parents. Many schools alternate the use of written grade reports with the conduct of such conferences. The teacher-advisor program facilitates this process, since the teacher advisor monitors the total progress of each advisee. In some secondary schools, teacher-student-parent conferences are led by students, thus providing for self-assessment and student participation in decision making. Still other secondary schools alternate the use of teacher-student-parent conferences with only teacher-parent conferences. Regardless of the specific plan used, parent conferences enhance direct, two-way communication between the school and the home.

In schools with teacher-advisor programs, the contact between the school and the home is not confined simply to grade reporting. Parents realize that if they have any questions about how their child is progressing, then the teacher advisor can be contacted. This relationship is not only beneficial to parents who wish immediate responses to their concerns, but also to teachers and the total school. Increased formal and informal contacts with parents allow teachers to advise parents of any potential difficulties that may arise, and conversely. Thus, the school is viewed favorably because it is responsive to the concerns of teachers, students, and parents. Moreover, appropriate attention can be paid to helping each student plan systematically to meet educational and career goals.

In addition to the formal and informal contacts between teachers and parents, the teacher-advisor program expands teachers' school-community relationships. In providing educational advisement, teacher advisors come to know, understand, and work with the larger community. As described in Chapter 5, the programs in some secondary schools include experiential learning in the community as well as within the the school. As teacher advisors become familiar with the total program of the school, therefore, their understanding and appreciation of the contribution of community agencies to the educational enterprise, in general, and to the development of their advisees, in particular, are increased.

ENHANCING PERSONAL-SOCIAL
DEVELOPMENT

The fourth function of an effective teacher-advisor program is that of enhancing the personal and social development of students. In so doing, teacher advisors help their advisees learn more about themselves and their relations with others.

Traditionally, concerns about the personal and social development of students have been the domain of the guidance and counseling staff of the secondary school. But how can the guidance staff do an adequate job of helping hundreds of students in the area of personal and social growth and development? In traditional schools, the counselor-student ratio typically is so large that only a few students are able to have meaningful personal interaction with counselors. By contrast, in schools with teacher-advisor programs all students work continually with an informed and concerned adult.

Schools that have used teacher-advisor programs to enhance the personal and social development of students have been successful only by carefully preparing teachers to work with students in this domain. Of all the functions that a teacher advisor fulfills, none is more likely to cause greater anxiety than the expectation that teachers will help students in personal-social development. Typically, teachers say, "I'm not trained to be a counselor." While this may be true, it contains two fallacies. First, the role of teacher-advisor does not require teachers to fulfill the role of the professional counselor. Counselors are still the people who work with students needing specialized assistance. Counselors must be able to exercise their expertise so that teachers can refer students with particular problems to them, just as counselors may refer students with severe problems to other agencies. The second fallacy is that in order to serve as an advisor, the teacher must have extensive training. Instead, the teacher-advisor program simply requires staff members to understand the role of advisor and be willing to serve as responsible resource people. If students need in-depth assistance beyond what the teacher can comfortably provide, appropriate procedures must be used for proper referral. As professionals, teachers should be willing and able to help young people beyond simply conducting classes.

To help teachers become comfortable as advisors, some schools have devised comprehensive programs for fostering the personal and social development of students. For example, in many schools teacher advisors are given complete plans for activities to enhance personal and social growth. These plans, which resemble typical lesson plans, contain step-by-step instructions regarding activities that are appropriate at different times during the school year and how the activities should proceed. At Webster Transitional School, for example, the total staff participated in developing and selecting exercises included in the teacher advisor's resource guide. In addition to certain activities used schoolwide, such as respect for the rights of others, care of school property, and skills in individual decision making, optional activities may be elected and used. Adequate planning time is provided each week for the team of teacher-advisors to select appropriate activities, to plan for the use of their advising time, and to evaluate the effectiveness of the advising activities. Such planning ensures that all students, regardless of advisor, are exposed to appropriately selected activities during their three years in the school. Then, if a student changes his or her advisor there is continuity across the various advisor groups in the school.

To see how the functions of educational advisement, schoolwide communication, home-school-community relations, and personal-social development are fulfilled in middle, junior, and senior high schools, we describe the arrangements for teacher-advisor programs used in four selected secondary schools.

ALTERNATIVE ARRANGEMENTS FOR TEACHER-ADVISOR PROGRAMS

In this section we describe teacher-advisor programs as they are organized and operate in four secondary schools—two senior high schools, a junior high school, and a middle school. Each example includes a brief description of the school, the organizational arrangements for advising, and the operation of the teacher-advisor program. Since the schools represent a wide range in size, location, and clienteles served, their teacher-advisor programs also differ.

Wilde Lake High School, Columbia, Maryland

Wilde Lake High School is located between Washington, D.C., and Baltimore, Maryland. It is a comprehensive senior high school

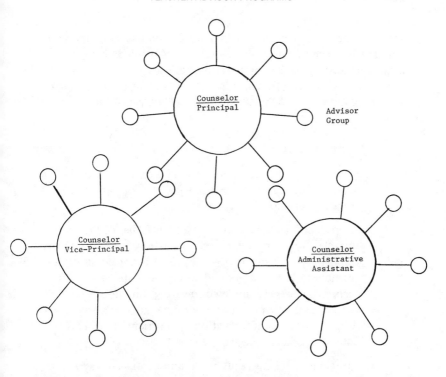

Figure 10.1 The Organization for Advising at Wilde Lake High
School, Columbia, Maryland

that enrolls about 900 students in Grades 9 through 12. Approximately 80 percent of the students enter college after graduation. The
school is housed in a circular, open-concept building, the hub of
which includes administrative and counseling offices, a staff planning area for teacher offices, and the instructional media center. The
staff is comprised of the principal, a vice principal, and an administrative assistant; two media specialists; three guidance counselors;
and approximately 60 certificated and classified staff.

As shown in Figure 10.1, the school is organized for advising into
three clusters, each of which is under the direction of a counselor.
Each counselor coordinates the activities of advisor groups within
his or her cluster. An administrator also serves as a resource to each
cluster. Each teacher advises 15 to 20 students. Teacher advisors meet

with their advisees in group sessions for 20 minutes each day. Other contacts between advisors and advisees are scheduled before or after school or during teacher preparation periods.

At Wilde Lake, careful consideration was given to specifying the following duties of teachers as advisors (*Handbook for Teachers*, 1979-80, p. 2):

All advisors will:

1. Keep accurate records on attendance and tardiness to school, and assume responsibility for an advisee's whereabouts during advisor period.

2. Keep a confidential file on each advisee. The file should contain the following items: (a) the official progress record (report card) of the advisee, (b) records and notes of conferences with the advisee and/or his/her parents, (c) official record of courses completed toward graduation, (d) an up-to-date and accurate schedule of the advisee's week, and (e) personal data information re: participation in student activities, special projects, etc.

3. Inform all advisees regularly of announcements and information from the administration, guidance, and elsewhere.

4. Monitor each advisee's academic progress by keeping the report card up-to-date and accurate and by conferencing with each advisee at least once per month.

5. Serve as a liaison between:
   a. The advisee and his/her parents;
   b. The school and the parents;
   c. The advisee and the cluster counselor (referring advisees who need information or help to the cluster counselor).

6. Serve as an interested, caring person to whom each advisee knows he/she can bring academic and personal problems if he/she wishes to do so.

7. Assist each advisee to develop responsible behavior by holding him/her accountable to school policies and by helping him/her learn to plan a course of action and to evaluate the results.

8. The advisor, in close conjunction with the guidance counselor, will also:
   a. Assist advisees in making course selections that will meet both state requirements for graduation and career needs.
   b. Assist advisees in gaining information about tests (PSAT, SAT, GATB, etc. See Teacher-Advisor Handbook for dates for testing.).
   c. Update each advisee's permanent record at the end of the school year.

9. Become familiar with official background information housed in the cumulative record file in the counseling area. Early in the year, advisors should arrange with their cluster counselor to schedule time in the records room to review the cumulative folder on each advisee.

The extent to which the above are fulfilled is formally monitored and evaluated through monthly reports of teacher advisors.

During the daily advisor sessions attendance and announcements are first handled. Then, advisors engage the group in activities suggested by their cluster counselor or they work with individual students. Advisors use this time to review each student's academic progress. Advisement folders are maintained for this purpose. Advisors update these folders which contain a record of student performance and progress in each unit of instruction in each subject.

At Wilde Lake, the matching of a student with a particular advisor is done through a process shared by both students and school officials. While students are enrolled in one of the middle schools, they are able to select three possible high school teachers, in order of preference, to serve as their future advisors. Administrators and counselors review these preference lists and, if possible, honor student choices. The student typically stays with the same advisor for all four years.

How is it possible for students who are still enrolled in a middle school to select their advisors? First, many students are somewhat familiar, through reputation, with a large number of the high school teachers. Frequently, a student's brothers or sisters who have attended the high school suggest the same advisor that they had. Second, the high school counselors go to the middle schools and make presentations concerning the staff of the school and its advisement program. Brief vitae of the high school teachers also are distributed. Middle school counselors also suggest possible advisors. Even so, students later have the opportunity to change advisors after the first semester of the ninth grade.

Advisor groups are multiaged. Wilde Lake has deliberately adopted the policy of mixing students from all grade levels into the same advisor groups because it is felt that the older students often serve as useful role models for the younger ones.

Wilde Lake has experienced only minor difficulties with its advisor program. One problem is that of helping teachers new to the school in understanding the functions and operation of the advisor program. Teachers who worked in the school at the beginning of its program received inservice training regarding the role of the teacher advisor. New teachers, however, have had to learn their advising role primarily from the experienced staff. Hence, additional orientation and preparation are needed for new staff members. Another perplexing issue is that of deciding what time of the day is most appropriate for scheduling the teacher-advisor period. At Wilde Lake it now meets at the end of the first regularly scheduled period. A third difficulty actually grows out of the success of the teacher-advisor program. Graduates of Wilde Lake often return to the school to visit and consult their former advisors. Although this indicates the power of the relationships formed, it presents some complications to teachers who, because they are in demand by former students, may have less time to spend with their current advisees.

From the description of the arrangement for the teacher-advisor program at Wilde Lake High School we now turn to that in another senior school wherein the program operates quite differently.

Irvine High School, Irvine, California

Irvine High School is a comprehensive school enrolling over 1,800 students in Grades 9 through 12. It is located in a suburban area south of Los Angeles. Approximately 60 percent of the students enter college after graduation. The school is built on the campus plan with separate buildings for instructional and other activities. As shown in Figure 10.2 and as described earlier in Chapter 8, Irvine High School is organized into subschools. Each of these schools, or units, is composed of approximately 600 students, 30 teachers, a

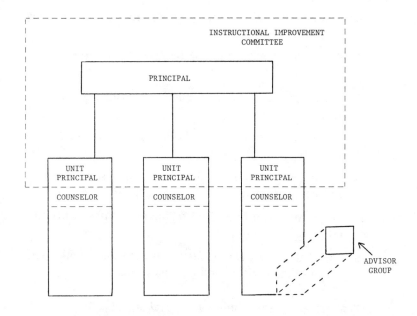

INSTRUCTION AND ADVISORY UNITS

Figure 10.2 The Organization for Advising at Irvine High
School, Irvine, California

counselor, and an assistant or unit principal. Each subschool or unit
consists of approximately 28 advisor groups. The number of
subschools can change from four to three or four to five, depending on the total school enrollment.

At Irvine, the teacher-advisor program is important to the success of the school. The following are the major categories of responsibility of all staff members who also serve as advisors (*Irvine High
School Advisement*, pp. 2-5):

Program Planning

Any activity dealing with the act of choosing school courses,
such as course selection, evaluation of course schedule or ten-

tative long-range educational planning. In program planning it is assumed that:

1. The student has some long-range career education and life goals.

2. The parent has some long-range career education and life goals.

3. These two sets of goals have been compared for similarities and differences.

4. The student has assessed his or her learning style, interests, and past performance.

5. The student is aware of all the many options in learning programs.

6. The student has matched his or her goals and abilities with courses that students and parents choose.

That is program planning. It takes an advisor with responsibility for only a few students to assure that the courses each student "registers for" are just the last step in a very thorough process.

Parent Relations/Conferences

Those special activities designed to increase parent participation in the schooling process of their children and to ensure frequent positive contact among the advisor, student, and parent.

Feedback/Evaluation

That information that a school needs to hear, formally or informally, so that it can change itself to better suit the needs and desires of the people it serves. This category does not mean feedback to the student. It means feedback a student gives to the school.

Decision-Making Skills

The conscious application of a process to make decisions. Although decision making is woven into activities in many categories, it also is a distinct category to aid advisors in teaching the process.

Career Planning/Preparation

Activities to help students select and prepare for a career.

School/Community Issues

Activities concerned with the human aspect of individuals working together. Included are human development activities and group skills. This area also includes any discussions needed about current schoolwide issues that might arise during a school year, such as vandalism, a special decision the school needs to make, or any shared concern.

The advisor and advisee may do activities selected from these eight broad areas, depending upon the time of year and the particular circumstances of the advisee. Sometimes the activities will be formal; other times they may be but a brief personal interaction.

At Irvine, all staff members—administrators, counselors, teachers, and paraprofessionals—serve as advisors to groups of approximately 15 students. In this way, the size of advisor groups is smaller than in a typical class. Moreover, opportunities are provided for all staff members to maintain continuing contact with individual students.

The daily schedule of the school allots 35 minutes midmorning as advising time. Advisor groups meet during the first 15 minutes. Agendas include announcements and attendance and specific activities appropriate for the total advisor group. For the remaining 20 minutes, advisors may either continue with their total advisor groups or schedule individual conferences. During these conferences students may meet with their advisor or their other teachers or take a midmorning break.

Whereas at Wilde Lake advisor groups are multigraded, at Irvine the groups are single graded. This is viewed by the staff as preferable because opportunities are provided for students of the same grade to interact concerning issues relating to their interests and activities. For example, some issues, such as graduation plans and college admissions, are of concern primarily to juniors or seniors, whereas other topics, such as orientation to the school, are appropriate for freshmen. Typically, freshmen or sophomores require more advising time than do juniors and seniors. To assist advisors with monitoring the progress of their advisees, a folder for each student is used which includes a checklist of activities appropriate at each grade level.

At Irvine, as at Wilde Lake, students remain with their same advisor throughout their four years in the school. Such continuity is important, so that meaningful relationships can be established among advisors, advisees, and their parents or guardians.

At Irvine, attention has been paid to the issue of how best to form advisor groups. When the program began, students were assigned randomly. Later, students were allowed to select their advisors. Both approaches worked well, but a better way was sought to match advisors with advisees. Since most of the ninth graders come from the same middle school which also has an advisor program, middle school advisor groups now move intact to the high school. When students are in the eighth grade they meet with the high school teacher who will be their advisor the following year. The teacher advisor explains Irvine's instructional program and helps students in selecting their high school courses. This helps students make the transition from one level of schooling to the next by providing students a familiar group to identify with in high school. It also improves communication and promotes a sense of unity across the schools of the district.

Irvine has paid attention to deciding what is the best time of the day for conducting the teacher-advisor program and in finding new staff members with the requisite training or experience to serve as teacher advisors. Currently, the midmorning advising period is working well. To enable the staff to work comfortably as teacher advisors, inservice training for the staff is continually updated.

Having examined the organization and operation of teacher-advisor programs in senior high schools, we now examine those used in junior high and middle schools.

Coolidge Junior High School, Phoenix, Illinois

Coolidge Junior High School in Phoenix, Illinois, south of Chicago, enrolls about 250 seventh and eighth grade students. The principal and administrative assistant provide leadership to a staff of 18 teachers. As shown in Figure 10.3, the staff and students are

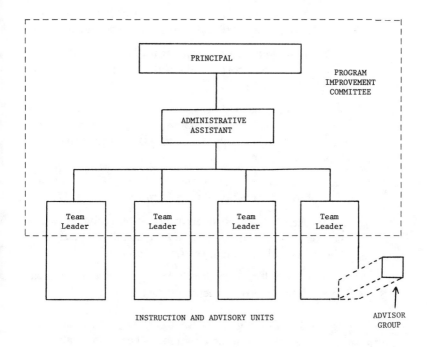

Figure 10.3 The Organization for Advising at Coolidge Junior
High School, Phoenix, Illinois

organized into four Instruction and Advisory (I & A) units. Each
unit is headed by a team leader who serves on the schoolwide Program Improvement Committee which is chaired by the principal.

The staff at Coolidge has devoted sustained attention to identifying the needs of junior high school students. Their program is designed to meet student needs for participation, responsibility, recognition, a positive self-concept, peer and adult approval, self-expression,
and creativity. Each teacher serves as advisor to approximately 15
of the students assigned to the I & A unit. In Coolidge it is expected
that (*Handbook for Teachers*, Coolidge School, pp. 8-9):

1. The teacher shall know his/her children well in order to provide effective individualized instruction. The teacher will:

   a. Diagnose what the child needs for better learning.
   b. Seek and use information on the child—his/her past learning experiences.

2. The teacher will be held responsible for all records pertaining to his/her students. Advisor-advisee periods are an important part of our daily program. Use this time to get to know your advisee.

3. The teacher will protect the rights of students from infringement by other students, teachers, or others.

4. The teacher shall receive directly all questions about his/her decisions and about his/her instructional practices. All children and their parent(s) are the teacher's clients.

5. The teacher will actively seek help in those areas in which he/she feels a need or there is evidence of a need.

Advisor groups at Coolidge meet twice each day—10 minutes in the morning and 20 minutes in the afternoon. The morning advisory period is similar to the familiar homeroom for checking attendance, making announcements, and the like. The afternoon time is usually used for the systematic review of student progress in all academic areas. This review usually takes place in individual conferences between the advisor and the advisee or it may be scheduled at other available times.

Coolidge's advisor program fulfills the major functions of educational advisement, schoolwide communication, home-school-community relations, and personal-social growth of students. One of the main functions emphasized in the teacher-advisor program at Coolidge is that of improving home-school-community relations. Teacher advisors monitor the progress of each advisee. Teacher advisors also are responsible for conducting information nights held at the school throughout the year. Parents go to the advisor for an explanation of their child's academic progress in all curricular areas. Teacher advisors also keep contact with parents via telephone, mail, or home visits throughout the year. Such continuous interaction between teachers and parents has been a major force for building an unusually high degree of understanding and support for Coolidge Junior High School on the part of parents and citizens throughout the community.

Webster Transitional School, Cedarburg, Wisconsin

Located north of Milwaukee in Cedarburg, Wisconsin, Webster Transitional School is a middle school that enrolls about 700 students in Grades 6 through 8. The school is structured into eight academic instructional units, an allied arts team, and a support team. Each academic unit is composed of 75 to 100 students and a team of 3 to 4 teachers. Five of the academic units are composed of 6th and 7th graders while three include only 8th graders. The teachers of each academic team are responsible for instruction in language arts, reading, mathematics, science, and social studies. The allied arts team is compooosed of 12 teachers, including industrial arts, home economics, art, music, and physical education. The support team includes the director of the instructional materials center, the guidance counselors, a reading consultant, and the special education teachers.

As shown in Figure 10.4, the organization for advising at Webster Transitional School is somewhat unique. Advisory groups of five to seven staff members are formed as allied arts teachers and support unit staff members join the academic unit teachers for advising. In this way, all teachers and counselors serve as advisors, hence advisor groups are reduced to an average of 12 to 16 students. Also, productive relationships for planning, implementing, and evaluating the teacher-advisor program are established by including the total staff as advisors.

At Webster the program also is based on the unique needs of the early adolescent which the staff has defined as follows (Webster Transitional School, *Three-Year Progress Report*, 1977, pp. 8-9):

Needs of Adolescents

1. Early adolescence is the most traumatic period in the life of a human being.

2. Early adolescence is a time of rapid, irregular growth and development.

3. Biological changes taking place alter not only the physical child but also his or her social and emotional status.

4. Mental maturation, like physical development, is in transition during the middle school years.

5. Early adolescence is marked by the youngster's transition from dependence upon the family for security to a similar dependence on the peer group.

6. The early adolescent is overwhelmed with self-adjustment problems, with the problem of ego resynthesis. Ego is the all-absorbing interest for the early adolescent.

7. Adolescents need to understand their growth changes and become aware of the effect which personal growth changes have relative to others.

8. The school must help reduce the personal anxieties of the early adolescent period if it is to attain his or her motivation in the learner's role.

Keeping in mind the many areas of student development—intellectual, physical, social, and emotional, we have established the following goals which aim for the development of the total student. These goals are the culmination of the expressed desires of the community, the faculty, and the parents.

Goals of the School

1. The middle school promotes growth in basic learning skills and academic concepts.

2. The middle school guides the child toward proficiency in independent learning, keeping in mind the continuing need to learn throughout life.

3. The middle school provides a wide variety of curriculum experiences involving the child in situations which will develop social skills and cultural understanding.

4. The middle school develops self-discipline and responsibility through a variety of enriching activities.

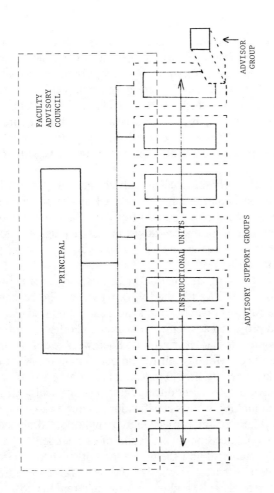

Figure 10.4 The Organization for Advising at Webster Transitional School, Cedarburg, Wisconsin

5. The middle school encourages each pupil to understand and accept his or her role as a developing adolescent—an individual with personal needs, values, and shared social responsibilities.

To help in meeting the above goals, students at Webster select their advisors from staff of their advisor group based on mutual interests. Early in the school year, staff members share their interests with students in total advisory group meetings to assist them in selecting advisors. Following such sessions, students list advisor group staff with whom they feel compatible. Likewise, advisors select students with whom they feel they can work effectively. During initial advisor group meetings, students also share their interests with group members.

All functions of an effective teacher-advisor program are fulfilled at Webster, but particular emphasis is placed on the personal and social development of adolescents. To fulfill this function, the staff developed a handbook for teacher advisors that includes structured activities which emphasize the development of skills required for personal and social growth.

At Webster, provisions are made for the advisory staff to work on planning their activities for the following week. The academic, allied arts, and support team members meet each Wednesday afternoon to discuss projected advisement activities and other operational matters relating to their advisor groups. Each week, advisors meet with their advisees on Monday during the last 15 minutes of the day and on Thursday mornings for 30 to 60 minutes. Large group, small group, and individual activities during these sessions deal with goal setting, decision making, values clarification, career awareness, and other matters. Many of the projects and activities are designed to increase the personal decision-making skills of each student. The objective is to help students know themselves and others better. Group projects are often used to emphasize the need for cooperation, awareness of personal skills, and recognition of strengths possessed by others. Some of the group activities concern schoolwide issues, such as consideration for others in the lunchroom and throughout the school. As students within advisor groups become well acquainted, they celebrate birthdays and send "get well" cards to members of the group. Thus, the teacher-advisor program has served to increase students' concerns for others and create a positive atmosphere throughout the school.

In reporting to parents, teacher-student-parent conferences are regularly scheduled at Webster. These conferences are led by students who assume responsibility for synthesizing and reporting their progress in all areas. Thus, teacher advisors, students, and parents enjoy continuing mutually supportive relations. Evaluations of the program show that students are well informed about their educational progress and are able to report it meaningfully to their parents, have a positive self-concept, demonstrate group cohesiveness, and show pride in their school.

ISSUES IN IMPLEMENTING TEACHER-ADVISOR PROGRAMS

We have shown four examples of how teacher-advisor programs have been organized and implemented in secondary schools. We have also seen that the purposes and operation of each program are quite different and especially between high schools and middle schools. Despite these differences, the staff of each school has had to pay sustained attention to certain basic issues before they attempted to implement their teacher-advisor programs. Here, we outline the issues that must be addressed by the staff of any secondary school in terms of its own philosophy, needs, and capabilities if the teacher-advisor program is to be successful. These basic issues are as follows:

1. How much planning of the program and preparation of the staff are required?

2. Which grade levels should be included in advisor groups?

3. How should advisor groups be formed?

4. Which staff members should serve as advisors?

5. When, how often, and for how long should advisor groups meet?

6. How much staff time is required for advising?

Planning for Advising

The staff of any secondary school considering a teacher-advisor program must regard the program as a major educational change.

As such, considerable attention must be paid to the amount of time and resources and the activities required to plan and implement the program effectively. Moreover, appropriate people must be involved at each step in the planning and decision-making process.

A description of the major activities followed by the staff of Irvine High School in planning, implementing, and evaluating its teacher-advisor program is instructive. After the decision was made to establish a teacher-advisor program, an advisement committee was selected, consisting of representative students, counselors, teachers, and others. This committee reviewed relevant literature, visited other schools, and synthesized the information by defining the developmental needs of students, the role and competencies of the teacher advisor, the role of the counselor, and the competencies of advisees. Staff and student needs were assessed; staff development activities were conducted; and materials and strategies for advisement were planned, submitted for approval, and then implemented. Subsequently, the program has been evaluated continually both by the staff and by outside consultants regarding the extent to which it meets the needs of students, teachers, counselors, parents, and others. Through feedback, the results of such evaluations are recycled to serve as the basis for continued improvement of the teacher-advisor program.

Undoubtedly, staff members who initially participate in the planning process are well prepared to understand and implement the program and are also committed to its effective implementation. Yet in each school, subsequent staff changes require that new staff members must be appropriately oriented to and prepared for their expanded role as teacher advisors. Increased attention in inservice meetings to revisiting the philosophy, organization, and operation of the teacher-advisor program can be beneficial to both "old" and "new" staff members.

Determining Advisor Group Membership

What should be the composition of advisor groups? Should advisor groups be single-graded or multigraded? Again, answers must be determined locally. As we saw earlier, advisor groups at Wilde Lake High School are multigraded, so that older students can serve as role models for younger ones. By contrast, Irvine High School has single-graded advisor groups because it is felt that advisory sessions often concern problems related to a particular grade level.

Whatever choice is made relative to the grade levels of advisor groups, several other factors must be considered. Advisor groups should be heterogeneous enough to ensure that groups are neither all male nor all female, no groups are composed only of athletes, no groups are composed only of the academically talented, and no groups include only students experiencing academic problems. In this regard, we are reminded of one principal who, during the teacher-advisor period, proudly pointed out the window to a group of students cleaning up the parking lot and observed, "There are the real 'rummies' of the school—all in Mr. X's advisor group. He surely knows how to handle those kids!" Such formal or informal labeling is inimical to the basic purposes of an effective teacher-advisor program.

Forming Advisor Groups

In forming advisor groups, the staff of a school must consider the question, "How are students to be matched with their advisors?" Answers will largely depend on the maturity level of the students as well as the size of the school. In this regard, middle and junior high schools often assign students to I & A units or teams within which a choice of advisors is made, whereas senior high students are usually given considerably wider choice of advisors.

In small communities, where incoming students have some acquaintance with teachers, students may be able to select their advisors. By contrast, in large urban schools this is impossible. Such schools often combine arbitrary placement and student choice. In Irvine Senior High School, for example, incoming freshmen are initially assigned administratively with their middle school advisory groups, but later are allowed to choose different advisors.

The extent to which students are able to transfer from one advisor to another must also be considered. Some schools follow a "no-transfer" policy, particularly if the student has a choice in the initial selection process. Others allow one or more changes to be made by mutual consent of the student, the current advisor, and the new advisor. Since advisor-advisee compatibility is desirable, students and teachers should be consulted. Whatever the policy for matching or transferring advisees, some freedom of choice should be allowed so that staff-student relations can be enhanced.

Scheduling Advisor Group Meetings

The issues of how often, for how long, and when in the day advisor groups should meet depend on the breadth and depth of expectations held for the teacher-advisor program. In many senior high schools, the advisor period is held daily, usually for 10 to 30 minutes. In other middle and junior high schools, such as in Webster Transitional School, advisor periods are held only a few days each week and usually for longer periods of time. Even so, in all secondary schools, students are encouraged to arrange time outside of the regular advisory period to talk with their advisors as needed. Such individual conferences are important, since group sessions are often devoted to administrative matters or other planned activities. Adequate time must be provided so that both group and individual contact between advisors and advisees can fulfill the functions of the teacher-advisor program.

Schools have experimented widely with determining the best time of the school day for scheduling advisor group meetings. In middle schools this issue may not be so critical, since their schedules are often quite flexible. In junior and senior high schools, however, the trend has been toward scheduling advisor-advisee contact mid-morning, both as somewhat of a change in the routine of regular classes and as a device for acting on problems or issues during the remainder of the school day.

Deciding Who Will Serve as Advisors

To what extent should all staff members—administrators, counselors, specialists, teachers, or paraprofessionals—serve as teacher advisors? This is a perplexing issue, indeed. Previously, the idealized norm has been "the wider the participation then the better," since such total participation tends to increase staff awareness and involvement, as well as to reduce the advisor-advisee ratio. Experience has shown, however, that such widespread involvement poses some problems. For example, administrators or counselors may need to be available during the advisement period to monitor the implementation of the program or to serve as specialized resources. In some schools, shared responsibilities for joint advising of an advisee group have been devised for administrators and counselors. In other schools, all staff members except the principal serve as teacher advisors. In still other schools, counselors are kept free during the advisement period to receive referrals. In the schools of some states paraprofessionals are prohibited from serving as advisors despite the fact that they may possess the professional and personal qualifications for doing so. In any event, the issue of who will serve as a teacher advisor must be determined.

If only as a footnote, some observations also should be made regarding qualitative and quantitative changes in the role of the guidance counselor in schools having effective teacher advisor programs. Regarding qualitative change, the counselor in a school with a teacher-advisor program generally becomes a resource person or facilitator, available to help not only students with problems that require the specialized training of the counselor, but also teachers in becoming competent to serve as advisors. In schools with effective teacher-advisor programs, the counselor assumes a new leadership role in directing and sustaining the program. Counselors often are responsible for assessing schoolwide needs and suggesting various activities for teacher-advisor groups. Counselors also help in planning the materials and procedures for effectively operating the program. In schools with teacher-advisor programs, the ideal that "all teachers are counselors" is more nearly approached.

Regarding quantitative change in the counselor's role, in many schools each counselor must serve 300 or more students. Thus, there is not enough time for counselors to work with individual students. However, when teacher advisors are able to take care of some of the activities formerly handled by counselors, there is more time for counselors to assist referred students having particular, previously-assessed needs. Therefore, professional counselors generally enthusiastically endorse and provide leadership to the development of effective teacher-advisor programs.

Allocating Time for Advising

Since a teacher-advisor program represents a major change in secondary education, adequate time must be allocated for planning the program. Many staffs have targeted their staff development resources in this direction. Beyond the planning process, however, basic decisions must be made regarding the allocation of staff time to implement the teacher-advisor program effectively.

In most middle and junior high schools and in some senior high schools student advising is viewed as a normative function of the typical teacher's role. Therefore, the teacher-advisor program simply formalizes and facilitates achieving the goals of the school. In many complex, comprehensive high schools, however, the degree of teacher specialization, the concern with already heavy work loads, the lack of staff preparation for advising, and many other organizational and personalistic factors mitigate against establishing effective teacher-advisor programs. If the four basic functions of teacher-advisor programs are to be fulfilled effectively, then the demands placed on the staff are undoubtedly equivalent to those of a typical class. Hence, we recommend that such load equivalence be granted, that the teacher-advisor responsibilities be defined, and that the staff be evaluated in part on the basis of their performance as teacher advisors. To those who would decry the cost of a teacher-advisor program on these terms, we simply point to the previously defined inadequacies of our secondary schools, many of which might be remedied through an effective teacher-advisor program.

SUMMARY

In this chapter we first defined the four functions of a teacher-advisor program: promoting educational development, increasing schoolwide communication, improving home-school-community relations, and enhancing personal-social development. Four alternative organizational arrangements for teacher-advisor programs in middle, junior, and senior high schools were depicted and described.

The chapter concluded by stressing the need for the staff of each local school to give systematic attention to planning its teacher-advisor program. Among the major factors to be considered are preparing the staff for advising; determining advisor group membership; forming advisor groups; determining the length, frequency, and scheduling of advisory group meetings; deciding who will serve as advisors; and allocating adequate time and resources for advising.

Attention given to planning and implementing teacher-advisor programs should help improve quality of education in secondary schools, both immediately and in the years ahead.

PART IV: COMMUNITY, SUPPORT ARRANGEMENTS, RESEARCH

CHAPTER 11

HOME-SCHOOL-COMMUNITY RELATIONS

John C. Daresh

How can the varied interests and concerns of parents and citizens be channeled to assist the secondary school in carrying out its educational improvement efforts? How can persons in the school formulate ways for improving communication that takes place between the school and community groups? How can the school tap the rich resources of its surrounding community to promote educational practices that address the needs and interests of individual students? Answers to these questions concerning home-school-community relations are considered in this chapter.

The purpose of this chapter is to clarify the comprehensive and enabling objectives of Component 8 of the design for improvement—Home-School-Community Relations:

Comprehensive Objective:

Effective communication and cooperative educational efforts between the school and the community are carried out as part of a program of home-school-community relations.

Illustrative Enabling Objectives:

A comprehensive program of home-school-community relations:

Is formulated and monitored by a school committee composed of representative school staff, parents, and students.

Provides for frequent and effective communication between the school and community.

Encourages the school staff to participate in the analysis of the home and neighborhood conditions of their students.

Encourages parents and other community persons to participate in in-school educational activities and to provide suggestions to aid in decision making.

Involves parents in planning the individual educational program of their child.

Provides for student progress to be reported to parents regularly and effectively.

In this chapter, we consider the importance and aims of effective home-school-community relations, some examples of programs designed to increase community involvement, and finally, the relationship between effective home-school-community relations and the other components of the design for secondary school improvement described throughout this book.

IMPORTANCE OF HOME-SCHOOL-COMMUNITY RELATIONS

A major purpose of developing effective home-school-community relations is to enable parents and other citizens to participate in the educational activities of the school. Another purpose is to increase communication between the school and the community by encouraging staff members to participate in the analysis of home and neighborhood conditions of students. Effective home-school-community relations encourage parents to become involved in the educational processes of the school by working with teachers in planning the individual educational programs of their children each semester. Communication is increased because parents, as active participants with their children in educational programming, work together with students in monitoring progress made in course work and other aspects of the educational process.

The importance of the development of effective home-school-community relations by schools has been underscored by a good deal of recent research. For example, in a longitudinal study reported by Klausmeier and Allen (1978), the relationship between a number of variables and rapid and slow cognitive development by children was studied. The results show that, for Grade 12 students, a positive relationship exists between the rate of cognitive development and a number of variables related to home life and the family, including the perceptions of the parents regarding their children and the school (Klausmeier & Allen, p. 198).

Figure 11.1 shows the home and family variables which were associated with rapid and slow cognitive development. As shown in the figure, several variables in the area of home and family were found to differentiate between rapid and slow developers in Grade 12. Klausmeier and Allen concluded that rapid developing students hold positive attitudes toward parents, family, and the home in general, and parents of rapid developers hold positive attitudes toward the school and education, and are concerned and interested in their child's school, teachers, and curriculum.

Slow developers, on the other hand, had parents who typically demonstrated little involvement with their child and with the school and expressed negative attitudes toward the school and education.

Research also shows the importance of the school establishing positive interactions with the home and the community. In a review of literature included in her study of school-community relations in secondary schools, Oinonen (1980) cited studies which discovered relationships between effective programs of home-school-community relations and student performance. For example, Sestak and Frerich (1968) and Hunter (1967) found that good school-community relations had a positive impact on student progress. Hobson (1976) found a significant positive correlation between parent involvement in school activities and student achievement. Brookover, Lapere, Homachek, Thomas, and Erickson (1965), in a study of junior high school students and their parents, found that when parents are involved in school activities, their children showed significant progress in mathematics, reading, and language arts. Research also indicates that parental involvement in the educational process can greatly enhance a child's prospects for academic success (Keeves, 1971; Baker, 1977).

Findings from studies such as these provide convincing evidence that a school turning its attention to developing effective home-school-community relations is not merely an attempt to improve public relations and get "good press." To be sure, a political purpose is served by involving parents in the activities of the school; but even more important is the educational value to be attained.

In earlier chapters of this book we have shown that the involvement of parents and other community members is essential in improving educational practice. We now consider a framework for understanding specific ways in which a fruitful relationship between the school and its surrounding community may be established.

AIMS OF HOME-SCHOOL-COMMUNITY RELATIONS

After synthesizing the results of several studies of the relationship between schools and their communities, Bowles and Fruth (1976) developed 10 assumptions about effective school-community relations:

1. Home-school-community relations involve more than the effective use of media. Communications media are definitely part of a successful program, but their use should not comprise the total program.

2. The benefits of any instructional or organizational change must be made visible and tangible to the various subpublics in the school community. Thus, members of school subpublics must be involved early in the implementation efforts and answers to questions must be in concrete, specific, and understandable terms.

3. An effective program of home-school-community relations involves working very closely with parents. This includes parent volunteers, home-school visits, and parent participation in educational decision making.

4. School staff members should use the educational resources available in the community. This action will both enhance the instructional program and increase the staff's knowledge of the community.

5. Members of the school staff must expand their concepts of community. Educational affairs should not be considered in isolation from community affairs and municipal issues.

6. Children are the most important subpublic in a school. They are a primary source of information for their parents, they affect the way that their parents and other adults respond, and the way they perceive their education now will influence their view of schools when they are adults.

Figure 11.1 Variables Associated with Rapid and Slow Cognitive Development

Variables	Sixth Grade	Twelfth Grade
Self		
IQ Score	Yes	Yes
Self-Esteem	Yes	Yes
Internalized Responsibility for Learning	No	No
Attitudes toward School	Yes	Yes
Attitudes toward Curriculum	Yes	Yes
Achievement Motivation	Yes	Yes
Self-Directedness of Behavior	Yes	Yes
Peer Relations	No	Yes
Attitudes toward Parents-Home	No	Yes
School/education		
Absenteeism[c]	Yes	Yes
Grades (A-F)	Yes	Yes
Curriculum (Courses Taken)[c]	No	Yes
School Involvement-Activities	No	Yes
Extracurricular Activities:		
TV Viewing[c]	No	Yes
Reading	Yes	Yes
Sports	No	No
Hobbies	Yes	Yes
School Structure[b]	No	No
Classroom Structure[b]	No	No
Home-School Interaction	No	Yes
Rapport with Teachers	No	Yes
Home/family		
Demographic:		
Socioeconomic Status of Parents	Yes	Yes
Marital Status of Parents	No	No
Number of Children in Family	No	No
Parental Attitudes toward School-Education	Yes	Yes
Parental Expectations for Child	Yes	Yes
Parental Involvement with Child	No	Yes
Parental Supervision-Control of Child	No	Yes
Intellectual Climate of Home	Yes	Yes
Child's Home Responsibilities	No	No
Parental Child-Rearing Attitudes	No	No

[a]Based on Mize and Klausmeier, 1977, p. 220.

[b]The rapid and slow developers in each grade group went to the same schools and also had their instruction in the same or similar classroom arrangements.

[c]Variable was higher or more positive for rapid developer unless marked with c.

7. The relationship between the school and its community should be continuous and ongoing. Crisis-management should be avoided since a program is easier to build and maintain during times of tranquility than in times of torment.

8. Home-school-community relations is not the same as the use of community advisory committees. While advisory groups, ad hoc parental committees, and study groups are useful, they are but a small part of a comprehensive program.

9. Many diverse subpublics are not showing an increased interest in the schools. Provision should be made to ensure adequate communication, to increase community involvement in school activities, to provide for participation in educational decision making, and to develop ways of resolving actual or potential conflicts among the subpublics, the school, and the home.

10. Educators do not hold a monopoly on the expertise about educational practices. Citizens are better informed, more knowledgeable, and more sophisticated than in the past (adapted from Bowles & Fruth, 1976; Fruth, Bowles, & Moser, 1977).

These assumptions were incorporated in a model which holds that effective home-school-community relations are a product of the processes of analysis, communication, involvement, participation, and eventual resolution of community issues by school policy makers (Bowles & Fruth, 1976). Bartels (1976) defined each of these processes as follows:

Analysis is the process by which issues and members of the community are identified and related.

Communication is the process which utilizes many forms of interaction among various members of the community, and between the school and the community members.

Involvement is the process through which various community members contribute time, energy, expertise, and other resources to a school.

Participation is the process which provides entry to the decision-making processes of a school.

Resolution is the process which is designed to solve problems and to reduce actual or potential conflicts among the home, the school, and the community.

These five processes are further reduced to a set of three aims to be addressed by a systematic approach to home-school-community relations. First, there must be opportunities for parents and other citizens to have input, as appropriate, in making decisions related to the school. Second, effective two-way communication must take place between the school and its community. Third, the school must utilize appropriately the resources of the larger community to enhance the educational program. Let us now examine each of these three aims in greater detail.

Involvement in Schoolwide Shared Decision Making

Schoolwide shared decision making is improved when groups both within and outside of the school have opportunities to participate appropriately in the decision-making process. Administrators, teachers, counselors, students, and other staff members are the people within the school who ordinarily serve as members of educational improvement committees, councils, or cabinets. Parents and citizens should also be involved regularly in making decisions related to the school's total educational program. When arrangements for shared decision making are first formulated, attention must be paid not only to involving the proper combinations of representatives from within the school, but also to including representatives of groups outside the school.

Three basic arrangements have been used in schools to increase decision involvement by people outside the school. First, decision making groups such as an educational improvement committee might include parents and other community representatives as regular members. Watkins (1978) found several advantages to this type of arrangement:

1. The presence of parents on such committees adds parental and community perspectives to issues.

2. Continuous interactions with parents cause professional educators to be more client-centered in their thinking.

3. Participation by parents and other citizens in the school's decision-making processes assists in legitimizing decisions in the eyes of the community.

A concern, of course, in involving community members in schoolwide decision making on a continuing basis is that many meetings of educational improvement committees or councils deal with issues having little immediate interest to parents. For example, when the agendas of committee meetings are filled almost entirely with daily operational issues, parents become disenchanted with discussions that concern areas directly related to the professional staff's normal interest or expertise.

The second way to involve parents and citizens in the school's decision-making processes is through ad hoc participation. In this way, parents and others become involved only in those issues in which they are specifically interested. An example of this would be the establishment of an ad hoc task force composed of teachers, students, administrators, counselors, and parents for the purpose of preparing a student handbook.

A third way to promote participation in shared decision making is for the school to establish permanent special advisory groups to enable parents and other citizens to have an on-going role in making recommendations regarding issues of particular interest.

Fostering Effective Two-Way Communication

Typically, communication between the school and its community has consisted of using techniques such as newsletters, bulletins, and announcements in the media—newspapers, radio, and television (Fruth, Bowles, & Moser, 1977). Relying on these approaches is but a small part of establishing and fostering effective communication because they are only one-way communication devices—the school "tells" only its side of the story.

Needed are ways of making sure that there are open lines of communication from the community to the school. Traditional two-way communication devices include open houses, "back-to-school nights," parent-teacher association meetings, and parent conferences. These activities are useful, but often they do not assist citizens interested in the educational process to come together to share mutual concerns.

Home-school-community relations and its aim of fostering more effective two-way communication must be an integral part of the philosophy and standard procedures of the school, not a haphazard arrangement where parents and other community members are occasionally invited into the school.

Utilizing Community Resources

The third aim of home-school-community relations is to utilize the resources of a community to enrich the quality of the school's educational program. Previously, we suggested that schools by themselves can no longer be expected to provide students with all the skills and knowledge required to cope with the complexities of our modern world. The experiences of many people, in addition to professional educators, must be tapped and made available so that each student may be prepared as adequately as possible to deal with the future. Making use of the community as an educational resource may take two forms. First, community representatives may be invited into the school to serve as resource persons. Second, the school may send its students out into the community for programs of experiential learning and career education. In both cases, there is a strengthening of the bonds between the school and its community.

In this section, the three major aims of a program of home-school-community relations have been presented and explained: Involving parents and other citizens in shared decision making, fostering effective two-way communication, and utilizing community resources to enrich the school's total educational program. The next section includes descriptions of home-school-community relations programs in three secondary schools and one district which address these aims.

EXAMPLES OF PROGRAMS OF
HOME-SCHOOL-COMMUNITY RELATIONS

In this section, the ways in which three secondary schools—one middle school, one junior high school, and one senior high school—and a school district have developed systematic approaches to the aims of home-school-community relations are described. Each has been selected because it has a unique approach to one of the first two aims, involving parents and citizens in the school's decision making processes, and fostering effective two-way communication. Examples of schools which address the third aim—utilizing community resources to enrich the school's educational program—were presented earlier in Chapter 5.

Irvine High School, Irvine, California

Irvine High School, located in a suburban area south of Los Angeles, is a comprehensive senior high school enrolling more than 1,800 students in Grades 9 through 12. The teachers and students are organized into administrative units, or subschools, each of which is under the direction of one of the school's assistant principals. The principal is responsible for providing leadership to the entire school and coordinating the activities of the three units.

Irvine has a schoolwide shared decision-making group called the Instructional Improvement Council. Its major responsibilities include stating curriculum policy, assessing educational needs, adopting new programs, allocating finances, and setting schoolwide goals and objectives. The membership of the Council consists of the principal, an assistant principal, five teachers, four students, and a classified staff member. In addition, opportunities exist for parents to participate in the ongoing decision-making process of the school because the membership of the Instructional Improvement Council includes at least three parent representatives.

Membership in the Instructional Improvement Council as a parent representative implies continued participation in the Council's shared decision making. The organizational structure of Irvine also provides for the ad hoc involvement of parents and other citizens on one or more of the standing committees of the Council, and also on task forces that are created periodically to deal with specific issues in the school. Examples of standing committees are the Budget Advisory Council and the School Advisory Forum. The Budget Advisory Council has the primary responsibility for preparing the school's total budget, an important task because the Irvine district philosophy provides for each school to enjoy considerable autonomy in developing its annual operating budget. Through the Budget Advisory Council, representative Irvine parents, teachers, and students have a voice in determining budgetary allocations to programs and activities in the school.

The School Advisory Forum is a group which encourages parents and others to express their views about the school, and also as a place where representatives from the school are able to go for feedback concerning their suggestions and proposals. There is a link between this Forum and the Instructional Improvement Council because some parent members of the Forum also serve on the Council. As a result, parent concerns which are heard in the Forum are communicated to the Council. In effect, the School Advisory Forum provides a setting where dialogue occurs between the school and parents, thus reducing misinformation resulting from informal and inaccurate communication being circulated around the community.

Coolidge Junior High School, Phoenix, Illinois

Coolidge Junior High School is located in Phoenix, Illinois, a suburb south of Chicago. It enrolls approximately 250 students in Grades 7 and 8. Coolidge also has a schoolwide decision-making group, the Program Improvement Committee. At Coolidge, however, parents and other community members do not serve as regular members of the Committee. Attendance by people from these constituencies at regularly-scheduled meetings of the Committee is encouraged, however.

Another structure has been created at Coolidge expressly for the purpose of improving the quality of communication among the school, home, and community. This organization, the Coolidge Common Council, is composed of four teachers, four parents, and four students. It meets monthly with the school principal to discuss and recommend policy changes for the school. Discussion covers a wide variety of topics, including schoolwide objectives, student activities, behavioral concerns, school regulations, and other issues.

The principal then relates the concerns and suggestions to the Program Improvement Committee. This arrangement allows decisions in the school to reflect input from administrators, teachers, parents, and students. At the same time, parents are able to be involved in issues of greatest immediate concern.

Another key to effective home-school-community relations at Coolidge is the school's teacher-advisor program. This program serves as an important link between the Coolidge staff and parents. Because each parent knows his or her child's teacher-advisor, there is always someone to whom the parent can turn with specific questions or concerns about the educational program of the school.

Another unique feature of the Coolidge program of home-school-community relations is the position of home-school coordinator. This full-time staff member serves as a community liaison person. The coordinator visits the homes of many families in the school attendance area and, at times, brings to the school parents who would ordinarily be unable to attend parent meetings. Due to these and other efforts by school personnel, Coolidge has enjoyed a record of having at least 90 percent of all parents attend parent-teacher conferences each semester. This frequent contact between parents and staff fosters effective two-way communication. In addition, individual teachers frequently go out in the community and make home visits. Activities such as these ensure that parents and others are kept well-informed of the activities and programs of the school.

Webster Transitional School, Cedarburg, Wisconsin

Webster Transitional School, a middle school that enrolls approximately 700 students in Grades 6 through 8, is located in Cedarburg, Wisconsin, a suburb of Milwaukee. All the major aims of home-school-community relations are fulfilled at Webster. The school, however, takes special care in addressing the aim of promoting effective two-way communication between the school and the home. This is best illustrated through the parent-student-teacher conferences held throughout the school year.

According to school policy, teachers as advisors of students meet with parents at least twice each school year, at the end of the first and third quarters. Two afternoons and one evening are set aside for this purpose, thus providing opportunities for parents to find a convenient time to visit the school. Students are required to be present at the conferences and, in most cases, actually conduct the conferences.

The specific purposes of the parent-student-teacher conferences are:

1. To develop trust, cooperation, and communication between the school and home.

2. To gain an understanding of each student's background.

3. To discuss academic progress and performance.

4. To discuss social and affective development of students.

5. To develop responsibility and accountability through self-evaluation of progress and performance, and joint goal setting with parents and students.

Evaluations of students by teachers and the students themselves serve as the basis for each conference. The student rates himself or herself on class and test work, ability to work in groups, neatness, responsibility, and goal setting. Teachers evaluate students using the same criteria. The evaluation serves as the basis for the conference with parents and replaces conventional report cards for the first and third quarters.

The parent-student-teacher conferences at Webster are an illustration of how a school has been able to implement an arrangement to increase two-way communication by encouraging face-to-face encounters among teachers, parents, and students on a regular basis. As is true of the other schools described in this chapter, Webster uses a variety of other techniques to keep parents and other citizens informed about and involved in what is going on in the school. For example, each month the school publishes the *Webster Newsletter* which contains general school news as well as specific information about upcoming school activities. There is also a Parent Advisory Committee which encourages parents to comment on the development of new school policies and programs. This organization meets throughout the school year. Finally, there is also an emphasis on bringing about a high degree of community involvement in the academic program of the school. Parents volunteer their time to work in the Instructional Materials Center, chaperone field trips, and help as tutors or volunteer aides.

Milwaukee, Wisconsin, Public Schools

An example of a systematic effort by a large urban district to develop more effective home-school-community relations can be seen in the Milwaukee Public Schools.

A recommendation found in the 1975 court order to desegregate Milwaukee's public schools was that the Board of School Directors should establish more effective ways to involve community groups in the operation of the city's schools. In addition, the school district was directed to find new ways of keeping the Milwaukee taxpayers better informed about what was taking place in the schools.

Early in 1976, the Milwaukee Board of School Directors requested that the superintendent submit a proposal for community involvement in the planning for desegregation through the use of specialty, or "magnet" schools. The proposal was developed and approved for a community involvement organization to be formed. This organization, called the "Committee of 100," was given the charge of serving in an advisory capacity to the Board of School Directors.

Representatives to the Committee of 100 are elected from each of Milwaukee's 14 high school areas. Each area is allocated a certain number of positions, based on the number of students served in the area, which it may fill in the Committee of 100.

Among the accomplishments of the Committee of 100 since its establishment were:

> Advising the Board of School Directors and superintendent on desegregation plans for the Milwaukee Public Schools.
>
> Making suggestions to the Board on security and safety problems related to the busing of students.
>
> Recommending a policy on drug abuse to the Board.
>
> Making suggestions to the Board concerning the plan to change Milwaukee's junior high schools into middle schools.

Other ongoing concerns of the Committee have included such issues as determining the effectiveness of the district's desegregation plan, suggesting ways of inviting more parent and citizen involvement in the schools, and recommending to the Board ways of combatting violence and vandalism in the schools.

The Committee of 100, as is true of many other similar organizations in school districts across the nation, has enjoyed varying degrees of success as a strategy designed to increase community involvement in the schools. Predictably, a higher degree of citizen involvement and interest in the activities of the Committee are shown when more visible and volatile issues such as possible neighborhood school closings are being considered. At other times, interest is not as great. Nevertheless, the Committee does represent an effort on the part of an urban school district to increase involvement by a diverse big city population. As issues arise that are viewed as important to the Milwaukee Public Schools, the Committee of 100 will continue to serve as the primary link between community concerns and public policies.

RELATIONSHIP BETWEEN HOME-SCHOOL-COMMUNITY RELATIONS AND OTHER AREAS OF EDUCATIONAL IMPROVEMENT

In this chapter, examples of programs of home-school-community relations have been presented. Each program addresses the major aims of involving parents and other citizens in educational decision making, increasing two-way communication, and utilizing community resources to enrich the school's educational program.

The design for secondary school improvement, as described in Chapter 1, serves as the organizing theme of this book. Each chapter has explained specific components of the design, including examples of how concepts have been put into practice in middle, junior, and senior high schools of varying size and location. In this section, the relationship between effective home-school-community relations and each of the other components is explained.

Educational Programming for the Individual Student

In Chapters 2 and 3, the concept of arranging a total educational program of courses and other activities to meet the needs of each student, and also designing an instructional program in each course for each student was described. It must be recognized that a foundation of this type of educational programming is a strong relationship between the home and the school. In arranging a total educational program for each student and also an instructional program in each course, teachers must work closely with parents as well as students, and keep parents informed of the progress that their child is making throughout the educational program. Teachers also need to be aware of the types of home and community backgrounds that each student has so that courses and other activities selected may take into account such variables in the student's home background.

Curricular Arrangements

The development of a comprehensive and flexible curriculum that takes into account not only state and district requirements but also student characteristics was the subject of Chapter 4. Again, an important relationship between the local school and its surrounding community is implied.

Recent Gallup public opinion polls show that parents and other citizens typically are not interested in directly planning the curriculum of their schools. Such findings may reflect the fact that curriculum development has traditionally been viewed as a process wholly controlled by professional educators. To develop a more comprehensive and flexible curriculum, however, existing resources of the larger environment may need to be explored by the school. To accomplish this, it is probable that professional educators will need to seek more participation by the public in reviewing changes in the curricular offerings of their schools.

Experiential Learning and Career Education

Tied directly to the needed relationship between curriculum development and community involvement is the establishment of experiential learning and career education. In Chapter 5, the concept of expanding opportunities for learning beyond the confines of ordinary classes was detailed. To provide such opportunities, the school must have a solid program of home-school-community relations which keeps parents and other community members informed and involved, and which also makes extensive use of the expertise of community members as a way to supplement conventional learning experiences of students. Furthermore, through systematic attention to school-community issues, schools can increase the likelihood that the community is receptive to efforts to place students in work and other career education experiences as an integral part of their growth and development.

Student-Decision Making Arrangements

The secondary school needs to provide instruction to students in how to improve their decision-making skills, and also to make opportunities available for students to make increasingly important decisions as they proceed from one grade level to another. It is crucial that a spirit of collaboration and cooperation exist between the school and parents if these decision-making skills are to be addressed completely. Parents need to be informed of the rationale for allowing students to make their own decisions, and parents also need to lend their support by providing guidance to their child as he or she begins the process of making choices and learning of the accompanying accountability and responsibilities associated with each decision. An attempt by the school to enable students to make progressively more important decisions can only be successful if an environment of mutual trust exists between parents and the staff of the school.

Evaluation of Student Learning and Educational Programs

Although the evaluation of student learning and educational programs is essentially an activity conducted by the staff within the school, it has a major impact on the quality of the interaction between the school and its surrounding community. School staffs have traditionally viewed educational evaluation which yields results that can be made public only when favorable to the school program. The problem with this is that when the public becomes aware of any evaluation finding that is not favorable to the school, then the strength of the negative finding is often magnified. School personnel then must expend considerable time and effort in responding to criticisms of the school by the public.

By considering and perhaps adopting some of the concepts and practices related to the systematic evaluation of student learning and educational programs, the school is able to make judgements and modifications of instructional practices based on data and other solid evidence. This may alleviate the frequent "crisis response" by schools to the community. Second, effective evaluation practices can serve as a solid basis for developing open communication among school staff, parents, and other citizens.

Administrative Arrangements

Because one of the three aims of effective home-school-community relations is to involve parents and other community members in the ongoing decision-making processes of the school, there is a clear relationship with the component of administrative arrangements for shared decision making. A basic premise of that component holds that those who have a "stake" in the outcome of a decision should have the opportunity to participate in its initial formulation. To facilitate arrangements where parents and others have the opportunity to be part of the schoolwide decision making process is at the heart of the "participation" stage of the model of home-school-community relations described earlier in this chapter. The need to keep parents and other taxpayers informed and to promote active participation can be seen as a major supportive factor which enables the maintenance of any educational improvement effort.

Organization for Instruction and Advising

One function that needs to be incorporated in any organization for instruction is a mechanism for reporting student progress to parents. This function complements the aim of promoting effective two-way communication through home-school-community relations. Reporting to parents should not consist only of using such traditional techniques as grade report cards and infrequent parent-teacher conferences. Instead, reporting student progress to parents should be a continuous, active process where a high level of communication is maintained so that parents know the objectives of courses and the extent to which their children are meeting those objectives before problems arise. The essence of keeping parents informed lies in the practice of telling what will be done in the future, not what should have been done in the past.

Teacher-Advisor Programs

A major function of teacher-advisor programs is that of improving home-school-community relations. Examples of how this function is fulfilled in different secondary schools are numerous. At Webster Transitional School, for example, the teacher-advisor program serves as the basis for parent-student-teacher conferences held during the school year—an important way of establishing effective two-way communication. At Coolidge Junior High School, the Community Council and the home-school coordinator are features which allow the school to maintain positive relationships with its community.

SUMMARY

In this chapter, the importance of home-school-community relations was shown through a brief review of relevant literature and research. Second, assumptions concerning home-school-community relations and aims based on these assumptions were listed and explained. Next, the ways in which these aims were addressed in a senior high school, a junior high school, a middle school, and a large urban school district were described. Finally, relationships between home-school-community relations and other components of the design for the improvement of secondary education were traced.

References

Baker, J. L. *An empirical study investigating parent participation/involvement and its effect on the achievement scores of follow-through children in the Oakland public schools.* Unpublished doctoral dissertation, University of Oregon, 1977.

Bartels, L. I. *Simformation 2: Organizing volunteer programs in IGE schools.* Madison: Wisconsin Research and Development Center for Cognitive Learning, 1977.

Bartels, L. I. *Supports and constraints to home-school-community relations in an urban, inner-city IGE school* (Technical Report No. 488). Madison: Wisconsin Research and Development Center for Individualized Schooling, 1978.

Blumenberg, E. The school-community advisory council: For better or for worse? *Journal of Secondary Education*, February 1971, *46*.

Bowles, B. D. *School-community relations: Community support and student achievement: A summary of findings*. Madison: Wisconsin Research and Development Center for Individualized Schooling, 1980.

Bowles, B. D., & Fruth, M. J. Improving home-school-community relations. In J. M. Lipham & M. J. Fruth (Eds.), *The principal and individually guided education*. Reading, MA: Addison-Wesley, Inc., 1976.

Brookover, W. B., Erickson, E. & Joiner, M. *Self concept of ability and school achievement III* (Cooperative Research Project 2831). East Lansing, MI: Bureau of Educational Research Services, College of Education, Michigan State University, 1967.

Bureau of School Programs Evaluation. *Which school factors relate to learning*? Albany, NY: University of the State of New York, State Education Department, 1976.

Hobson, P. J. W. *Structured parental involvement: An analysis of a Title I summer parent guided AT-HOME project*. Unpublished doctoral dissertation, George Washington University, 1976.

Hunter, M. C. Home-school communication. *National Elementary Principal*, November 1967, *47*.

Keeves, J. P. The home, the school, and achievement in mathematics and science. *Science Education*, 1975, *59*, 439-460.

Kim, J. E., Fruth, M. J. & Bowles, B. D. *Home-school-community relations: The state of the art* (Theoretical Paper No. 61). Madison: Wisconsin Research and Development Center for Cognitive Learning, 1976.

Klausmeier, H. J., & Allen, P. S. *Cognitive development in children and youth: A longitudinal study*. New York: Academic Press, 1978.

Klausmeier, H. J., Rossmiller, R. A. & Saily, M. (Eds.), *Individually guided education: Concepts and practices.* New York: Academic Press, 1977.

Lipham, J. M., & Fruth, M. J. *The principal and individually guided education.* Reading, MA: Addison-Wesley Publishing Company, 1976.

Oinonen, C. *The relationship between school-community relations and student achievement in elementary and secondary schools* (Technical Report No. 552). Madison: Wisconsin Research and Development Center for Individualized Schooling, 1980.

Sistak, M. D., & Frerich, D. D. The principal's role in school-community relations. In National Education Association (Eds.), *Selected articles for principals.* Washington, D.C.: National Education Association, 1968.

Watkins, A. N. *Decision making processes in senior high schools that individualize instruction* (Technical Report No. 460). Madison: Wisconsin Research and Development Center for Individualized Schooling, 1978.

Suggestions for Further Reading

Cervone, B. T., & O'Leary, K. A conceptual framework for parent involvement. *Educational Leadership*, November 1982, *40*(2), 48-49.

Presents a model for describing effective strategies to increase parent involvement as active and passive participants in the educational program of the school.

Davies, D. (Ed.). *Communities and their schools.* New York: McGraw-Hill, Inc., 1981.

Includes a collection of readings concerning the most significant issues related to increasing involvement by parents and citizens in public schools.

CHAPTER 12

SUPPORT ARRANGEMENTS

John C. Daresh

Throughout this book, a design for the improvement of secondary education has been presented. Suggestions for increasing the effectiveness of instructional, curricular, organizational, administrative, and advising practices have been given, along with examples of successful efforts from schools across the nation. Once improvement efforts have been started, however, and new practices are first implemented, staffs of secondary schools committed to systematic renewal must address the issue of how to ensure that an effort can be maintained over time. Support arrangements both within and outside of each local school must be identified and cultivated to enable a school to keep effective practices going and become a self-renewing organization.

This need for constant attention to be paid to systematic support for educational improvement serves as the basic theme of this chapter which has as its primary purpose the clarification of the following comprehensive and enabling objectives of the design for the renewal of secondary education:

Comprehensive Objective:

The environment for learning and instruction in the school and for work and other educative experiences in the community is enriched through the intellectual, technical, and material support provided by school and school district groups, and by external groups, such as the state education agency, intermediate agencies, teacher education institutions, and professional education associations.

Illustrative Enabling Objectives:

The school district and local school make provisions for:

The *Educational Improvement Committee,* or other group, to meet weekly during school hours to plan and carry out its activities.

Each teaching team, or other group, to have a common time for carrying out their preparation, planning, evaluation, and other activities.

Each advisor to meet regularly with his or her advisee group and individual advisees.

Teachers to receive assistance in carrying out their educational improvement activities.

The state education agency takes initiative with the local school districts for activities such as:

Developing strategies for stimulating the educational improvement activities of local schools.

Providing financial and technical support to local schools in carrying out their educational improvement activities.

Encouraging job descriptions to be changed, if necessary, to enable teachers to participate in student advisement and in educational improvement activities.

Reviewing and changing the licensing requirements of currently licensed educational personnel and developing new licensing programs to meet changing societal conditions and related demands on education.

Teacher education institutions, working cooperatively with local schools and the state education agency, take initiative for activities such as:

Evaluating their programs to prepare administrators, counselors, teachers, and other educational personnel; revising existing programs; and developing new programs to meet changing societal conditions and related demands on education.

Developing and offering credit and noncredit courses designed to meet the needs of prospective educational personnel and inservice personnel to participate effectively in educational improvement activities.

Arranging with local schools for cooperative preparation of student teachers and interns.

Professional education associations at the local, state, and national level take initiative for activities such as:

Providing leadership to their members in carrying out educational improvement activities.

Identifying and publicizing local schools that demonstrate educational improvement.

Influencing local, state, and federal legislation to support educational improvement.

Encouraging the adoption of contract provisions which facilitate educational improvement.

This chapter begins with a brief description of why support arrangements are essential for promoting and maintaining improvement activities in the schools. Next, the nature of required support arrangements, as indicated in the Comprehensive and Enabling Objectives, will be examined. Particular emphasis will be placed on the responsibilities of groups such as the local school and district, state education agencies, universities, and professional associations. The chapter concludes with some brief examples of support arrangements for local educational improvement efforts which are already in place.

NEED FOR SUPPORT ARRANGEMENTS

Given the current constraints facing educators such as declining enrollments and tax bases, disappearing state support and federal assistance, schools can no longer afford to embark on projects of widespread school improvement without first examining carefully their capacity to support not only initial implementation and planning activities, but more importantly, the maintenance of a project once it has begun. Too many false starts by public educators will not be tolerated by taxpayers.

Recent research on school improvement and change in educational organizations makes it clear that the most effective way to proceed toward an improvement effort is to address local school needs and priorities. Long-lasting change will not result from externally mandated programs. However, even with this emphasis on local efforts, it is equally clear that the long-term maintenance of a change effort for improvement will not be possible unless strategies are developed to make certain that sufficient support is available from agencies found in the environment of each school. Generally speaking, major groups which comprise this environment include the school district administration, the state education agency, and the federal educational community. Attention must be paid to the influence of local, state, and national professional associations, and also by institutions of higher education. Each of these groups which exist beyond the walls of the individual local school plays an important role in supporting educational improvement. School staffs must not only be aware of the presence of such groups, but also how best to make use of them in planning, implementing, and maintaining local school improvement activities.

NATURE OF SUPPORT

The design for the renewal and improvement of secondary education provides individual secondary school staff with a conceptual framework which may be used to assess conditions in their schools and then make plans to carry out improvement activities in one area or another. The design does not attempt to prescribe a single way of doing things in all schools. Because of this flexibility, and also due to the fact that educational improvement is assumed to be an ongoing, dynamic activity, there is a special responsibility for local schools to ensure that the conditions needed to permit and promote improvement activities are first established. A facilitative environment for improvement must be created within each school and in each district, and this environment must address an important issue such as how to provide staff with adequate time and other resources needed to plan for renewal and improvement. In addition, attention must be paid to such important factors of effective schools as how to promote meaningful staff development and provide organizational arrangements to encourage the broad-based involvement and sense of collegiality needed to ensure that a school staff will take ownership for improvement activities.

Time and Other Resources

The maintenance of improvement efforts in local secondary schools does not require extraordinary amounts of additional financial and other resources from the school district or other agencies, once an effort has been first started (Daresh, 1978). However, it is reasonable to expect that some additional assistance be provided in the earliest stages of educational improvement, and it is critical that planners of any activity be aware of and take into account the need for some specialized resources. These resources generally fall into three distinct categories: time, additional staff, and money. All three types of resources are linked very directly to one another.

The greatest single resource needed by local schools and districts to assist those engaged in educational improvement is time. This time is necessary at three different points in the school improvement process. First, staff members need time while they are engaged in the important activities related to preplanning for an improvement effort. For example, teachers and others require time during the normal school day to get together for inservice activities that may be needed to increase their understanding of a particular improvement practice. A second point where staffs require additional time is in the actual preparatory activities prior to starting an improvement effort. Teaching schedules need to be arranged so that teachers and others can meet during a regularly scheduled time to continue to plan their strategies for implementation, share concerns, and prepare whatever additional materials may be needed. Finally, additional time is also required during the critical first-year implementation of an improvement effort so that teachers, administrators, and counselors are able to continue to spend time working together to monitor and evaluate their activities.

Another important resource needed to facilitate school improvement activities is the allocation of additional support staff. Administrators and school boards obviously cannot extend the number of working hours available to school staffs each day or week. Simply increasing the number of hours that teachers and others must spend in schools without additional pay is neither a practical nor effective approach to addressing the basic need for more time available to school staffs. It is conceivable, however, that arrangements can be made so that time presently allocated to staff is restructured to permit more opportunities for planning improvement activities.

Such arrangements can be worked out within the parameters of the present school day in many cases. For example, substitutes might be used to replace teachers in their typical non-instructional tasks such as supervising corridors and cafeterias. Utilizing paraprofessionals to perform these and similar tasks so that teachers have more time to work on improving the quality of instruction in their school would appear to be a wise use of resources. Again, however, additional resources in this area of personnel allocation implies that support and commitment be provided by the district administration and school board throughout the preplanning, preparatory activities, and initial implementation of any educational improvement effort.

The third major category of resources that may be required to ensure proper initial implementation and long-term maintenance of educational improvement activities is additional finances. Teachers and other staff must be provided with sufficient incentives to work on improvement activities. Work will often need to be done at a time outside of the regular working hours for school staff members. Assuming that even the most dedicated educators need compensation for their time beyond the contract day, school boards must also become involved in providing additional resources to support the improvement effort.

School improvement activities can be started and maintained only if sufficient time, personnel, and money are made available for the important stages of preplanning, preparing, and initial implementing of any necessary program changes. One of the most discouraging things that can possibly occur in school improvement is to find that an effort must be discontinued soon after it has been started solely because the amount of resources needed were underestimated in the first place. Related to this is the fact that school district officials and school boards need to realize that their commitment to local school improvement must be deep and involve the allocation of real resources. Strategies in each school and district are required to ensure that sufficient time, personnel, and financial resources are available for the support of educational improvement activities. Regardless of the exact approaches developed to provide these resources, there are no short-cuts, and improvement will not be cheap.

Staff Development and Inservice Opportunities

During the time of great growth in our schools in the 1950s and 1960s, there was tremendous mobility among teachers. People moved freely from one school or district to another during their careers. In addition, there was a constant need for more new teachers to work in the nation's schools. Consequently, there was a steady stream of new people with new ideas being infused into schools. With the enrollment declines faced by most school districts, and also the decrease in the number of teachers needed, the present situation is considerably different.

Now, few teachers move to new schools once they have found a position in a building. Teachers tend to stay in the profession longer than they did in the past. As McLaughlin and Berman (1977) noted, "More and more districts are faced with the reality of fewer students, a decreased budget, and consequently a stable and possibly stale staff. Districts have fewer opportunities to 'hire' enthusiasm and new ideas, but instead must consider the professional development needs of the staff they already have." Staff development and inservice education, therefore, are no longer "frills" to be carried out by school districts and local schools. Instead, continuing professional development opportunities for staff are viewed as an essential ingredient to be included in any school improvement effort. It is through the development and utilization of effective inservice that teachers and other educational personnel are able to receive assistance in carrying out their educational improvement activities.

Care is needed to ensure that three important issues are addressed when developing strategies for effective staff development and inservice. First, attention must be paid to the ways in which professional development opportunities are made available within school districts. Second, the content of staff development must be carefully reviewed. Finally, delivery systems utilized in the presentation of inservice and staff development need consideration by planners of educational improvement.

Some changes might be necessary regarding professional development provided by school districts. For example, the traditional view of staff development and inservice education being orchestrated almost exclusively from a districtwide perspective is rapidly being replaced by the fact that each individual school must be responsible for determining its own priorities for inservice. The Rand Change

Agent Study (McLaughlin & Berman, 1976) made it clear that local school staff development needs are of a higher priority and will ensure greater staff involvement and satisfaction than attempts to meet only school district goals. This observation has an important implication with regard to potential policy changes in many school districts. At present, resources for inservice are controlled almost exclusively by the central office. It is important that the staffs of local schools be brought into the decision-making process that goes along with how these professional development resources are actually allocated to schools. Teachers engaged directly in planning and carrying out educational improvement activities are the best judges of the types of additional training they might need. The decentralization of control over inservice education is a highly desirable practice within school districts.

The limited research concerning the content of inservice has given us a fairly clear description of the most desired types of inservice. First, major reviews completed by Lawrence (1974) and Joyce and Associates (1976), as well as a large number of doctoral dissertations, have shown that inservice is generally viewed in a more positive light when content is based on the expressed needs of participants in the local school, and not handed down from the district office. Needs classified most frequently as important were, not surprisingly, those which dealt with issues and concerns of most immediate concern to practitioners. Teachers, in particular, believe that it is most important for inservice programs to offer what they view as "practical" advice (Frahlich, 1981). Second, although many different background characteristics of staff have been investigated to determine possible relationships with desired inservice content, the only characteristic that seems to be related is the experience level of an individual. For example, Burden (1979) found that first year teachers expressed a need for inservice that helped them to increase their initial awareness of teaching activities and the teaching environment, and also addressed their feelings of uncertainty, confusion, and insecurity; more experienced teachers wanted inservice directed toward helping them to increase their insights regarding the characteristics of children as learners, and to enhance their professional confidence, security, and maturity.

A third finding concerning the content of inservice is that while the specific topics listed as desirable by staff are quite diverse, they fall into discernible categories. Using Katz' (1955) notion that people in organizations need, at various times, technical, human, or conceptual skills, a review of research on the content of inservice reveals that staff have a great desire for technical and human relations skill development, but show little interest in inservice programs that treat primarily conceptual issues. This may suggest that there is a high demand for content related to the increase of knowledge and skills needed for immediate problems, but little desire for inservice that addresses long-term solutions to complex problems.

The final important issue regarding inservice and staff development deals with the appropriate delivery systems that are to be used. Nicholson, Joyce, Parker, and Waterman (1977) noted five primary ways in which inservice education is carried out:

1. *Job-embedded inservice* (professional growth derived from normal activities associated with a job. For example, teachers learn valuable skills when they participate on an assigned curriculum committee);

2. *Job-related inservice* (training that is not strictly associated with prescribed job responsibilities. For example, teachers might participate in some type of outside workshops);

3. *Credential-oriented inservice* (the teacher is cast as a student of higher education, taking courses and pursuing a degree, much as he or she did as an undergraduate in college);

4. *Professional organization-related inservice* (courses and other learning experiences are promoted by teachers' and administrators' professional associations for the purpose of providing renewal and updating members with new skills);

5. *Self-directed inservice* (individual teachers fulfill their own professional development needs by reading educational journals, visiting schools, or participating in other individual activities).

Each of these five delivery modes is valuable to the staff of a school engaged in educational improvement activities. What must also be done by the school to enable this type of professional development to take place is to provide sufficient incentives, either in the form of supplementary pay or as released time, to staff members so that they might utilize whatever approach to inservice may be appropriate at a particular time.

In summary, it is essential that the issue of providing assistance to staff in the form of inservice education and staff development become a regular part of the operation of any school interested in engaging in educational improvement.

Increased Decision Involvement

An important ingredient to be included in any systematic approach to educational improvement is the development of opportunities for teachers, administrators, and other staff members to participate in decision making. Utilizing shared decision making to develop a spirit of collegiality among staff members has the advantage in that such collaboration and the sense of ownership derived from it can serve as a type of "insurance policy" which enhances the probability that an improvement effort will be maintained over time. If one assumes that the leadership of the principal is indeed the key factor supporting school improvement, as noted by many writing on school effectiveness (Edmonds, 1981; Lipham, 1981; Mortimer, et al., 1979; Austin, 1979), the question must be asked as to what happens to improvement activities if the principal leaves a particular school. The answer to this may depend largely on whether or not the improvement effort has been internalized by the staff, how well the staff understands the effort, and whether the staff views the effort as having a positive effect on the school. Whenever norms of cooperation are created, the possibility of successful implementation of an improvement effort is enhanced (Bell, Wyant, & Schmuck, 1979).

Collegiality can be developed through the utilization of shared decision making within each school. In addition, collaborative efforts can be encouraged by agencies external to the individual school. School improvement is a complex process requiring possible modification of many areas in a school's program. It is hard to imagine a single school or district which alone possesses all of the expertise needed to carry out sweeping revisions in such diverse areas as curriculum development, administrative reorganization, or modification of evaluation practices. External assistance may be required by the local school to carry out improvement in these and other areas. Interorganizational collaboration is needed to allow schools to "maintain quality programs, maximize limited resources, and avoid wasteful and inefficient duplication of services" (Northwest Regional Educational Laboratory, 1980). Neale, Bailey, and Ross (1981) observed that, as educational institutions must adjust to such conditions as declining enrollments and dwindling financial support, collaborative partnerships among educational agencies are not merely "good ideas," but rather essential features needed to ensure that schools may continue their improvement and renewal efforts.

The need to develop opportunities for increased decision involvement and the spirit of collegiality among staff may bring about modifications in existing conditions in and around schools. For example, the mere creation of decision-making groups is an empty exercise if policies in a school or district are not altered so that time is made available for groups to meet. Interest by staff members in participating in a school's decision-making processes will be minimal indeed if the experience represents just "serving on another committee" after school hours. All efforts to build support for improvement will be unsuccessful if policies are not revised to provide support for serious cooperative planning. Outside of the school, it is essential that linkage relationships among institutions with stakes in improving educational quality be encouraged. Partnerships involving local schools and districts, state education agencies, universities, and professional education associations must be offered. In this way, several agencies are able to work together to share expertise as a way to increase technical support for schools.

Specifically, ways in which these organizations external to the local school may assist in the support for educational improvement might include the state education agency providing financial and technical support, encouraging staff job descriptions to be changed, if necessary, and reviewing and changing state certification requirements to prepare personnel needed by schools attempting improvement activities and other changing educational needs. Universities can cooperate with local school improvement efforts by periodically evaluating their preservice training programs for teachers and administrators, developing credit and noncredit inservice courses for practitioners in the field, and arranging with local schools for cooperative preparation of students teachers and interns. Local, state, and national professional education associations are able to support local educational improvement by giving publicity to local schools that engage in exemplary programs, engaging in the political processes needed to influence local, state, and federal legislation to support improvement efforts, and encouraging the adoption of contract provisions which will facilitate and lead to continuing school improvement.

EXAMPLES OF SUPPORT ARRANGEMENTS

Throughout this chapter, the importance of arrangements for continuous educational improvement has been stressed. A brief explanation of the major factors that are addressed by effective school districts has been presented. In this section, examples of how two secondary schools and two state education agencies, one in a collaborative effort with a state university, have enhanced improvement efforts by developing strategies to provide ongoing support.

Steuben Middle School, Milwaukee, Wisconsin

In 1972, Steuben Middle School in Milwaukee was reorganized from a traditional junior high school to a middle school. One of the major changes which occurred involved the development of interdisciplinary Instruction and Advisory units to replace subject departments. This organization for instruction enabled teachers to replace subject departments. This organization for instruction enabled teachers of required academic subjects (reading, language arts, mathematics, and social studies) to work together cooperatively to plan new instructional strategies, the use of materials, and the advising of students. Until recently, however, this objective was only partially attained. The school time schedule did not initially provide teachers with an opportunity to meet together on a regular basis. Although teams were formed, provisions were not made for common planning time. As in most schools, teacher preparation and planning periods were given to staff independent of other team members' time.

In 1977, changes in the Steuben Middle School schedule were made to facilitate the development of common team planning time for all teachers in each unit. The way in which this was accomplished was to modify the bell schedule for the school, particularly during lunch periods. The number of students at lunch at any single time was reduced slightly by increasing the number of lunch periods. Teachers were released from most of their lunchroom supervisory responsibilities and given more time to work on instructional planning while students from their units were in the cafeteria. No instructional time was lost because five to eight minutes were added to the first three class periods of each day. Another feature of this arrangement was that teachers were given preparation periods which were in common with the other members of their teaching teams.

These changes at Steuben have allowed the arrangement of organizing teachers and students into units to reach its full potential. Greater opportunities now exist for teachers and others to work together to share expertise and resources on a daily basis.

Webster Transitional School, Cedarburg, Wisconsin

In many ways, Webster Transitional School, a middle school near Milwaukee, is organized for instruction and student advising in a way similar to Steuben. However, from the earliest stages in the development of the Webster program in 1972, an arrangement has been in place to facilitate the sharing of educational decisions by all teachers working as teams in the school's Instruction and Advisory units.

Teachers in the units at Webster share the teaching of required academic subjects. Students continue to move as groups to classes in other subjects offered in the school's curriculum—music, art, physical education, and allied arts. Each day, the students from each unit move as a group for a two-hour block of time to receive instruction in one or another of these curricular areas. The teachers of each unit are thus provided with a duty-free common block of two hours each day for the purpose of planning for instruction and student advisement. This common planning time is highly valued by the Webster staff because it provides them with the opportunities to develop necessary strategies and materials for carrying out effective educational programming for each student.

On yet another level, the arrangements at Webster provide a natural setting for the other factors mentioned as important conditions for supporting educational improvement. First, inservice education and staff development are carried out each time that the teachers are able to meet and work together. As a result, professional development has become a continuing process, not an isolated event. Second, the organization for instruction and advisement at Webster provides considerable opportunities for staff members to participate in shared decision making and develop the type of collegial spirit that is an important supportive factor for educational improvement.

Pennsylvania School Improvement Program

An example of an arrangement where a state education agency has devised a way to deliver ongoing support to local schools can be seen in the Pennsylvania School Improvement Program (PSIP). It was funded largely by the National Institute of Education and operated from July 1976 to January 1980. The primary focus of this program was to increase classroom use of research and development products in schools across the State of Pennsylvania, thereby improving educational practice. The primary strategy used by PSIP was to link state level resources directly with local schools, and not to involve district-level officials in the improvement process.

The Pennsylvania School Improvement Program was initially designed as a problem-solving process which could be used directly by local schools—elementary and secondary—as a way of identifying areas for improvement, principally in the basic skills areas of reading and mathematics. The objectives of PSIP were to assist local schools:

1. To analyze basic skills needs;

2. To improve student performance in basic skills through the best available programs and techniques produced in research and development.

The original purpose of the PSIP was to link the Pennsylvania Department of Education, two county intermediate educational units, and three research and development agencies—Research for Better Schools, Research and Information Services for Education, and the Learning Research and Development Center at the University of Pittsburgh—with schools in ten pilot school districts. By the end of the Program, there were seven intermediate units and schools from 29 school districts involved.

During the course of the three and one-half years of the Program, support to local schools was provided in three distinct phases. During the first year, intensive on-site assistance in the form of working sessions involving school assistance teams and local school action teams took place. Representatives of R & D agencies made frequent visits to participating schools to explain the nature of available products. In addition, during the first year, field testing of workshops and some materials to be used in conjunction with PSIP was conducted. During the second phase, emphasis was placed on the development of additional materials and workshops to assist the staffs at local schools in the strengthening and maintenance of their educational improvement efforts. The final 18 months of the Program were characterized by refinements to and adaptations of the initial PSIP process and model to meet the needs of local schools.

It has been clear from analysis of this Program that through the technical assistance provided primarily through the Pennsylvania Department of Education, it was possible for local schools to work with external support agencies such as the intermediate service units and R & D agencies to go from conducting initial needs assessment to devising plans for the implementation of school improvement activities within a fairly short period of time. The primary group responsible for assessing needs and planning improvements is still the local school educational improvement committee. However, the PSIP is a demonstration of the positive influence that an external agency, in this case a state education agency, can have in the process of facilitating educational improvement.

Wisconsin Secondary School Improvement Council

A second model of an effort made at the state level to support local secondary school improvement is the Wisconsin Secondary School Improvement Council, a council organized by Herbert J. Klausmeier of the University of Wisconsin in 1981. The council is composed of the organizations that are responsible for education in Wisconsin. Charter members of the Council are the Wisconsin Department of Public Instruction, the Wisconsin Association of School Boards, state universities, and professional education associations for teachers and administrators. The mission of the Council is to focus state leadership, resources, and initiatives on the improvement of secondary education in Wisconsin (Klausmeier, 1981).

The council was formed to carry out the following and other specific activities on a regular basis:

1. Formulate ideas and strategies directed toward the improvement of secondary education in Wisconsin.

2. Prepare position papers and descriptive statements regarding secondary education.

3. Assemble and disseminate listings of successful improvement programs, including specific information on how to obtain more detailed information of publicized programs.

4. Provide a listing of training programs, resource people, speakers, films, and other inservice and staff development programs which Council members have utilized and have found to be effective.

5. Identify significant research results, and also needed areas of research, which could assist members improve educational programs.

6. Disseminate a semi-annual listing of forthcoming workshops, conferences, and training programs that would be accessible to members.

7. Foster improvement of preparation programs for secondary school teachers, administrators, and counselors.

8. Foster improvement of the inservice education of secondary school teachers, counselors, administrators, and other school personnel.

The Wisconsin Secondary School Improvement Council is an interesting model of interorganizational collaboration to improve existing educational practices. It is a loosely-knit organization where member organizations pay no dues and assume the costs of participating in periodic meetings. At the same time, it is bound together by a common interest in improving secondary education in a state. This combination of bringing together very fine technical and con-

ceptual skills at a minimal cost is an intriguing idea that has implications for improvement efforts in other states as well.

A recent development derived from this earlier work in the Wisconsin Secondary School Improvement Council has been the formation
of a consortium for improving secondary schooling in Wisconsin.
Under the direction of the state superintendent of public instruction,
a consortium composed of the Department of Public Instruction,
six state universities, and three intermediate education agencies or
Cooperative Educational Service Agencies (CESA) was formed. The
universities and CESAs cooperate in providing the initial education
of improvement teams from schools and school districts of their
geographic areas, and then in providing follow-up activities in the
form of credit courses, noncredit seminars and workshops, and individual consultations.

SUMMARY

In this chapter, support arrangements for local secondary school improvement were explained. First, the need for such arrangements
was described in some detail. Next, the nature of important supportive factors was explained. These factors included providing sufficient time and other resources, leading effective inservice and staff
development activities, and developing increased staff collegiality
through increased shared decision making. Finally, the chapter concludes with examples of two secondary schools which have made internal organizational changes to facilitate the concepts described here
for assisting educational improvement, and two state education agencies which have taken the initiative for providing ongoing technical
assistance to local schools.

The major theme of this chapter is that, because improvement efforts require a good deal of energy in order to be successful, many
conditions and forces both within the school and outside of it must
be harnessed to make sure that not only a facilitative environment
exists for starting an improvement effort, but even more important,
making sure that such an effort can be maintained over time.

References

Bell, W. E., Wyant, S. H., & Schmuck, R. A. *Diagnosing a school's readiness for change.* Santa Clara, CA: Central California Facilitator Project, 1979.

Berman, P., & McLaughlin, M. W. Implementation of innovation. *Educational Forum*, March 1976, 345-370.

Burden, P. R. *Teacher's perceptions of the characteristics and influences on their personal and professional development.* Unpublished doctoral dissertation, Ohio State University, 1979.

Daresh, J. C. *Facilitative environments in senior high schools that individualize instruction* (Technical Report No. 457). Madison: Wisconsin Research and Development Center for Individualized Schooling, 1978.

Frahlich, L. M. *Staff development program analysis: Designing characteristics.* Unpublished doctoral dissertation, University of Southern California, 1981.

Joyce, B. R., Howey, K. R., Yarger, S. H., Hill, W. C., Waterman, F. T. Vance, B. A., & Baker, M. G. *Issues to face* (Inservice Teacher Education Report 1). Palo Alto, CA: Stanford Center for Research and Development in Teaching, 1976.

Katz, R. L. Skills of an Effective Administrator. *Harvard Business Review*, 1955, *33*(1), 33-42.

Klausmeier, H. J. *Charter of the Wisconsin secondary school improvement council* (mimeographed paper). Madison, WI, 1981.

Lawrence, G. *Patterns of effective in-service.* Tallahassee, FL: Florida State Department of Education, 1974.

McLaughlin, M., & Berman, P. Retooling staff development in a period of retrenchment, *Eduational Leadership,* February 1977, 34(5), 21-28.

Neale, D. C., Bailey, W. J., & Ross, B. E. *Strategies for school improvement.* Boston, MA: Allyn & Bacon, 1981.

Nicholson, A. M., Joyce, B. R., Parker, D. W., & Waterman, F. T. *The literature on inservice education: An analytic review* (Inservice Teacher Education Report 3). Palo Alto, CA: Stanford Center for Research and Development in Teaching, 1977.

Northwest Regional Educational Laboratory. *Interorganizational arrangements for collaborative efforts: Literature review.* Portland, OR: Northwest Regional Educational Laboratory, 1980.

Suggestions for Further Reading

Hager, J. L., & Scarr, L. E.   Effective schools—effective principals: How to develop both. *Educational Leadership,* February 1983, 40(5), 38-40.
Presents a description of a model where administrators in a school district in the State of Washington were shown how to spend more of their daily time involved directly with the support of effective instructional practices.

Joyce, B. R., Hersh, R. H., & McKibbin, M.   *The structure of school improvement.* New York: Longman, 1983.
Describes major practical and conceptual issues to be faced by local schools and school districts in developing strategies for long-term school improvement activities.

Neal, D. C., Bailey, W. J., & Ross, B. E. *Strategies for school improvement.* Boston, MA: Allyn & Bacon, 1981.
Presents a model for establishing collaborative school improvement partnerships which include teachers, administrators, university professors, state education agency representatives, and others.

CHAPTER 13

RESEARCH-BASED EDUCATIONAL IMPROVEMENT

Herbert J. Klausmeier

Nine of the 10 components of the design for improving secondary education have been described in the preceding chapters. Practices from a number of schools have been presented for illustrative purposes. This chapter deals with the last component of the design, educational research and development. The comprehensive objective and illustrative enabling objectives for this component are as follows:

Comprehensive Objective:

Knowledge is extended regarding learning, instruction, school structures and processes, and other factors related to schooling through research and development conducted by school personnel and cooperating individuals and agencies.

Illustrative Enabling Objectives

The school staff:

> Develops the capability for carrying out its own evaluative research and related improvement activities.

> Participates with district personnel and other individuals and agencies in research and development specifically directed toward education improvement in its school.

> Participates with individuals and agencies in research directed toward extending knowledge concerning schooling and the educative process.

Research to increase our understanding of planned change, administrative leadership, and shared decision making has been reported in the earlier chapters of this book by Lipham and Daresh.

In this kind of research, local schools provide information to the researcher about a particular research question. The researcher takes initiative for identifying the question, conducting the research, and reporting the results. Most of the research reported by Lipham and Daresh is of this type.

Another kind of research is directed toward improving education in local schools (Klausmeier, 1982). This kind of research is planned and conducted cooperatively with the schools. The schools work with the researcher in all aspects of the research, including identifying and delimiting the problem area, planning the research, gathering the data, and analyzing the results. As the schools work with the researcher, they gain considerable autonomy in conducting their own improvement-oriented educational research. In other words, they develop the capability for conducting their own evaluative research and for planning and conducting related improvement activities as described in Chapter 7 and later in this chapter. The author of this chapter planned and then conducted this kind of improvement-oriented educational research from 1977-78 through 1980-81 with Steuben Middle School (SMS), Webster Transitional School (WTS), Carl Sandburg Junior High School (CSJHS), Cedarburg High School (CHS), and Hood River Valley High School (HRVHS). This research provided the evidence regarding the effects of implementing the improvement strategies and also regarding the school structures and processes that facilitated the implementation of the improvement strategies. Hereafter, 1977-78 is referred to as Year 1 (Y1) of the project, 1978-79 as Y2, 1979-80 as Y3, and 1980-81 as Y4.

This chapter was written to enable you:

To understand the purposes of the cooperative research project.

To understand the research method and the improvement strategies that were employed.

To learn the effects of implementing the improvement strategies on student outcomes.

To identify the structures and processes of the participating schools that facilitated implementation of the improvement strategies.

To identify the nature of a school's permanent educational improvement capability.

To gain information about conducting evaluative research independently and improvement-oriented research cooperatively with an external agency.

PURPOSES OF THE COOPERATIVE RESEARCH PROJECT

The cooperative research project was conducted with five schools. The overall goal of the project was to determine the usability and effectiveness of the design for the renewal and improvement of secondary education. This required both development and research.

The objective of the development was for each school to develop its own improvement capability by starting or refining three improvement strategies and by starting or refining school structures and processes that would enable it to implement the strategies. These improvement strategies and school structures and processes are incorporated in the design and have been explained in the prior chapters of this book.

The research had four purposes. One was for each school to maintain a satisfactory level of student achievement from year to year and to raise an unsatisfactory level through implementation of the three improvement strategies. Maintaining or raising achievement in English, mathematics, and reading was a common concern of the five schools. A second purpose was to determine the extent to which each school could carry out its own data collection and data analysis and then plan and carry out improvement activities based on the results of the data analysis. A third objective was to relate the changes that occurred in student achievement from year to year to the implementation of the improvement strategies and to unanticipated events that occurred and that influenced student achievement. The fourth objective was to relate the organizational structures and processes of each school to its implementation of the strategies.

School structures, also referred to as organizational structures, is a term used to indicate not only administrative arrangements and the organization for instruction and advising but also other schoolwide programs and arrangements, for example, the curriculum and the program of home-school-community relations. Moreover, each school is considered as a unique social organization. Accordingly, each school has a culture of its own that, although similar to other schools of a district or state, is not identical to any other school. Therefore, it is presumed that no two schools will implement the improvement strategies in an identical manner nor will the school structures be identical.

With this view regarding secondary schools, the research and development activities were conducted as five case studies. No two schools used identical data gathering tools and procedures. Similarly, no two schools implemented the improvement strategies in an identical manner. The intent was for each school to use the evaluation procedures and the improvement strategies that it would continue to use after the project ended and thereby maintain its improvement capability. Since the data gathered were not identical in the schools, no statistical comparisons were made between any two schools. Instead, conclusions were drawn by examining the results across the five schools. Schools from a small town, a suburban community, and a large city were selected to enhance the generalizability of the findings.

RESEARCH PROCEDURES

Each school gathered and analyzed data annually regarding student outcomes, including achievement in English, mathematics, and reading; student attitudes toward various aspects of schooling; and attendance. Some schools also collected other data that they desired, for example, other areas of student achievement, student self-concepts, and discipline referrals. Each school analyzed the achievement data and also the mental ability information for the students of each grade and, in some cases, for the students of each teaching team. An achievement profile, as well as daily attendance, was available for each individual student. After the first year of data collection, the schools used the information to evaluate the effectiveness of their initial improvement activities and to plan and carry out improvement activities for the ensuing year. Project personnel provided consultation to the schools regarding the analysis and interpretation of the data on student outcomes and, to a much lesser extent, regarding their improvement activities.

Each school provided the project with information that was used in describing the school as it was functioning in Y1. The 10 components of the design that have been explained in earlier chapters of this book were employed in preparing the description. Each year thereafter each school provided the project information regarding its annual planned improvements that were designed to maintain or to raise student achievement or to improve any other student outcome desired by the school. Two other kinds of information were provided to the project by each school. One was the planned improvements that were not related to the selected student outcomes, for example, raising student achievement in science. The other was unanticipated events that occurred which may have influenced achievement of the desired student outcomes.

After the last data collection, the achievement and mental ability information that each school (except CHS) collected on each student was analyzed by the project both on a cross-sectional and a longitudinal basis. For reasons to be indicated later in the results section, the CHS data were analyzed on a longitudinal basis only. In the cross-sectional analysis, the mean achievements of the total students and of the boys and girls of the same grade across the four years were compared, for example, the means of the Grade 10 students of HRVHS of Y1, Y2, Y3, and Y4. Analysis of covariance, with mental ability the covariate, was used in this analysis. Analysis of covariance made it possible to take into account differences in mental ability among the successive classes and between the males and females. Where a difference among the means of the total students or the boys or girls for the four years was found to be significant at or beyond the .05 level, post-hoc comparisons were made of the means of each two years; i.e., Y1 with Y2, Y3, Y4; Y2 with Y3, Y4; and Y3 with Y4.

A longitudinal cohort consisted of a group of students who entered the first grade of a school, took all the tests, and remained through the last grade. Comparisons were made of the achievements of the quarters in mental ability and the males and females of each cohort, averaged across the times of testing. The gain in achievement of the males and females and of the four quarters in mental ability from one time of testing to the next was also compared. Repeated measures analysis of variance was used to test the significance of the difference in the mean achievements and in the mean gains. Where a difference significant at or beyond the .05 level was found, post-hoc comparisons were performed. We note that this analysis was performed for each cohort.

Each school had two or three longitudinal cohorts during the four years whose achievements and gains in achievement were compared. Analysis of covariance, with mental ability the covariate, was performed to determine the significance of the differences among the mean achievements and the mean gains of the cohorts and the males and females. The mean achievements of the four quarters in mental ability of the different cohorts could not be compared since mental ability was used as the covariate. Although extensive analyses of the longitudinal data were made, only a brief summary of the findings is presented later in this chapter. The detailed findings for each school are reported in Klausmeier, Serlin, and Zindler (1983).

Data regarding student attitudes, attendance, and dropouts were analyzed, using descriptive statistics. Tests of statistical significance were not performed.

The last phase of the research was to relate the changes in student outcomes that occurred from year to year to the planned improvements that were made and the unanticipated events that occurred. Each school's structures and processes were also related to its implementation of the improvement strategies.

IMPROVEMENT STRATEGIES

The design for the improvement of secondary education incorporates three strategies for maintaining or raising student achievement. The schools either developed or refined these strategies during the project. An overview of the kinds of improvement activities that were planned and carried out in implementing each strategy follows. Information regarding specific activities is presented later with the research results for each school.

One strategy (see Chapter 2) is to arrange an appropriate total educational program of courses and other educational activities for each student each semester. Here the student's career goals and interests are considered by the student and the student's advisor, as well as the prior characteristics. To arrange a more appropriate total educational program in the academic subjects *for students achieving below expectancy* in terms of mental ability, activities such as the following were carried out:

> Advising the high school student to take more academic courses.

> Advising the middle school, junior high, and high school student to take more units of academic courses.

Advising the high school student to take advanced rather than elementary academic courses.

Advising the middle school, junior high, and high school student to take advanced rather than elementary units of academic courses.

Advising the middle school, junior high, and high school student to spend more time at school and/or out of school on course-related activities.

Encouraging the middle school, junior high, and high school student to attend classes regularly.

Advising the high school student to spend less time on an out-of-school job and/or extracurricular activities and to take more courses and/or units of courses in the academic subjects.

The second strategy is to arrange an appropriate instructional program in each course for each student (see Chapter 3). This calls for the teacher to take into account each student's motivation, learning styles, and other characteristics. In arranging more effective instruction in the academic subjects for individual students, some teachers in all five schools carried out activities such as the following:

Encouraging students to use the entire class period in active learning.

Adapting the content and instructional materials to the student's capability for learning the particular subject matter.

Using available instructional materials flexibly and securing additional materials, especially to provide better for different learning styles and interests.

Using individual assignments, small-group work, and whole-class instruction to take into account individual student's learning styles and interests and also the nature of the subject matter.

Providing for out-of-class, course-related activities, including homework.

Modeling enthusiasm for the subject matter and the students.

Securing greater effort on the part of the students achieving below expectancy.

Getting students of low motivation to take more initiative to learn.

Providing encouragement and other social reinforcements, especially to the lower-achieving students.

The third strategy (see Chapter 7) is to set goals for the total group of students of a grade or of a team, or for certain quarters of it in mental ability, and to plan and carry out improvement activities to achieve the goals. This strategy was implemented in the various schools except CHS by carrying out activities such as the following:

Applying the individual educational programming strategy to the existing courses and curriculum.

Applying the individual instructional programming strategy in the existing courses.

Increasing the amount of time allocated for instruction for all the students of the grade in the course or curricular area where achievement was low.

Changing the content and objectives of the course or curricular area for all the students of the group where achievement was low.

Requiring another course and/or a unit of an existing course to be taken by all the students in the subject field where achievement was low.

Arranging for out-of-class instruction, e.g., computer-assisted instruction during the school day, after-school study, and/or summer classes, mainly for students experiencing specific difficulties.

EFFECTS OF IMPLEMENTING THE IMPROVEMENT STRATEGIES ON STUDENT ACHIEVEMENT

To determine the effects of each school's implementation of the improvement strategies, the annual changes in the achievements of the students of the same grade were related to the changes in the annual implementation of the improvement strategies and to the unanticipated events that occurred. Changes in the mean achievements of the later longitudinal cohorts of each school were also related to the implementation of the strategies. A significantly higher mean achievement by a later grade or longitudinal cohort is interpreted as a positive effect of implementing the strategies, and a significantly lower achievement is regarded as a negative effect unless there was some unanticipated event that offset the positive effects. Similarly, a nonsignificant difference is regarded as neutral unless there was some unanticipated event that offset the positive results of implementing the improvement strategies.

Steuben Middle School (SMS)

SMS is an integrated urban school located in Milwaukee, Wisconsin. The racial composition of the student body is about 48% Black, 10% Hispanic, 3% Native American, and 39% White. The socioeconomic level of the student population qualified SMS for ESEA Title I programs and services.

The total enrollment in Grades 7 and 8 was 751 in Y1, 830 in Y2, 851 in Y3, and 874 in Y4. The Grade 6 enrollment dropped from 92 to 36 during the four years as Grade 6 was being phased out. For this reason the data for Grade 6 were not analyzed.

In Y1 all of the SMS teachers of language, reading, math, science, and social studies and the students were organized into Instructional and Advisory Units (I & A units) consisting of four academic teachers and about 120 students. Each team of four academic teachers had its 120 students for a block of time each day and provided the instruction in language, math, reading, science, and social studies.

The administrative arrangement employed at SMS to plan, monitor, and implement its research and improvement activities was an Instructional Improvement Committee that was formed in Y1.

This consisted of the principal, the learning coordinator, and at least one teacher from each of its I & A units.

During the four years of the project, some changes were made in the administrative arrangements of the school. In Y2 a school research committee was formed from the membership of the Instructional Improvement Committee to review and interpret the annual test results. The departmental chair positions were eliminated in Y4 and their duties were assumed by the school's learning coordinator. Some of the I & A units were reorganized from year to year to take into account changes in the Grade 6, Grade 7, and Grade 8 enrollments. The major staff change was the loss of six aides in Y4.

The individual instructional programming strategy was being implemented in the academic subjects in Y1, and it was refined each year thereafter. Individual educational programming was being implemented only indirectly in Y1 inasmuch as the same academic subjects were required of all the students and in these subjects individual instructional programming was being implemented. Starting in Y2 and continuing thereafter the educational programs of only a few of the students were monitored and evaluated each semester. Goal setting, planning, and carrying out related improvement activities were started on a trial basis by about one-third of the I & A unit teams in the second semester of Y2 and by all of the I & A unit teams in Y3 and Y4. Accordingly, individual instructional programming and goal setting were implemented quite fully for the first time in Y3, while individual educational programming was implemented to a much lesser extent.

Mental ability scores were available for most of the students, based on administration of the Otis-Lennon Mental Ability Test when the students were in Grade 5. The Metropolitan Achievement Tests were administered in May of each year, starting in Y1. The results of this Y1 testing were not summarized and interpreted by the school staff until the first semester of Y2. Hence, only minor refinements were made in implementing the instructional programming strategy in the second semester of Y2. Accordingly, the Grade 7 and Grade 8 classes of Y2 did not experience any major planned improvements. However, a strong effort was made by the staff to raise the Grade 7 and Grade 8 achievements in Y3, the year in which the goal setting strategy was implemented for the first time in all of the I & A units.

The complete data regarding SMS (and the other schools) are summarized in a monograph by Klausmeier, Serlin, and Zindler (1983). Included are the mean scores for each grade each year, the standard deviations, the percentile scores equivalent to the mean scores, and the results of the tests of significance. Similar information is provided for each longitudinal cohort. Because of the large amount of space required, the tables are not provided here. Instead, only the results of the tests of significance and illustrative percentile ranks are indicated.

The means of the Y2 Grade 7 and Grade 8 classes in reading total, language, spelling, and math total were significantly higher than those of the Y1 classes in two instances, significantly lower in one instance (reading total), and not significantly different in five instances. On the other hand, the means of the last two Grade 7 and Grade 8 classes were significantly higher than the means of one or both of the first two classes in 17 instances and not significantly different in 15 instances. The smallest change in percentile scores was from 30 to 34 and the largest was from 30 to 44 for the instances in which the later mean was significantly higher than an earlier one.

The results of the three longitudinal cohorts support these for the successive grades. In all areas except reading total, the mean achievements of the second and third cohorts were significantly higher than those of a prior cohort. Similar positive results were obtained on a locally constructed mathematics test.

These consistently positive results that started in Y3 are attributable to the concurrent implementation of the goal-setting strategy and to providing better instructional programs for the individual students. Based on these achievement test results and the information regarding the implementation of the improvement strategies and the school structures and processes, we conclude that the improvement capability of SMS was quite well established by the third year. It became more effective in the fourth year.

Carl Sandburg Junior High School (CSJHS)

CSJHS enrolls students in Grades 7 and 8. It is the only junior high school in the Mundelein Elementary (K-8) School District, Mundelein, Illinois, a suburban district northwest of Chicago. There are four elementary schools in the district, but there is no senior high school. The community consists mainly of white collar, middle class Caucasians. The student enrollment of CSJHS was 380 in Y1, 346 in Y2, and 322 in Y3. The school changed its test battery in Y4 in accordance with a plan worked out by a district committee in Y1; therefore data were not analyzed for that year.

In Y1 the academic teachers and students were organized into four I & A units. The teachers had the students for a block of time each day and provided their instruction in language, math, reading, science, and social studies. The research and improvement activities of this small school were administered by the principal through meetings with the teachers of each of the I & A units. There was no educational improvement committee; rather, the principal and teachers functioned as a principal-faculty committee.

During the three years of the project no change occurred in the administrative arrangements of the improvement program. However, the number of I & A units was reduced from four to three in Y3 because of the declining enrollment. Further, in Y3 both of the Grade 8 language arts teachers were new to the school and there were three fewer teachers. In addition to these changes, a new gymnasium was built and some rooms of the regular building were remodeled during Y1 and the first semester of Y2. In Y3 the principal worked to gain community support not to close the junior high school. Both of these activities took a great deal of the principal's time.

The teachers implemented individual educational programming indirectly starting in Y3, but did not plan and monitor the individual educational programs of their students. They were already arranging individual instructional programs for the students in the academic subjects, all of which were required of all the students. Individual instructional programming was refined each year thereafter. Goal setting and planning and carrying out related improvement activities were started for the first time in Y3. Thus, both goal setting and individual instructional programming were implemented for the first time in Y3 and individual educational programming was implemented only indirectly.

The Grade 7 students were administered the Otis-Lennon Mental Ability Test and the Grade 7 and Grade 8 students were administered the Metropolitan Achievement Tests in May of each year. The first testing was done in May of Y1. The results, however, were not summarized and interpreted by the CSJHS staff until the first semester of Y2. Accordingly, only minor improvements were attempted in the second semester of Y2. Thus, the changes in achievement between Y2 and Y1 do not reflect the effects of implementing the improvement strategies.

The mean achievements of the Y2 Grade 7 and Grade 8 classes in reading total, language, spelling, and math total were not significantly different from the means of the earlier Y1 classes in any of the eight comparisons. On the other hand, the means of the Y3 classes were significantly higher than those of the two earlier years in seven comparisons and not significantly different in the other nine. The smallest change in the percentile rank from Y1 to Y4 was from 45 to 50 and the largest was from 49 to 61 for the four instances in which the Y4 mean was significantly higher than the Y1 mean.

The mean of the Y3 Grade 8 class was not significantly higher than the mean of the Y1 Grade 8 class in language, reading, and spelling. The lack of higher Grade 8 achievement in these areas very likely resulted from the new Grade 8 language arts teachers not being familiar with the CSJHS curriculum and the implementation of the improvement strategies.

The results for the two longitudinal cohorts support the preceding results. The students of the second cohort achieved significantly higher than the first one in mathematics total and not significantly different in reading total, language, and spelling.

The positive results for Y3 are attributed to more effective implementation of the individual instructional programming strategy and the concurrent implementation of the goal-setting strategy. Based on these positive effects of implementing the strategies and the information regarding the school structures and processes, we can conclude that CSJHS had established an improvement capability that was functioning effectively in the third year.

Hood River Valley High School (HRVHS)

HRVHS enrolls students in Grades 10, 11, and 12. It is the only high school in Hood River County, Oregon. There are two junior high schools in the district. The area is small town and rural. The economy is based on agriculture and forestry. The community is mainly middle class, Caucasian, with a few families of Asian background. There is a considerable amount of transient labor. Student enrollment dropped from 785 in Y1 to 607 in Y4.

The teachers of HRVHS were organized into broad fields. There were no departmental chairpersons; however, each broad field had a coordinator. Broad fields that had more than five teachers had at least one team leader in addition to the coordinator.

The administrative arrangement employed to plan, monitor, and implement the improvement activities involved an existing curriculum committee and a school cabinet. The curriculum committee consisted of the principal and seven elected teachers. The school cabinet consisted of the administrative team, five teachers, each of whom served as a coordinator of a broad curriculum field, five teachers, each of whom was a team leader from one of the five broad fields, and the IMC coordinator.

The administrative arrangement for the improvement activities did not change from year to year nor did the broad fields arrangement. The loss in student enrollment was accompanied by a substantial reduction in the teaching staff in Y4.

In Y1 each teacher, administrator, and counselor served as an educational advisor, or guide, to approximately 15 students. In implementing the individual educational programming strategy, these guides consulted with their advisees weekly or more often regarding units of courses in which to enroll, but they did not evaluate the effectiveness of their advisees' educational programs at the end of the semester or year.

To arrange more appropriate educational programs for students, the following changes were made from year to year:

Starting a Grade 10 mathematics placement program in Y2.

Requiring a semester course in English for all Grade 10 students instead of permitting English to be elective starting in Y3.

Increasing the attention given to reading in all the content subject fields starting in Y3.

Advising all students regarding math and English courses by math and English teachers starting in Y4; requiring students to complete three successive units of a course with a grade of C or higher rather than only one starting in Y4; and increasing the requirements in the academic subjects for high school graduation and decreasing the electives and the "survival skills" requirements in Y4.

The preceding changes in the requirements for high school graduation did not apply to the Grade 12 class of Y4.

Throughout the project the teachers arranged individual instructional programs for each student enrolled in their courses. Goal setting and planning and carrying out related improvement activities were started in Y3 and continued in Y4. Thus, all three strategies were implemented concurrently in the last two years.

The General Aptitude Test Battery was administered to the students when in junior high school in Grade 9. The Stanford Test of Academic Skills was administered annually in the spring to all students. The spring test results of Y1 were not summarized and interpreted until the first semester of Y2. Accordingly, only minor improvements were made in the spring of Y2. Therefore, the changes in student achievement from the first to the second year do not reflect changes or refinements in the implementation of the improvement strategies.

The means of the Grade 10, Grade 11, and Grade 12 classes were not significantly different from the means of the Y1 Grade 10, 11, and 12 classes in any of the three areas—English, math, or reading. However, the means of the last two Grade 10 classes were significantly higher than the means of the first two classes in 9 of 12 comparisons and not significantly different in the other three. The changes in the percentile scores from Y1 to Y4 for Grade 10 were from 74 to 80 in reading, 46 to 60 in English, and 54 to 62 in math.

The mean achievements of the last two Grade 11 classes were significantly higher than those of the first two classes in five comparisons and not significantly different in the other seven. The changes in the percentile scores from Y1 to Y4 for Grade 11 were from 54 to 65 in reading, 45 to 55 in English, and 56 to 66 in math. The means of the two later Grade 12 classes were not significantly different from the means of the two prior Grade 12 classes.

The higher achievements by Grades 10 and 11 are accounted for by the prior planned changes made for Grade 10 that were also made for Grade 11. The fact that the Grade 10 group achieved significantly higher in Y3 than in Y1 in all three subjects, while the Grade 11 group did not until Y4 is accounted for in terms of the cumulative effects of the planned changes. For example, the Grade 11 class of Y3 did not take the required English class when in Grade 10 but the Y4 Grade 11 class did. On the other hand, the Grade 12 class of Y4 did not experience the planned changes in the curriculum, advising, and instruction when in Grades 10 and 11 that the Grade 10 and Grade 11 classes of Y4 did.

There were two Grade 10-11-12 longitudinal cohorts. The mean achievement of Cohort 2 was significantly lower than the mean of Cohort 1 in reading but not significantly different in English and math. These results reflect the lack of significantly higher achievement by the last two Grade 12 classes and the second to the last Grade 11 class.

The positive results for the Grade 10 and Grade 11 classes are judged to have resulted from the planned changes made in connection with concurrently implementing the three improvement strategies, starting in Y3. Lack of significantly higher achievement by the last Grade 12 classes is presumed to have resulted from these Grade 12 students not having experienced the planned changes when in Grades 10 and 11. Based on these findings and taking into account the information regarding the school structures and processes, we conclude that HRVHS had established an improvement capability by 1979-80 and strengthened it in 1980-81.

Webster Transitional School (WTS)

WTS is the only middle school in the Cedarburg School District, Cedarburg, Wisconsin. It enrolls students in Grades 6, 7, and 8. Cedarburg is about 20 miles from Milwaukee. Nearly all of the students are Caucasian. The socio-economic level of the community is middle and upper-middle class. The student enrollment dropped from 761 in Y1 to 712 in Y4.

The teachers of language arts, reading, math, science, and social studies and the students were organized into I & A units. Each team had its students for a block of time each day and carried out the instruction in language, math, reading, science, and social studies. The administrative arrangement to plan, monitor, and implement its improvement activities was its existing Faculty Advisory Committee that was already functioning in Y1. This consisted of one teacher from each of the I & A units, three guidance counselors, two teachers from the allied arts team, one teacher from the supportive services team, and the leadership team consisting of the principal, the dean of students, and the instructional consultant.

Several changes occurred in the administrative and organizational arrangements. In Y2 a teacher-advisor task force was formed to assist in establishing a teacher-advisor program that focused on individual educational programming. In Y3 a research and development committee was established to lead the school's goal-setting strategy. The number of teachers and students changed from year to year with the changes in student enrollment. The total number of teachers decreased as enrollment dropped.

The teachers of WTS were already arranging individual instructional programs for their students in the academic subjects in the fall of Y1, and they refined their practices each year thereafter. In Y2 they started planning and monitoring the individual educational programs of their student advisees in Grades 6 through 8. Goal setting and planning and carrying out related improvement activities were started by all of the I & A unit teams in Y3. Accordingly, the three improvement strategies were being implemented in all grades in Y3 and Y4.

A locally constructed language arts test and a locally constructed mathematics test were administered to all the students each year in the fall, the spring, or both. The Gates-MacGinitie Tests of Reading were administered only in the spring of each year. The Short Test of Educational Ability was administered in Grade 7. The test scores of individual students were available for final analysis for Grade 6 starting in Y1, Grade 7 in Y2, and Grade 8 in Y3. Accordingly, data were available for three Grade 6, three Grade 7, and two Grade 8 classes as well as two Grade 6-7-8 longitudinal cohorts.

The results pertaining to reading comprehension and reading vocabulary as measured by the Gates-MacGinitie Tests are most interesting. The mean in reading comprehension of Grade 6 of Y3 was significantly higher (percentile score of 67) than the mean of Grade 6 of Y1 (percentile score of 60). However, the means were not significantly different in reading vocabulary. The mean in reading comprehension of the last Grade 7 class was significantly higher (82nd percentile) that the mean of the first Grade 7 class (70th percentile); however, the reverse occurred in reading vocabulary where the mean of the last Grade 7 class was significantly lower (60th percentile) than the mean of the first Grade 7 class (67th percentile) and also lower than the second Grade 7 class (71st percentile). The pattern for the first and last Grade 8 classes was the same as that for the Grade 7 classes—71st vs. 65th percentile for reading vocabulary and 69th vs. 80th percentile for reading comprehension.

The Grade 6 class was administered the criterion-referenced tests in parts of speech, sentences, language total, and math total only in the fall. These results reflect the students' elementary school achievement and are not discussed further. The means of the last Grade 7 class in the four areas listed above were significantly higher than the means of the first Grade 7 class in 6 of the total of 7 comparisons and not significantly different in the other one. The last year Grade 8 means were significantly higher in 4 of a total of 5 comparisons and not significantly different in the other one. (The mathematics test was not administered to Grade 7 in the spring while the three language arts tests were not administered to Grade 8 in the fall. The other tests were administered in both the fall and spring.)   The mean achievement of Cohort 2 was significantly higher than that of Cohort 1 in mathematics and reading comprehension, significantly lower in reading vocabulary, and not significantly different in the three language areas. The negative finding regarding reading vocabulary is related to a fundamental deficiency in the school district's language arts curriculum that extends from the primary school into the high school. Insufficient attention is given to reading vocabulary at all of the school levels, and the middle school staff because of districtwide policy could not make the changes in the curriculum that were necessary to overcome the deficiency.

The consistently higher achievements by the later Grade 6, 7, and 8 classes are attributable to the concurrent implementation of all three improvement strategies. Inasmuch as WTS was able to implement the strategies to achieve these desired student outcomes and since its school structures and processes did not change much during the four years, we conclude that it had established a functional improvement capability.

Cedarburg High School (CHS)

CHS enrolls students in Grades 9, 10, 11, and 12. It is the only high school in Cedarburg, Wisconsin. About 80% of the entering Grade 9 students come from the one public middle school in the district and about 20% from parochial schools. While there is some industry and some farming in the district, the community is mainly white collar, middle and upper-middle class Caucasians who work in nearby Milwaukee.

Starting with the Grade 9 class of Y1, the Cedarburg teachers and students were organized into one of three programs: a beginning program for potential dropouts, a program called Progress in Continuous Alternative Education (PACE), or a traditional program that was continued from the prior year. The PACE alternative was the one in which the improvement strategies were implemented. In Y1 there were 30 entering Grade 9 students in the program for potential dropouts, 99 in PACE, and 210 in the traditional program. All of the Grade 10, 11, and 12 students were enrolled in the traditional program in Y1. The district plan was to extend the PACE alternative upward by one grade each year and to have a new Grade 9 PACE group start each year. The total enrollment of the school dropped from 1376 in Y1 to 1214 in Y4.

There was a total change in the administrative staff from Y1 to Y4. The assistant principal, who was the coordinator of the PACE program, resigned at the end of Y2. The assistant PACE coordinator, a teacher employed on a half-time basis, attempted to refine the Grade 9 and Grade 10 program and to extend the program upward into Grades 11 and 12. The principal resigned in the middle of Y3. A district committee coordinated the activities until a new principal was employed in the fall of Y4. Accordingly, the PACE program was not extended into Grade 11 in Y3 nor into Grade 12 in Y4 in the manner in which it had been initially planned.

The Grade 9 PACE students and their four academic teachers were organized into an I & A unit in Y1. The four academic teachers taught the PACE students English, math, science, and social studies in classes only for the PACE students. Each teacher and the PACE coordinator served as an educational advisor to about 20 PACE students. This same pattern of instruction and advising for the PACE students was employed in Grades 9 and 10 in Y2 and each year thereafter, but not in Grades 11 and 12. In Grade 11, only part of the PACE students were taught in PACE classes, mainly English and social studies, and in Grade 12 there were very few classes for PACE students only. The educational advising continued into Grade 11 but not into Grade 12.

Individual educational programming was implemented effectively with the first Grade 9 and Grade 10 students during Y1 and Y2. Individual instructional programming also was implemented for these

Grade 9 and Grade 10 PACE students quite effectively, except for a curriculum constraint. The curriculum constraint was that the PACE students had to use the same textbooks and study the same content as the traditional students in all courses, even though the PACE students entered Grade 9 with considerably higher mean achievement and mental ability than the traditional students. Goal setting was not carried out systematically with any PACE classes.

Since the Grade 10, 11, and 12 students of Y1 continued in the traditional program, there were no baseline classes for these grades. However, there were two PACE and two traditional longitudinal cohorts. The first cohort was tested when enrolled in Grades 9 through 12 and the second one in Grades 9 through 11. The Short Test of Educational Ability was administered in Grade 9 annually. The Iowa Tests of Educational Development were administered in October to all the Grade 9 students in Y1, the Grade 9 and 10 students in Y2, the Grade 9, 10, and 11 students in Y3, and the Grade 9, 10, 11, and 12 students in Y4.

Table 13.1 presents the adjusted means in language, math, and reading and the differences between the means of the PACE and the traditional cohorts. The adjusted means are based on fall tests. Thus, the differences between the PACE and the traditional cohorts in Grade 9 reflect the results of their education prior to Grade 9. The differences each year thereafter reflect the results of the prior year at CHS. These differences were not tested for statistical significance because the PACE students voluntarily chose to enter the Grade 9 program and had a higher mean mental ability and a higher mean entering achievement level than the traditional students. However, the size and consistency of the differences in the means are regarded as sufficient to be of practical importance.

The differences between the means of the first PACE cohort and the traditional cohort when in Grade 12 were consistently larger than in Grade 9 in reading, language, and math, favoring the PACE cohort. The same pattern held for PACE Cohort 2 and traditional Cohort 2 from Grade 9 to Grade 11. These differences consistently favoring the PACE cohorts suggest that the individual educational programming and the individual instructional programming carried out with the two PACE cohorts during Grades 9 and 10 had positive effects despite the curriculum constraint indicated earlier and the resignation of the PACE coordinator. The positive effects may be due in part to the higher ability of the PACE students. However,

Table 13.1 Adjusted Means and Differences Between Means for PACE and Traditional Longitudinal Cohorts 1 and 2: Cedarburg High School

	Comparison of Mean Gain by Each Cohort						
	Cohort 1				Cohort 2		
	Gr. 9 1977–78	Gr. 10 1978–79	Gr. 11 1979–80	Gr. 12 1980–81	Gr. 9 1978–79	Gr. 10 1979–80	Gr. 11 1980–81
Reading							
PACE	15.62	17.49	18.61	19.79	14.15	16.03	18.67
TRAD	13.37	15.39	15.70	16.93	14.11	15.82	17.75
Diff.	2.25	2.10	2.91	2.86	0.04	0.21	0.92
Language							
PACE	15.82	17.72	18.21	19.41	15.85	17.60	19.59
TRAD	13.19	15.18	15.54	16.01	14.95	16.48	18.45
Diff.	2.63	2.54	2.67	3.40	0.90	1.12	1.14
Math							
PACE	13.85	17.34	18.66	19.16	14.03	16.56	18.99
TRAD	12.76	14.98	15.11	16.24	12.93	14.96	16.61
Diff.	1.09	2.36	3.55	2.92	1.10	1.60	2.38
Student N							
PACE	61				87		
TRAD	122				130		

the traditional cohorts had a greater opportunity to raise their achievement since their mean achievements when in Grade 9 were consistently lower than the Grade 9 PACE means. Moreover, the possibility of topping out on the tests when tested in the fall of Grades 11 and 12 was greater for the PACE students.

Based on these findings, we conclude the CHS did not maintain an improvement capability after Y2. The administrative arrangements of the school did not facilitate the refinement and upward extension of individual educational programming and individual instructional programming after Y2, and the goal setting strategy was not implemented.

NOTES REGARDING ATTENDANCE,ATTITUDES, AND DIFFERENCES BETWEEN SEXES AND AMONG QUARTERS IN MENTAL ABILITY

1. Attendance and student attitudes toward various aspects of schooling were relatively stable from year to year except when a school made a systematic attempt to better either of these areas. When this was done, incidences of betterment occurred but not as frequently as for student achievement. At the same time, activities carried out to raise student achievement infrequently had any effect on attitudes or attendance.

2. The longitudinal cohorts of SMS and CSJHS gained significantly in each area tested from Grade 7 to Grade 8. The cohorts of WTS, HRVHS, and CHS gained in some subjects between each time of testing and in all subjects between at least two of three different times of testing.

3. The mean achievement of the girls was consistently higher than that of the boys in language and spelling in Grades 7 and 8 of SMS and CSJHS, in reading total and language total of Grades 9, 10, and 11 of CHS, and in English in Grades 10, 11, and 12 of HRVHS. No consistent pattern of sex differences was found in mathematics. The boys' achievement was significantly higher than the mean of the girls in math problem solving in Grades 7 and 8 at SMS; however, the mean of the girls was higher at CSJHS in math computation, math concepts, and math total in Grade 7. The mean of the boys was significantly higher than that of the girls in math in Grades 9, 10, 11, and 12 of CHS; however, the difference was not significant in Grades 10, 11, or 12 of HRVHS.

Neither sex gained more than another in mathematics from one time of testing to the next in any school, Grades 7 through 12. The girls of at least one cohort, but not all cohorts, gained more than the boys in spelling and reading from Grade 7 to Grade 8 and in English during one or more of the high school years. (The previous findings are based only on standardized test scores. WTS was not included in this analysis because it used locally constructed tests.)

4. The most surprising finding was that there were scarcely any differences in the gains in achievement made by the four quarters in mental ability. In four schools, only 26 of 684 comparisons that might have been significant were. None were significant at CHS.

Moreover, in a number of the 26 instances the lowest quarter gained more than one or both of the two highest quarters.

It cannot be established that the implementation of the improvement strategies was definitely associated with the lack of significant differences in the gains made by the girls and the boys or among the four quarters in mental ability. However, in all the schools the improvement strategies were implemented in the same manner for boys and girls and for the four quarters in mental ability. It is possible that this equal attention to individual students, regardless of sex or mental ability, contributed to the lack of differences in the gains.

CONCLUSIONS AND DISCUSSION

The cross-sectional analyses performed on the students' test scores showed that the mean achievements of the later grades of Y2 of SMS, WTS, CSJHS, and HRVHS typically were not significantly different from the means of the earlier grades of Y1. But, as noted earlier, these schools made only minor changes in implementing the instructional programming and the educational programming strategies in Y2. Accordingly, the mean achievements of the students were not expected to improve significantly in Y2.

The means of the Y4 grades of these four schools were significantly higher than the means of the earlier grades of Y1, Y2, and Y3 and the means of the Y3 grades were significantly higher than those of Y1 and Y2 in 67 instances and not significantly different in 69, and significantly lower in three (all in reading vocabulary in one school). The higher achievements of these later grades are due mainly to the improvement activities that were carried out in implementing the goal-setting strategy and to a lesser extent to the refinement of the instructional programming strategy and the educational programming strategy. The higher mean achievements of the later longitudinal cohorts in comparison with the first cohort support this conclusion. Thus, implementation of the goal-setting strategy appeared to be the determining factor in bringing about consistently higher student achievement while implementing the other strategies maintained the same level of achievement from year to year.

CHS implemented only the individual instructional programming strategy and the individual educational programming strategy in Grades 9 and 10 and to a lesser extent in Grade 11. The implementation of these strategies yielded positive results in terms of maintaining or slightly improving student achievement.

The results regarding student attendance and attitudes were positive in all five schools. Attendance and attitudes became slightly more positive from year to year when goals were set to improve them, and they remained relatively stable when this was not done. Activities carried out only to raise student achievement appeared to have relatively little effect on attitudes and attendance.

The preceding positive results must be interpreted in the context of the schools having a reduction in teachers or aides in one or both of the last two years. Also, the loss of both experienced language arts teachers in Y3 at CSJHS probably accounts for six Grade 8 language arts comparisons being nonsignificant rather than significant. Nine nonsignificant differences at HRVHS would probably have been significant had the later Grade 11 students of Y3 and the later Grade 12 students of Y3 and Y4 experienced the planned improvements that were made in Grade 10 after they had already completed Grade 10.

Two other points should be borne in mind regarding the changes from year to year. First, the achievements of students of age 13 and 17 in the academic subjects tended to go down during the 1970s, as shown by the National Assessment of Educational Progress (undated a, b, c, d, e). Accordingly, maintaining the same level of achievement rather than experiencing a loss from year to year might be interpreted as a positive rather than a neutral effect. Second, some of the nonsignificant differences occurred in Y4 after the means of the students of Y3 were already significantly higher than those of Y1 or Y2. Maintaining this higher level of achievement also might be considered as a positive rather than a neutral effect.

Based upon the consistently positive results, it is concluded that the design provides relevant guidelines for the renewal and improvement of secondary education. In this context, it is considered to be validated as both usable and effective. Even though the number of schools was small, the uniformity of the results across these schools of greatly different characteristics in different locales is noteworthy.

A few conclusions are in order regarding implementation of the design. The effects of implementing the improvement strategies were more consistent across the two middle schools and the junior high school than the two high schools. Moreover, the strategies, structures, and processes of the design appeared to be more readily adapted and implemented by the middle schools and the junior high school. Although this is the case, the improvement strategies and the organizational structures and processes of the design were found to be effective at the high school level in each grade in which they were implemented appropriately.

The schools set goals in terms of student achievement, and they used norm-referenced and criterion-referenced achievement tests to assess the attainment of the goals. They used the results of their mental ability tests to estimate the expected level of achievement of the students. The schools might have set goals in terms of other student outcomes in the cognitive domain, such as creativity or writing skills. Similarly, they might have employed other means of measuring student outcomes and might not have used the students' mental ability scores. The design is not prescriptive in this regard; rather, each school makes the decisions regarding desired outcomes and measurement tools.

The schools did not set goals to improve their advising, administrative, evaluation, or other school processes. However, this might have been done. The goal-setting strategy and the related planning and monitoring processes of the design are intended to be as applicable to school structures and processes as they are to improving student achievement.

The difference between implementing this design for the renewal and improvement of secondary education and acting on the findings from school effectiveness research warrants a brief discussion. The design focuses on how a school can bring about educational improvement, including how it establishes a permanent improvement capability. School effectiveness research has identified many characteristics of effective schools, including clear educational goals, good discipline, and expectations for high student achievement (Edmonds, 1982; Purkey & Smith, 1982). The descriptors of effective schools do not indicate the structures and processes that schools can use to become effective. For example, how a school with unclear goals, a lack of order, and low student achievement is to become goal-directed, orderly, and high achieving is not made clear. The design does not directly answer these questions either. Rather, it specifies organizational structures and processes by which a school identifies areas of desired improvement and then sets goals, develops plans, and carries out improvement activities to attain the goals. Thus, a school that has developed an improvement capability is able to address any characteristic of effective schooling that it may select as well as other areas of improvement.

POSTSCRIPT

When the last data on student outcomes were collected in the schools in Y4, it appeared that four schools had developed a permanent improvemen. capability. There was some uncertainty regarding CHS. During the next two years economic conditions worsened nationally and this was reflected in program reductions, staff reductions, or both. Accordingly, it might have been expected that the four schools would not maintain their internal improvement capability into 1982-83. This was not the case.

SMS was continuing all of its organizational arrangements in 1982-83 and was implementing the instructional programming and goal-setting strategies. Moreover, all of the prior junior high schools of Milwaukee had become middle schools and each one was developing an improvement capability similar to that of SMS as part of a district-wide school effectiveness project.

CSJHS was continuing in much the same pattern as in Y4. Enrollment had stabilized at about the Y4 level. Individual instructional programming and goal setting were being implemented. Students of each grade were being grouped for instruction according to their entering achievement levels in language arts and mathematics. This reduced the teacher's task in providing suitable instructional programs for each student. The facilitative organizational structures were continuing in the same pattern as earlier.

WTS was continuing its improvement strategies and school organizational structures and processes much as it had been in Y4. In the interim, a district committee had worked toward improving the district curriculum in reading vocabulary. A more clearly delineated performance-based program of education in language arts, math, and reading was being implemented. This started with Grade 6 in Y4 and had been extended into Grade 8 in 1982-83.

HRVHS was also continuing its organizational arrangements and its implementation of the three improvement strategies. Both individual instructional programming and individual educational programming had been refined and parental participation had markedly increased.

In 1982-83 the PACE and traditional alternatives of CHS had been discontinued as separate schools within the larger school. However, many features of the PACE program had been extended throughout the school. These included objective-based instruction, teachers serving as advisors to students and planning and monitoring the educational programs with the advisee, and reporting progress to the student and the parents in individual conferences. Also, an educational improvement committee had been formed and was functioning effectively. All of the academic teachers and students of Grade 9 were organized into academic units of four teachers and about 100 students. Implementation of the goal-setting strategy had begun. Thus, Cedarburg High School, also had established an effective improvement capability.

A statewide secondary school improvement program was started in Wisconsin in 1981. A Wisconsin Secondary School Improvement Council was formed under the present author's leadership to expedite the program. The charter members included the professional educational associations of Wisconsin, including those of teachers and administrators, the Wisconsin Association of School Boards, the Wisconsin Department of Public Instruction, seven teacher education institutions, and five other organizations directly concerned with secondary education. In August of 1982 the Superintendent of Public Instruction of Wisconsin endorsed the design and established an Office of School Improvement in the Department. This office is working with state universities and cooperative educational service agencies in using the design in the improvement of secondary education in Wisconsin.

References

Edmonds, R. R. Programs of school improvement: An overview. *Educational Leadership*, 1982, *40*(3), 4-11.

Klausmeier, H. J., Serlin, R. C., & Zindler, M. C. *Improvement of secondary education through research: Five longitudinal case studies* (Program Report No. 83-12). Madison: Wisconsin Center for Education Research, 1983.

National Assessment of Educational Progress. *Mathematical achievement: Knowledge, skills, understanding, applications.* Denver, CO: National Assessment of Educational Progress, undated (a).

National Assessment of Educational Progress. *National assessment results in social studies/citizenship.* Denver, CO: National Assessment of Educational Progress, undated (b).

National Assessment of Educational Progress. *Results of two national reading assessments: Some performance up; some down.* Denver, CO: National Assessment of Educational Progress, undated (c).

National Assessment of Educational Progress. *Three national assessments of science: Changes in achievement, 1969-77.* Denver, CO: National Assessment of Educational Progress, undated (d).

National Assessment of Educational Progress. *Writing achievement 1969-70: Results from the third national writing assessment.* Denver, CO: National Assessment of Educational Progress, undated (e).

Purkey, S. C., & Smith, M. S. *Effective schools—A review.* Madison: Wisconsin Center for Education Research, 1982.